RESTRICTED AN 01-85FA-1

F7F TIGERCAT
PILOT'S FLIGHT OPERATING INSTRUCTIONS

NAVY MODEL

F7F-1N • F7F-2N
F7F-3 • F7F-3N

Airplanes

by U.S. Navy

THIS PUBLICATION SUPERSEDES AN 01-85FA-1 DATED 15 FEBRUARY 1945
REVISED 15 MARCH 1945

PUBLISHED UNDER JOINT AUTHORITY OF THE COMMANDING GENERAL,
ARMY AIR FORCES, AND THE CHIEF OF THE BUREAU OF AERONAUTICS

Appendix I and II of this publication shall not be carried in aircraft on combat missions or when there is a reasonable chance of its falling into the hands of the enemy

NOTICE.—This document contains information affecting the national defense of the United States within the meaning of the Espionage Act, 50 U. S. C., 31 and 32, as amended. Its transmission or the revelation of its contents in any manner to an unauthorized person is prohibited by law.

©2008-2011 Periscope Film LLC
ALL Rights Reserved
WWW.PERISCOPEFILM.COM
ISBN# 978-1-935700-72-2

RESTRICTED

Pilot's Handbook
for
NAVY MODEL
F7F-1N • F7F-2N
F7F-3 • F7F-3N
Airplanes

THIS PUBLICATION SUPERSEDES AN 01-85FA-1 DATED 15 FEBRUARY 1945
REVISED 15 MARCH 1945

PUBLISHED UNDER JOINT AUTHORITY OF THE COMMANDING GENERAL,
ARMY AIR FORCES, AND THE CHIEF OF THE BUREAU OF AERONAUTICS

Appendix I and II of this publication shall not be carried in aircraft on combat missions or when there is a reasonable chance of its falling into the hands of the enemy

NOTICE.—This document contains information affecting the national defense of the United States within the meaning of the Espionage Act, 50 U. S. C., 31 and 32, as amended. Its transmission or the revelation of its contents in any manner to an unauthorized person is prohibited by law.

1 May 1946

RESTRICTED

POLICY GOVERNING DISTRIBUTION AND USE OF THIS PUBLICATION

Instructions Applicable to U. S. Navy Personnel:

1. Navy Regulations, Article 76, contains the following statements relating to the handling of restricted matter:

"Paragraph (9) (*a*). Restricted matter may be disclosed to persons of the Military or Naval Establishments in accordance with special instructions issued by the originator or other competent authority, or in the absence of special instructions, as determined by the local administrative head charged with custody of the subject matter."

"(*b*) Restricted matter may be disclosed to persons of discretion in the Government Service when it appears to be in the public interest."

"(*c*) Restricted matter may be disclosed under special circumstances, to persons not in the Government Service when it appears to be in the public interest."

2. The Bureau of Aeronautics Aviation Circular Letter No. 50-45 contains the following paragraph relative to the use of aeronautical technical publications:

"Paragraph 6. *Distribution to all interested personnel.* In connection with the distribution of aeronautic publications within any activity, it should be borne in mind that technical publications, whether confidential, restricted or unclassified, are issued for use, not only by officer personnel, but also by responsible civilian and enlisted personnel working with or servicing equipment to which the information applies."

3. Disclosure of technical information in this publication may not be made to representatives of foreign governments or nationals except in instances where those foreign governments have been cleared to receive information concerning all equipments, or other technical data covered by this publication.

Instructions Applicable to Army Personnel:

1. This publication is intended for technical aid and education of military and civilian personnel engaged in promoting the war effort. Its maximum distribution and use is therefore encouraged. However, since the publication is "restricted" within the meaning of AR 380-5, the following security regulations will be observed:

a. Members of Armed Forces and civilian employees of War Department will be given access to this publication whenever required to assist in the performance of their official duties (including expansion of their knowledge of AAF equipment, procedures, etc.).

b. Personnel of War Department contractors and subcontractors may be given possession of this publication, on a loan basis, or knowledge of its contents, only when required to assist in the performance of War Department contracts. Releases will be made in accordance with the requirements of T. O. No. 00-5-2.

c. Representatives of other governments will be given possession of this publication, or knowledge of its contents, only in accordance with AAF Letter No. 45-6.

2. This publication is restricted because the information contained in it is restricted. It does not follow that the physical article to which it relates is also restricted. Classification of the matériel or component must be ascertained independently of the classification of this document.

3. Neither this publication nor information contained herein will be communicated to press or public except through Public Relations channels.

---LIST OF REVISED PAGES ISSUED---

NOTE.—A heavy black vertical line, in the outer margin of revised pages (the left margin for left-hand columns, and the right margin for right-hand columns) indicates the extent of the revision. This line is omitted where more than 50 percent of the page is revised. A black horizontal line to the left of page numbers listed below indicates pages revised, added or deleted by current revision. The line is used only on second and subsequent revision.

BuAer

ADDITIONAL COPIES OF THIS PUBLICATION MAY BE OBTAINED AS FOLLOWS:

AAF ACTIVITIES.—Submit requisitions to the Commanding General, Fairfield Air Service Command, Patterson Field, Fairfield, Ohio, Attention: Publications Distribution Branch, in accordance with AAF Regulation No. 5-9. Also, for details of Technical Order distribution, see T. O. No. 00-25-3.

NAVY ACTIVITIES.—Submit requests to Chief, BuAer, Navy Department, Washington, D. C., Attn.: Publications Section on order form NAVAER-140. For complete listing of available material and details of distribution see Naval Aeronautic Publications Index, NavAer 00-500.

RESTRICTED

Pilot's Handbook
for
NAVY MODEL
F7F-1N • F7F-2N
F7F-3 • F7F-3N
Airplanes

THIS PUBLICATION SUPERSEDES AN 01-85FA-1 DATED 15 FEBRUARY 1945
REVISED 15 MARCH 1945

PUBLISHED UNDER JOINT AUTHORITY OF THE COMMANDING GENERAL,
ARMY AIR FORCES, AND THE CHIEF OF THE BUREAU OF AERONAUTICS

Appendix I and II of this publication shall not be carried in aircraft on combat missions or when there is a reasonable chance of its falling into the hands of the enemy

NOTICE.—This document contains information affecting the national defense of the United States within the meaning of the Espionage Act, 50 U. S. C., 31 and 32, as amended. Its transmission or the revelation of its contents in any manner to an unauthorized person is prohibited by law.

1 May 1946

RESTRICTED

POLICY GOVERNING DISTRIBUTION AND USE OF THIS PUBLICATION

Instructions Applicable to U. S. Navy Personnel:

1. Navy Regulations, Article 76, contains the following statements relating to the handling of restricted matter:

"Paragraph (9) (a). Restricted matter may be disclosed to persons of the Military or Naval Establishments in accordance with special instructions issued by the originator or other competent authority, or in the absence of special instructions, as determined by the local administrative head charged with custody of the subject matter."

"(b) Restricted matter may be disclosed to persons of discretion in the Government Service when it appears to be in the public interest."

"(c) Restricted matter may be disclosed under special circumstances, to persons not in the Government Service when it appears to be in the public interest."

2. The Bureau of Aeronautics Aviation Circular Letter No. 50-45 contains the following paragraph relative to the use of aeronautical technical publications:

"Paragraph 6. *Distribution to all interested personnel.* In connection with the distribution of aeronautic publications within any activity, it should be borne in mind that technical publications, whether confidential, restricted or unclassified, are issued for use, not only by officer personnel, but also by responsible civilian and enlisted personnel working with or servicing equipment to which the information applies."

3. Disclosure of technical information in this publication may not be made to representatives of foreign governments or nationals except in instances where those foreign governments have been cleared to receive information concerning all equipments, or other technical data covered by this publication.

Instructions Applicable to Army Personnel:

1. This publication is intended for technical aid and education of military and civilian personnel engaged in promoting the war effort. Its maximum distribution and use is therefore encouraged. However, since the publication is "restricted" within the meaning of AR 380-5, the following security regulations will be observed:

a. Members of Armed Forces and civilian employees of War Department will be given access to this publication whenever required to assist in the performance of their official duties (including expansion of their knowledge of AAF equipment, procedures, etc.).

b. Personnel of War Department contractors and subcontractors may be given possession of this publication, on a loan basis, or knowledge of its contents, only when required to assist in the performance of War Department contracts. Releases will be made in accordance with the requirements of T. O. No. 00-5-2.

c. Representatives of other governments will be given possession of this publication, or knowledge of its contents, only in accordance with AAF Letter No. 45-6.

2. This publication is restricted because the information contained in it is restricted. It does not follow that the physical article to which it relates is also restricted. Classification of the matériel or component must be ascertained independently of the classification of this document.

3. Neither this publication nor information contained herein will be communicated to press or public except through Public Relations channels.

―――――― LIST OF REVISED PAGES ISSUED ――――――

NOTE.—A heavy black vertical line, in the outer margin of revised pages (the left margin for left-hand columns, and the right margin for right-hand columns) indicates the extent of the revision. This line is omitted where more than 50 percent of the page is revised. A black horizontal line to the left of page numbers listed below indicates pages revised, added or deleted by current revision. The line is used only on second and subsequent revision.

BuAer

―― ADDITIONAL COPIES OF THIS PUBLICATION MAY BE OBTAINED AS FOLLOWS: ――

AAF ACTIVITIES.—Submit requisitions to the Commanding General, Fairfield Air Service Command, Patterson Field, Fairfield, Ohio, Attention: Publications Distribution Branch, in accordance with AAF Regulation No. 5-9. Also, for details of Technical Order distribution, see T. O. No. 00-25-3.

NAVY ACTIVITIES.—Submit requests to Chief, BuAer, Navy Department, Washington, D. C., Attn.: Publications Section on order form NAVAER-140. For complete listing of available material and details of distribution see Naval Aeronautic Publications Index, NavAer 00-500.

RESTRICTED

RESTRICTED
AN 01-85FA-1

TABLE OF CONTENTS

SECTION I
DESCRIPTION

	Page
1. AIRPLANE	1
2. POWER PLANT	2
a. General	2
b. Power Plant Controls	2
3. FUEL SYSTEM	5
a. Fuel Specification	5
b. Tanks and Capacities	5
c. Fuel System Controls	6
4. OIL SYSTEM	11
a. Oil Specification	11
b. Description	11
c. Oil System Controls	11
5. FLIGHT CONTROLS	11
a. Aileron and Elevator Controls	11
b. Rudder and Brake Control Pedals	11
c. Elevator, Aileron and Rudder Trim Tab Controls	12
6. HYDRAULIC SYSTEM CONTROLS	12
a. General	12
b. Emergency Control—L.G. Extension and Brake System	12
c. Landing Gear Control	12
d. Arresting Hook Control	13
e. Brake Control	13
f. Wing Flaps Control	14
g. Wing Folding Controls	16
h. Rudder Booster By-Pass Control	17
i. Gun Charging Controls	17
7. ELECTRICAL EQUIPMENT CONTROLS	17
8. MISCELLANEOUS CONTROLS AND EQUIPMENT	19
a. Cockpit Hoods	19
b. Pilot's Seat and Harness	19
c. Equipment Controls	20
d. Controls Lock	20
e. Chartboards	20
f. Map Cases	20
g. Relief Tubes	20
h. Anti-blackout Provisions	20

SECTION II
NORMAL OPERATING INSTRUCTIONS

	Page
1. BEFORE ENTERING THE COCKPIT	27
a. Flight Limitations and Restrictions	27
b. Obtain Gross Weight	28
c. Entrance to Airplane	28
2. ON ENTERING THE PILOT'S COCKPIT	28
a. Standard Check For All Flights	28
b. Special Check For Night Flights	28
3. FUEL AND OIL SYSTEM MANAGEMENT	28
a. Operation of Fuel System	28
b. Operation of Oil System	29
4. STARTING ENGINES	29
5. WARM-UP AND GROUND TEST	30
6. SCRAMBLE TAKE-OFF	31
7. TAXIING INSTRUCTIONS	31
8. TAKE-OFF	32
9. ENGINE FAILURE DURING TAKE-OFF	32
10. CLIMB	33
11. GENERAL FLYING CHARACTERISTICS	33
12. STALLS	34
13. SPINS	34
14. PERMISSIBLE ACROBATICS	34
15. DIVING	34
16. NIGHT FLYING	35
17. APPROACH AND LANDING	36
18. STOPPING ENGINES	37
19. BEFORE LEAVING PILOT'S COCKPIT	38
20. MOORING	38

SECTION III
FLIGHT OPERATING DATA

AIRSPEED CORECTION TABLE	39
POWER PLANT CHART	40-41

SECTION IV
EMERGENCY OPERATING INSTRUCTIONS

1. FIRE	43
2. ENGINE FAILURE	43
3. FORCED LANDINGS	43
4. EMERGENCY L. G. OPERATION	44
5. EMERGENCY BRAKE SYSTEM OPERATION	45
6. EMERGENCY ESCAPE FROM AIRPLANE	45
7. EMERGENCY OPERATION OF ELECTRICAL SYSTEM	45
8. EMERGENCY OPERATION OF HYDRAULIC SYSTEM	45
9. EMERGENCY OPERATION OF FUEL SYSTEM	48
10. EMERGENCY OPERATION OF CONTROLS	48

SECTION V
OPERATIONAL EQUIPMENT

1. ARMAMENT	49
a. Gunnery	49
b. Bombing Equipment	51
c. Rocket Projectile Provisions	52
d. Miscellaneous Equipment	52

RESTRICTED

RESTRICTED
AN 01-85FA-1

	Page
2. OXYGEN	53
a. Cylinder and Control	53
b. Regulator	53
c. Preflight Check List	53
d. Operating Instructions	54
3. COMMUNICATION AND ELECTRONIC EQUIPMENT	55
a. Communication Equipment Model F7F-1 Airplane	55
b. Radar Equipment (AN/APS)— Model F7F-1 Airplane	58
c. Communication Equipment Model F7F-2N Airplane	58
d. Radar Equipment—Model F7F-2N Airplane	61
e. Communication Equipment—Model F7F-3 Airplane	61
4. RADAR OPERATOR'S COCKPIT	63

	Page
SECTION VI	
EXTREME WEATHER OPERATION	67
APPENDIX I	
OPERATING CHARTS, TABLES, CURVES AND DIAGRAMS	
Protection Against Gunfire Diagram	69
Take-Off, Climb and Landing Chart	70-71
Dive Angle vs. Angle of Attack	72
Stalling Speed vs. Weight (Power Off)	72
Angle of Attack vs. Indicated Airspeed Curves	73
Operation Flight Strength Diagram	73
Engine Calibration Curves	74-75
APPENDIX II	
Preliminary Supplementary Operating Instructions	76

ILLUSTRATIONS

Figure	Page
1. F7F-1N Airplane—¾ Rear View—R. H. Side	iii
2. F7F-2N Airplane—¾ Front View—L. H. Side (Wings Folded)	iii
3. F7F-3 Airplane—¾ Rear View—R. H. Side	iv
4. F7F-3N Airplane—¾ Front View—R. H. Side	iv
5. Engine Control Quadrant	2
6. Ignition Switch	2
7. Primer and Starter Switches	3
8. Cowl Flaps, Carburetor Air and Oil Cooler Exit Duct Doors Controls	4
9. Propeller Feathering Controls	4
10. Fuel System Controls	6
11. Fuel System Diagram	7
12. Fuel System Control Diagram	8
13. Tank Pressurizing Release Handle	9
14. Fuselage Droppable Tank Manual Release	9
15. Oil System Diagram	10
16. Pedal Adjustment Ratchet	11
17. Tabs Controls Unit	12
18. Landing Gear Control	13
19. Arresting Hook Control	13
20. Wing Flaps Control	14
21. Hydraulic System Diagram	15
22. Wing Folding Control	16
23. Wing Folding Safety Lock Control	16
24. Pilot's Switch Box	17
25. Radar Operator's Cockpit Hood	18
26. Pilot's Cockpit Hood	18
27. Pilot's Heater and Defroster Control	19
28. Pilot's Seat and Harness	19
29. Controls Lock	20
30. Pilot's Main Instrument Panel	21
31. Pilot's Lower and Right Side Instrument Panels	22
32. Pilot's Cockpit—L. H. Side	23
33. Pilot's Cockpit—R. H. Side	24
34. Interior Arrangement Diagram	25
35. Ladder and Steps	28

Figure	Page
36. Airspeed Installation Correction Table	39
37. Power Plant Chart	40-41
38. Landing Gear Emergency Dump Control and Brake Air Gage	44
39. Emergency Brake Control	45
40. Hydraulic Hand Pump and Panel	46
41. Emergency Controls	47
42. Rudder Booster By-Pass Control	48
43. Gun Charging Controls	49
44. Armament Control Switches	49
45. Armament Installation	50
46. Gunsight Light Control	51
47. Manual Bomb Release Handles	51
48. Tow Target Control	52
49. Pilot's Oxygen Cylinder Control	53
50. Oxygen Regulator	53
51. Oxygen Equipment Diagram	54
52. Communicating Controls (F7F-1 Airplane)	56
53. Pilot's Communicating Controls (F7F-2N Airplane)	57
54. Radar Operator's Communicating Controls (F7F-2N Airplane)	58
55. Pilot's Communicating Controls (F7F-3 Airplane)	59
56. VHF Range vs. Altitude	62
57. Radar Operator's Cockpit—L. H. Side	64
58. Radar Operator's Cockpit—R. H. Side	65
59. Radar Operator's Cockpit—Looking Forward	66
60. Protection from Gunfire Diagram	69
61. Take-Off, Climb, and Landing Chart	70-71
62. Flight Operation Instruction Chart	72-73-74
63. Dive Angle vs. Angle of Attack	75
64. Stalling Speed vs. Weight (Power Off)	75
65. Angle of Attack vs. Indicated Airspeed	76
66. Operating Flight Strength Diagram	76
67. Engine Calibration Curves	77-78

RESTRICTED
AN 01-85FA-1

Figure 1—F7F-1N Airplane—¾ Rear View—R. H. Side

Figure 2—F7F-2N Airplane—¾ Front View—L. H. Side (Wings Folded)

RESTRICTED
AN 01-85FA-1

Figure 3—F7F-3 Airplane—¾ Rear View—R. H. Side

Figure 4—F7F-3N Airplane—¾ Front View—R. H. Side

SECTION I
DESCRIPTION

MAIN DIFFERENCES F7F-1N, F7F-2N, F7F-3, F7F-3N AIRPLANES				
DIFFERENCE	F7F-1N	F7F-2N	F7F-3	F7F-3N
EXTERNAL FEATURES	Single Place	Two Place	Single Place. Larger vertical fin.	Two Place. Larger vertical fin. Larger nose fairing.
ENGINE MODEL FUEL TANK CAPACITY (GALLONS)	R2800-22W or -34W Main ....210 Reserve ....150 Aux. ....60 ――― Total ....420 Droppable 600	R2800-22W or -34W Main ....210 Reserve ....105 Aux. ....60 ――― Total ....375 Droppable 600	R2800-34W Main ....210 Reserve ......*185 Aux. ....60 ――― Total ....455 Droppable ......600 *Removable Reserve 80	R2800-34W Main ....210 Reserve ....105 Aux. ....60 ――― Total ....375 Droppable 600

MAXIMUM ARMAMENT	4—.50 Cal.
	  1600 Rounds
	4—20 mm Cannon
	  800 Rounds
	1—2000# Bomb
	2—1000# Bombs
		4—.50 Cal.
		  1600 Rounds
		4—20 mm Cannon
		  800 Rounds
		1—2000# Bomb
		2—1000# Bombs
		8—5" Rockets
			4—.50 Cal.
			  1600 Rounds
			4—20 mm Cannon
			  800 Rounds
			1—2000# Bomb
			2—1000# Bombs
			8—5" Rockets
				4—20 mm Cannon
				  800 Rounds
				1—2000# Bomb
				2—1000# Bombs
				8—5" Rockets

STRUCTURE			Material change (To permit maneuvers with increased wt.)	Material change (To permit maneuvers with increased wt.)
COMMUNICATING EQUIPMENT	Radar—Pilot Operated	Radar (two man)	Day Fighter Equipment	SCR-720 Radar (two man)
NORMAL GROSS WEIGHT	21400	21700		

1. AIRPLANE.

The F7F series airplanes are twin engine, folding, high mid-wing fighters (class VF) equipped with tricycle landing gear and designed to operate from aircraft carriers and from regular landing fields. The landing gear, arresting hook, wing flaps, wing folding, brakes, rudder booster and gun chargers are operated hydraulically. The oil cooler duct doors, carburetor air duct doors and cowl flaps are operated electrically.

The F7F-1N model (single seater) carries a normal fuel load of 420 gallons in three self-sealing cells in the fuselage.

The F7F-2N model (two seater—second cockpit for navigator-radar operator) carries a normal fuel load of 375 gallons in three self-sealing cells. A spare kit, made up of a removable self-sealing tank of 80 gallons capacity with the necessary lines and fittings is supplied for use when the second cockpit is not manned.

The F7F-3 model (single seater—80 gallon removable tank in second cockpit) carries a normal fuel load of 455 gallons is four-self sealing cells in the fuselage.

The F7F-3N model (two seater—refer to F7F-2N above) carries a normal fuel load of 375 gallons in three self-sealing cells. The four .50 cal. fuselage machine guns are eliminated in this model because of the radar installation.

The armament, except as noted above, consists of four .50 cal. machine guns installed in the forward section of the fuselage and four 20 mm cannon installed in the wing inner panels. Provision is made to install eight five inch rockets, four under each wing outer panel on airplane Serial No. 80294 and subsequent. A gun camera is installed in the leading edge of the left wing. Three bomb racks and fittings are installed, one in the fuselage and one under each wing inner panel.

Normal Weight—F7F-1N 21400
            F7F-2N 21700
            F7F-3
            F7F-3N
Span (Wings Spread) .... 51' 6"
     (Wings Folded) .... 32' 2"
Fuselage Length .... 44' 8½"
Height (Over Tail at Rest)
  Serial Nos. 80259-80364 .... 14' 6½"
  Serial No. 80365 and subsequent .... 15' 8½"

2. POWER PLANT.

a. GENERAL. — F7F-1N and F7F-2N airplanes, Serial Nos. 80259-80358 inclusive are equipped with R2800-22W single stage, two speed, supercharged engines. F7F-3 airplanes, Serial No. 80359 and subsequent are equipped with R2800-34W engines. These engines are installationally interchangeable—the -34W model has an improved high blower performance.

Figure 5—Engine Control Quadrant

Figure 6—Ignition Switch

Full feathering, three bladed, Hamilton Standard Hydromatic propellers are used in both installations. Refer to Section III for operating instruction for each engine.

b. POWER PLANT CONTROLS.

(1) CONTROL QUADRANT.—The quadrant, located on the left hand side of the cockpit, carries the following controls:

(a) BOOST CONTROL (THROTTLE) LEVERS.—Large handles (paired) on top of quadrant. Inboard lever (right engine) carries microphone switch button. Airplanes not equipped with manifold pressure regulators have conventional throttles.

1. Move FORWARD to OPEN.
2. Move AFT to CLOSE.

In airplanes equipped with manifold pressure regulators, the throttle levers become "boost control" levers, and are used to set the regulators to maintain the manifold pressure desired. Once set in this manner, the regulators automatically control the carburetor throttles to maintain constant manifold pressure at any altitude below critical altitude. Above critical altitude, manifold pressure will vary just as it does at full throttle when a conventional throttle is used. The pilot is relieved of controlling manifold pressure as he changes airspeed, altitude or rpm, except that he must observe manifold pressure limits when setting the boost control levers and must guard against excessive manifold pressure when rpm is reduced. Forward movement of the boost control levers increases manifold pressure settings, aft motion reduces them. No harm will result from advancing the boost control levers to full forward position for take-off or military power, provided the water injection switch is "OFF", because the maximum manifold pressure available is controlled by the manifold pressure regulators.

With manifold pressure regulators installed, the throttle levers are connected to the regulators which in turn are connected to the throttles on the carburetors. The pilot sets the regulators for the desired manifold pressure through movement of the throttle levers in the cockpit, and the regulators by hydraulic servo operation of the carburetor maintain this setting for him. To do this, the regulators obtain hydraulic power from the main engine oil pressure. As a safety precaution the unit is so designed that in the event of failure of the oil supply to the regulator the pilot will have manual control of the throttle below 47" Hg. in high blower and 41" Hg. in low blower at 2800 rpm.

The manifold pressure limits allowed by the regulators on R-2800-22W engines are as follows:

Low Blower—Military Power—53.5" Hg.
High Blower—Military Power—48.5" Hg.
Low Blower—Combat Power—65.0" Hg.
High Blower—Combat Power—60.0" Hg.

The manifold pressure limits allowed by the regulators on R-2800-34W engines are as follows:

Low Blower—Military Power—54" Hg.
High Blower—Military Power—49.5" Hg.
Low Blower—Combat Power—65" Hg.
High Blower—Combat Power—60" Hg.

It should be noted that when making a military or rated power climb, the pilot can shift from low to high blower and the regulator will automatically reset the manifold pressure to the required value without requiring a change in the position of the boost (throttle) controls.

(b) MIXTURE LEVERS. — Marked (M) (paired) on inboard side.

1. Move FORWARD to AUTO LEAN, and FULL FORWARD to AUTO RICH.

2. FULL AFT to extreme aft sector (red) to IDLE CUT-OFF. Check for proper setting in AUTO LEAN and AUTO RICH.

(c) PROPELLER LEVERS. — Marked (P) (paired) aft of throttle levers.

1. Move UP to DECREASE RPM.

2. Move DOWN to INCREASE RPM.

(d) VERNIER CONTROL.—Knobs adjacent to levers, for synchronization.

1. Rotate CLOCKWISE to DECREASE RPM.

2. Rotate COUNTER-CLOCKWISE to INCREASE RPM.

(e) SUPERCHARGER LEVER. — On small quadrant outboard of propeller levers (one lever shifts both engines).

1. Move UP for HIGH BLOWER.

2. Move DOWN for LOW BLOWER.

(2) IGNITION SWITCH (BOTH ENGINES).—The switch is located on the left hand side panel.

(a) Master control — push-pull handle—push to ON—pull to OFF (CUT).

(b) Separate switch handles for each engine—three positions of each—L. Magneto, R. Magneto, both.

(3) PRIMER AND STARTER CONTROLS.

(a) GENERAL.—The primer and starter control switches are located on the top of the electrical distribution panel, primer switch forward, starter switch (with safety cap) aft.

Note

F7F-1 airplanes, serial Nos. 80259, 80260 and 80261 have Type III BR cartridge starters on the engines. The cartridge is fired electrically when the switch is moved to ON. The starter breeches are accessible for loading through the main wheel wells. Eight spare cartridges for each engine are stowed in containers adjacent to the starter breeches.

A direct cranking electric starter is installed on each engine and is controlled by a starter switch on the pilot's switch box on the right hand side of the cockpit. The switch when closed energizes a relay which in turn allows current to operate the starter.

(b) PRIMER SWITCH — (FORWARD SWITCH).—Flick intermittently to prime.

To LEFT for LEFT ENGINE.

To RIGHT for RIGHT ENGINE.

(c) STARTER SWITCH—(AFT SWITCH).—Equipped with safety cap—lift safety cap and hold switch ON.

To LEFT for LEFT ENGINE.

To RIGHT for RIGHT ENGINE.

Figure 7—Primer and Starter Switches

Note

Since ignition booster is energized only while switch is ON, hold starter switch ON until engine turns under own power, to utilize booster facilities.

CAUTION

1.

Continuous cranking must not exceed one minute. If the engine does not start, open the starter switch and allow the starter to cool for at least one minute. If the engine fails to start after the second attempt, check the engine.

2.

When the airplane battery is used as the source of power for starting, the engine must not be cranked continuously more than 30 seconds with a 30 second rest period before the next cranking.

(4) COWL FLAPS CONTROL.

(a) GENERAL.—The cowl flaps control switch is located on the upper left side of the lower control panel.

(b) OPERATION.

1. Switch UP—AUTOMATIC operation.
2. Switch to CENTER—OFF.
3. Switch DOWN to LEFT—MANUAL operation—cowl flaps OPEN.
4. Switch DOWN to RIGHT—MANUAL operation—cowl flaps CLOSED.

Movement of the cowl flaps is effected by electric screw jacks. When the switch is in AUTOMATIC, the motors operating the screw jacks are con-

Figure 8—Cowl Flaps, Carburetor Air and Oil Cooler Exit Duct Doors Controls

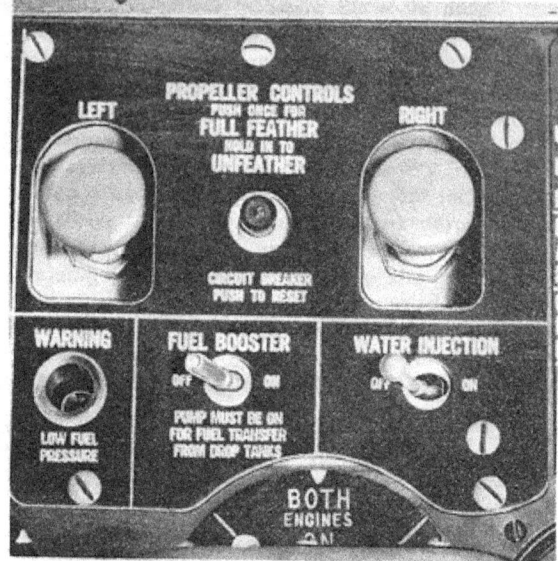

Figure 9—Propeller Feathering Controls

trolled by thermostats; as cylinder head temperatures increase, the cowl flaps are opened and as temperatures decrease the flaps close. The OFF position is to be used only in case of malfunctioning of the system or damage, and when the engine is stopped on the ground. In case of malfunctioning of the thermostats, or for other reasons, the cowl flaps can be operated by the pilot (switch in MANUAL) in accordance with instrument readings and visual inspection of the flap settings.

Note

To obtain intermediate settings, manually —switch to MANUAL, OPEN or CLOSED, as desired, then switch to OFF position when desired flap position is reached.

(5) CARBURETOR AIR CONTROL.

(a) GENERAL.— The carburetor air control switch is located on the lower panel above the oil cooler exit door and cowl flap control switches.

(b) OPERATION.

1. Switch UP to RIGHT—DIRECT (air under ram through duct from leading edge).
2. Switch LEFT—ALTERNATE (heated air from engine compartment).
3. Switch to CENTER—OFF.

The normal carburetor air (for each engine) is taken from an opening in the wing leading edge outboard of the nacelle and carried inboard through a duct in the leading edge and down into the carburetor. A door or butterfly valve operated by an electric screw jack is installed in the duct; when the switch is set at DIRECT, the door is horizontal and acts as a vane for air to the carburetor; when the switch is set at ALTERNATE, the door is swung to

block this source and a secondary door in the bottom of the duct is opened by engine suction to admit air from the engine accessory compartment. A small backfire relief door, installed in the butterfly valve plate, will open under the force of a backfire, when operating in ALTERNATE (duct blocked off). The OFF position of the switch is to be used only when the system is damaged or when the engines are stopped on the ground.

Note

Filtered air setting of switch on early models is inoperable—filters are not installed.

(6) PROPELLER FEATHERING CONTROLS.

(a) GENERAL.—The propeller feathering controls are located at the top center of the lower control panel (two controls—one each engine).

1. To FULL FEATHER—PUSH CONTROL IN AND RELEASE.

2. To UNFEATHER—PUSH CONTROL IN AND HOLD UNTIL RPM REACHES 1200, THEN RELEASE.

A circuit breaker reset button is located between these controls and should be checked for IN position. The controls operate electric pumps located in the nacelles which generate oil pressure to feather the blades. The oil supply is drawn through special lines from the oil tanks. Accumulators of 515 cu. in. capacity are installed in the propeller feathering oil lines to maintain pressure.

CAUTION

On unfeathering cycle, if button is held too long, propeller will feather again.

(7) WATER INJECTION SYSTEM CONTROL.

(a) The single toggle switch for control of the pumps for the anti-detonant equipment (one system for each engine) is located on the lower instrument and control panel, to the right of the fuel booster pump switch.

1. Move switch to RIGHT to ON.

2. Move switch to LEFT to OFF.

WARNING

To prevent water injection system pump from burning out, set switch to OFF as soon as fluid supply is exhausted.

Supply sufficient for five minutes (approx.) operation. Sharp drop in manifold pressure indicates that fluid supply has been exhausted.

Note

Water injection systems have been made inoperable in airplanes lacking manifold pressure regulators.

(b) The maximum tank capacity is 16 gallons (each tank). Each system consists of a tank, a pump, a water regulator, tubing and electric lines installed in the engine nacelle. When the switch is set at ON, fluid (Spec. AN-A-18) is pumped from the tank forward to the regulator unit mounted on the engine. A limit switch, installed on the throttle, opens solenoids to allow the fluid to flow to the blowers in the engines when the throttle is moved to FULL FORWARD.

3. FUEL SYSTEM.

a. FUEL SPECIFICATION AN-F-28.

b. TANKS AND CAPACITIES.—The normal fuel supply is carried in three (four) self-sealing cells installed in the fuselage. The MAIN and RESERVE cells are installed in the fuselage tank section aft of the pilot's cockpit—the AUXILIARY cell is installed in the nose; these three cells are similar in design, each being made up of a self-sealing liner supported in a soft hammock bolted to an aluminum alloy top-plate assembly. The fourth cell (80 gal. removable reserve) is a rigid cell installed to the reserve cell (day fighters only).

The normal fuel supply of the F7F-1N airplanes, Serial No. 80259 to No. 80293 inclusive, is 420 U.S. gals. (350 Imp. gals.); the normal fuel supply of the F7F-2N and -3N airplanes, (night fighters) is 375 U.S. gals. (312.5 Imp. gals.). The reduction in fuel supply in these airplanes is due to the introduction of the second cockpit over the reserve tank. A removable reserve tank of 80 U.S. gals. (66.5 Imp. gals.) capacity may be installed over the reserve tank if the second cockpit is not manned, increasing the normal fuel supply to 455 U.S. gals. (380 Imp. gals.). This tank is a standard installation for F7F-3 airplanes (day fighters).

TANK CAPACITIES

F7F-1N	U.S. Gals.	Imp. Gals.
Main	210	175
Reserve	150	125
Auxiliary	60	50
Total	420	350
F7F-2 and -3 (Day Fighters)		
Main	210	175
Reserve (Includes 80 gal. removable)	185	154
Auxiliary	60	50
Total	455	379
F7F-2N and -3N		
Main	210	175
Reserve	105	87.5
Auxiliary	60	50
Total	375	312.5

Note

Auxiliary tanks are not installed in airplanes Serial No. 80259 and no. 80260. Therefore the normal fuel load in these airplanes is 360 U.S. gals. (300 Imp. gals.)

Figure 10—Fuel System Controls

c. FUEL SYSTEM CONTROLS.—A de-fueling unit, strainer, electric auxiliary pump, tank selector and engine selector valves are installed in the fuselage below, and aft of the pilot's cockpit.

(1) FUEL QUANTITY GAGE.—Located on the right side of the pilot's lower control panel; has three indicators (main, reserve and auxiliary tank loads). The needle on the reserve tank dial registers FULL (185 gals.) only when the removable tank is installed.

(2) TANK SELECTOR VALVE.—The tank selector valve control handle is located on the lower control panel, and has six settings:

(a) Pointer UP—MAIN tank.

(b) Pointer UP to LEFT—RESERVE tank.

(c) Pointer DOWN to LEFT—AUXILIARY tank.

WARNING

This auxiliary tank is not installed on airplanes Serial No. 80259 and no. 80260. Do not use this setting or fuel supply will be cut off.

(d) Pointer DOWN — FUSELAGE DROPPABLE tank (150 or 300 U.S. gals., 120 or 240 Imp. gals.).

(e) Pointer DOWN to RIGHT — WING DROPPABLE tanks (300 U.S. gals., 240 Imp. gals.).

Note

A stop is installed on the dial to prevent the pointer being set on droppable tank settings when these tanks are not installed.

(f) Pointer UP to RIGHT—fuel supply OFF.

A stop is installed on the dial between the WING DROPPABLE and OFF position. The pointer must be returned through the other settings.

(3) WING DROP TANKS SELECTOR SWITCH.—A three position toggle switch—LEFT, RIGHT and OFF is installed on the pilot's lower instrument panel below the tank and engine selector valves. A circuit breaker reset button is installed on the inboard face of the pilot's switch box forward of the recognition light switches. When the tank selector valve is set at WING DROP TANKS and the auxiliary pump is set at ON, this switch permits the use of fuel from the left or right drop tank as desired.

CAUTION

Since there is no indication of the amount of fuel remaining in a wing drop tank it is important that the pilot switch from an almost empty tank before starving the engines. Refer to Flight Operation Instruction Charts, Appendix, for the rate of consumption of Fuel for specific conditions.

(4) ENGINE SELECTOR VALVE.—The engine selector valve control is located on the lower control panel to the right of the tank selector valve.

(a) Pointer UP—BOTH engines.

(b) Pointer LEFT—LEFT engine only.

(c) Pointer RIGHT—RIGHT engine only.

(d) Pointer DOWN—OFF.

CAUTION

The fuel system is not a cross feed type, and the selector valve is installed to cut off flow to a damaged engine.

The engine selector valve should be kept on BOTH except in cases of engine failure, when fuel flow must be cut off from the inoperative engine, or, in testing.

(5) ELECTRIC AUXILIARY FUEL PUMP.—The auxiliary fuel pump switch is located on the lower panel above the selector valve controls.

(a) Switch to LEFT—OFF.

(b) Switch to RIGHT—ON.

The pump is located in the tank section and acts as a booster to the engine driven pumps. The warning light glows when pressure drops below 17 psi.

Operate the auxiliary pump to build up initial fuel pressure to start the engines, to maintain fuel pressure at altitude, during critical periods of fuel system operation such as take-off, high power operation, landing, droppable tanks, (fuel transfer), changing tanks and for emergency in case of failure of the engine driven pumps.

CAUTION

Operate the auxiliary fuel pump when changing tanks, to prevent loss of fuel pressure.

(6) FUEL TRANSFER SYSTEM.—The transfer system replaces fuel used from the reserve tank during warm-up and take-off, with fuel from the droppable tanks. The installation consists of a line from the

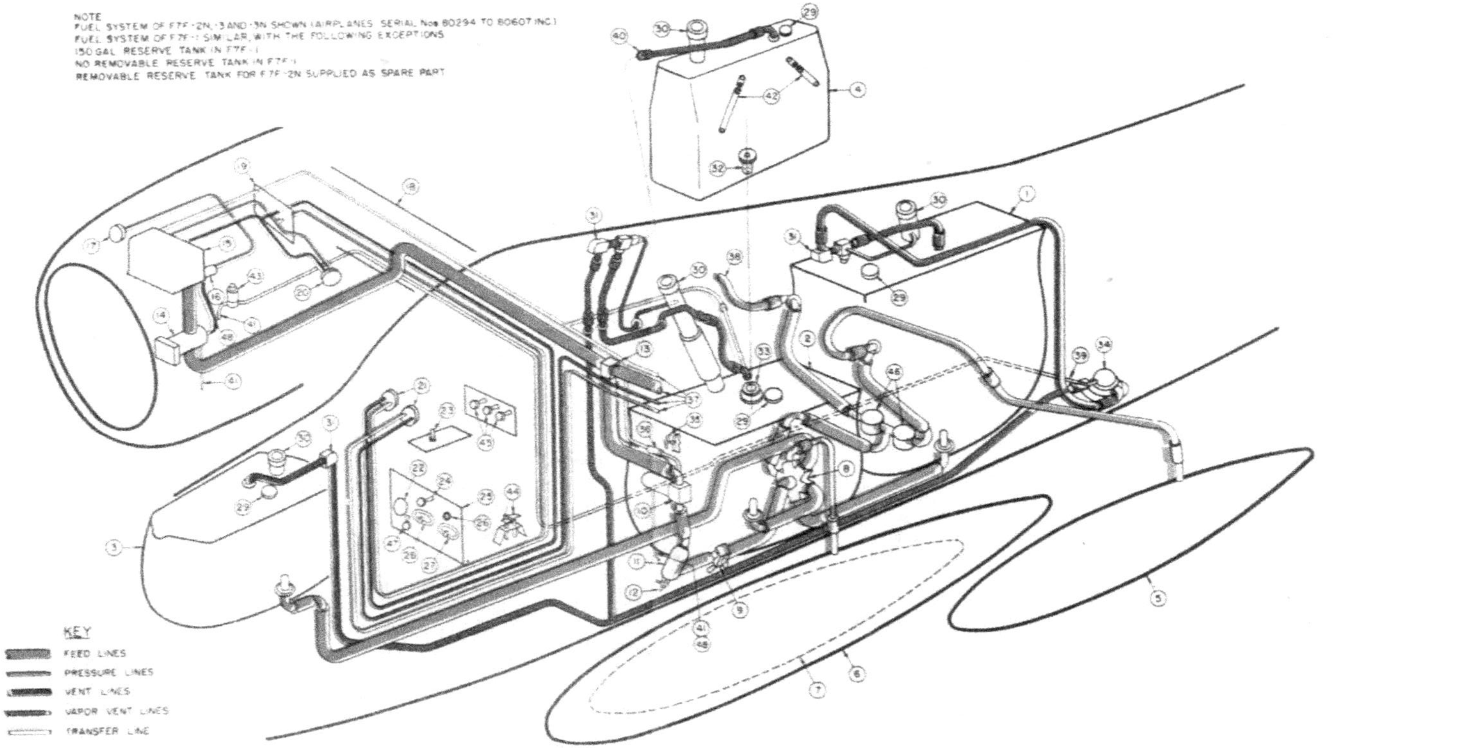

RESTRICTED
AN 01-85FA-1

NOTE
FUEL SYSTEM OF F7F-2N, 3 AND 3N SHOWN (AIRPLANES SERIAL Nos 80294 TO 80607 INCL)
FUEL SYSTEM OF F7F-1 SIMILAR WITH THE FOLLOWING EXCEPTIONS:
150 GAL RESERVE TANK IN F7F-1
NO REMOVABLE RESERVE TANK IN F7F-1
REMOVABLE RESERVE TANK FOR F7F-2N SUPPLIED AS SPARE PART

KEY
■■■ FEED LINES
■■■ PRESSURE LINES
■■■ VENT LINES
■■■ VAPOR VENT LINES
■■■ TRANSFER LINE

1. Main Tank
2. Reserve Tank
3. Auxiliary Tank
4. Removable Reserve Tank
5. 150 Gal. Wing Droppable Tank
6. 300 Gal. Fuselage Droppable Tank
7. 150 Gal. Fuselage Droppable Tank
8. Tank Selector Valve
9. De-Fueling Unit
10. Electric Auxiliary Fuel Pump
11. System Fuel Strainer
12. Strainer Drain Valve
13. Engine Selector Valve
14. Engine Driven Fuel Pump (2)
15. Carburetor Header
16. Primer Solenoid
17. Engine Primer Unit
18. Forward Face Wing Box Beam
19. Quick Disconnect Block
20. Fuel Pressure Warning Unit
21. Engine Gage Units
22. Fuel Quantity Gage
23. Primer Switch
24. Auxiliary Pump Switch
25. Lower Instrument and Control Panel
26. Fuel Pressure Warning Light
27. Tank Selector Valve Control Handle
28. Engine Selector Valve Control Handle
29. Fuel Level Transmitter
30. Tank Fillerneck
31. Vent Line Check Relief Valve (3)
32. Removable Reserve Tank Connector Fitting
33. Reserve Tank Connector Fitting
34. Tank Pressurizing Unit
35. Pressurizing Release Handle
36. Fuel Transfer Solenoid
37. Lines to Left Nacelle
38. Line to Right Wing Droppable Tank
39. Tank Pressurizing Line to Manifold Cut-off
40. Removable Tank Vent Line Connector
41. Drain Line
42. Attaching Straps—Removable Tank
43. Manifold Cut-off Valve
44. Droppable Tanks Manual Release Handles
45. Bomb-Droppable Tank Selector Switches
46. Wing Drop Tank Solenoid Valves
47. Switches for Wing Drop Tank Solenoid Valves
48. Pump Vent Lines

Figure 11—Fuel System Diagram

RESTRICTED

RESTRICTED
AN 01-85FA-1

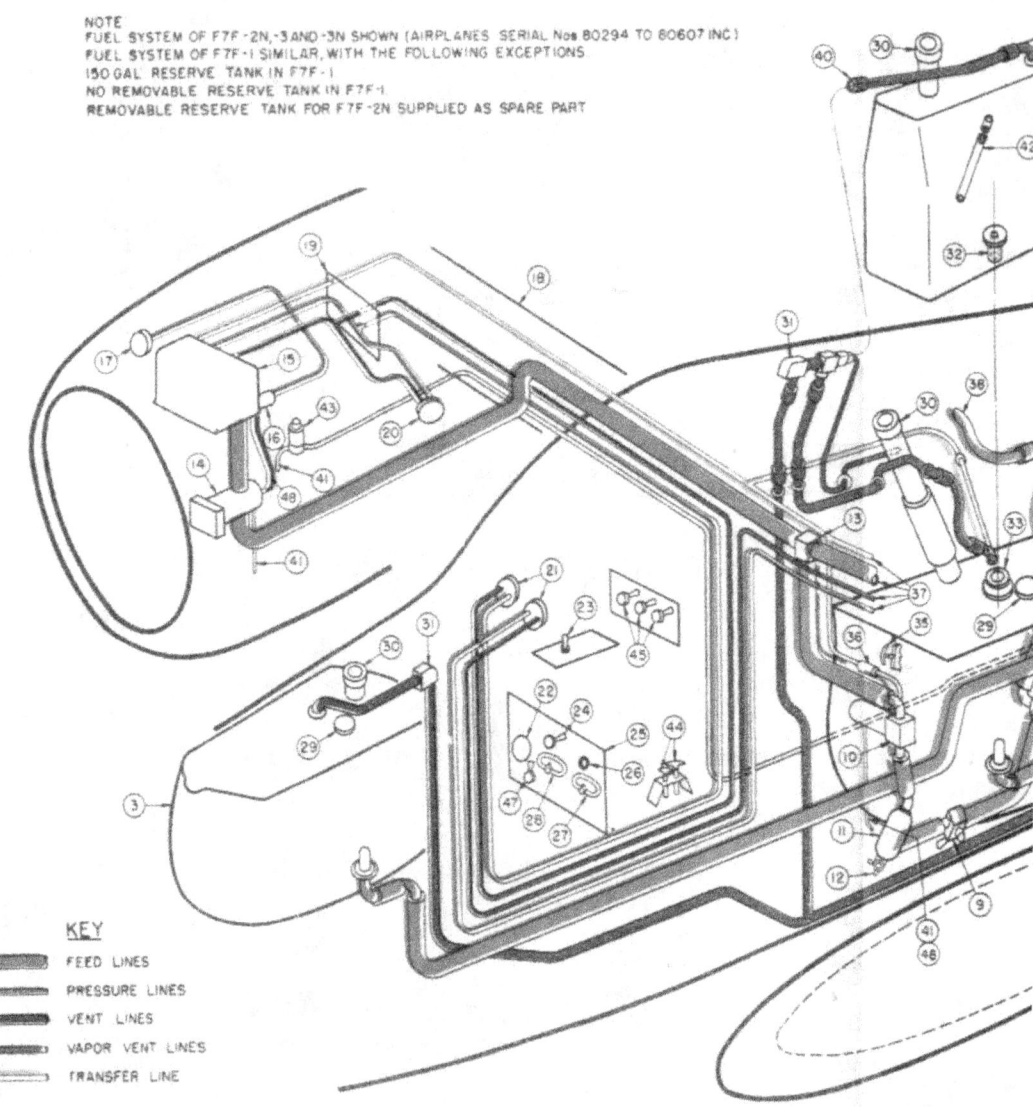

NOTE
FUEL SYSTEM OF F7F-2N,-3 AND -3N SHOWN (AIRPLANES SERIAL Nos 80294 TO 80607 INC)
FUEL SYSTEM OF F7F-1 SIMILAR, WITH THE FOLLOWING EXCEPTIONS.
150 GAL RESERVE TANK IN F7F-1
NO REMOVABLE RESERVE TANK IN F7F-1
REMOVABLE RESERVE TANK FOR F7F-2N SUPPLIED AS SPARE PART

KEY
- FEED LINES
- PRESSURE LINES
- VENT LINES
- VAPOR VENT LINES
- TRANSFER LINE

1. Main Tank
2. Reserve Tank
3. Auxiliary Tank
4. Removable Reserve Tank
5. 150 Gal. Wing Droppable Tank
6. 300 Gal. Fuselage Droppable Tank
7. 150 Gal. Fuselage Droppable Tank
8. Tank Selector Valve
9. De-Fueling Unit
10. Electric Auxiliary Fuel Pump
11. System Fuel Strainer
12. Strainer Drain Valve
13. Engine Selector Valve
14. Engine Driven Fuel Pump (2)
15. Carburetor Header
16. Primer Solenoid
17. Engine Primer Unit
18. Forward Face Wing Box Beam
19. Quick Disconnect Block
20. Fuel Pressure Warning Unit
21. Engine Gage Units
22. Fuel Quantity Gage
23. Primer Switch
24. Auxiliary Pump Switch
25. Lower Instrume
26. Fuel Pressure
27. Tank Selector
28. Engine Sele
29. Fuel Level Tra
30. Tank Fillernec
31. Vent Line Che
32. Removable Re
33. Reserve Tank
34. Tank Pressuri
35. Pressurizing R
36. Fuel Transfer

Figure 11—Fuel System Diagram
RESTRICTED

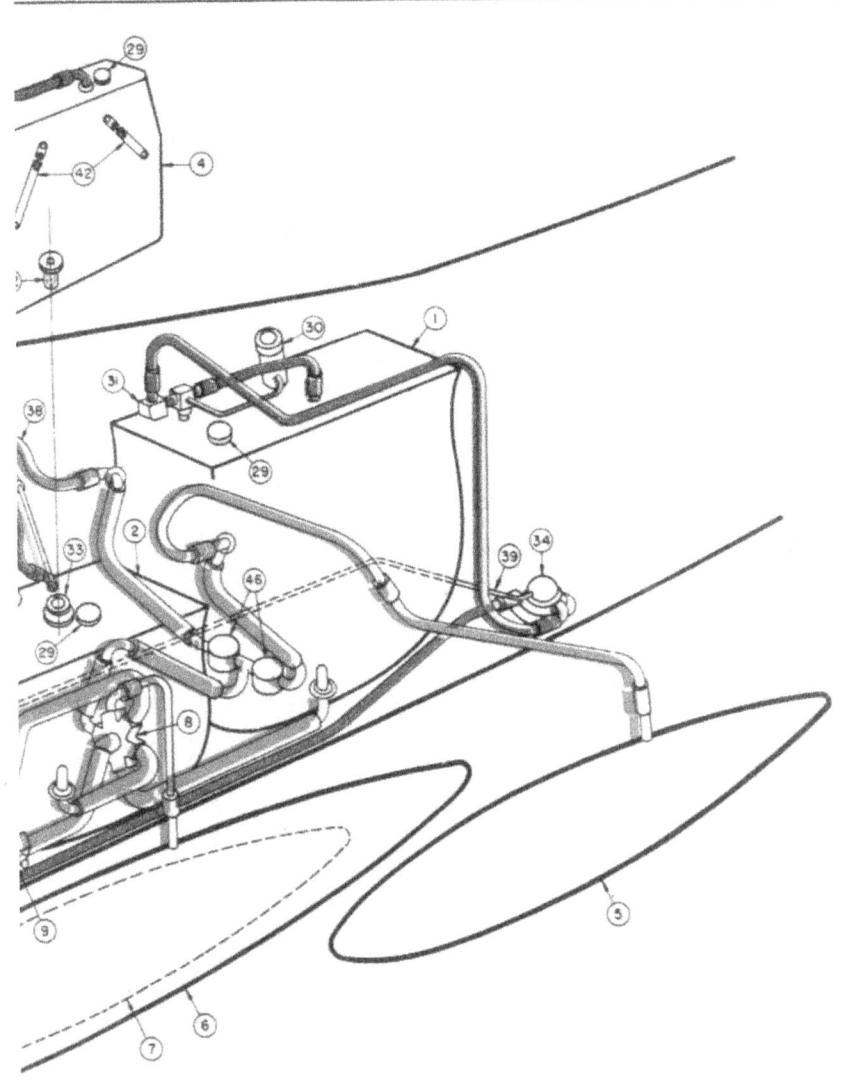

nstrument and Control Panel
essure Warning Light
elector Valve Control Handle
 Selector Valve Control Handle
vel Transmitter
illerneck
ine Check Relief Valve (3)
able Reserve Tank Connector Fitting
 Tank Connector Fitting
'ressurizing Unit
izing Release Handle
ansfer Solenoid

37. Lines to Left Nacelle
38. Line to Right Wing Droppable Tank
39. Tank Pressurizing Line to Manifold Cut-off
40. Removable Tank Vent Line Connector
41. Drain Line
42. Attaching Straps—Removable Tank
43. Manifold Cut-off Valve
44. Droppable Tanks Manual Release Handles
45. Bomb-Droppable Tank Selector Switches
46. Wing Drop Tank Solenoid Valves
47. Switches for Wing Drop Tank Solenoid Valves
48. Pump Vent Lines

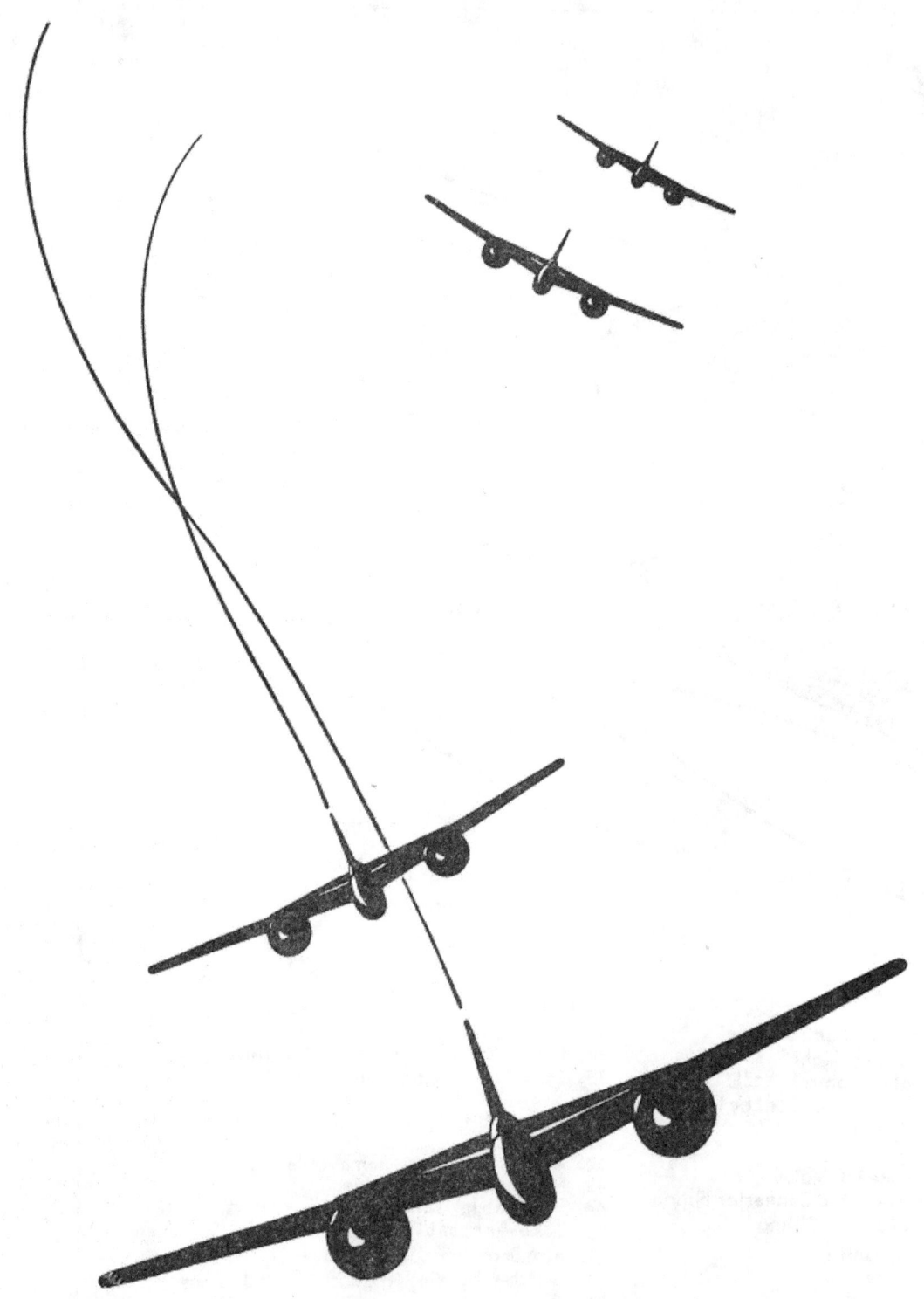

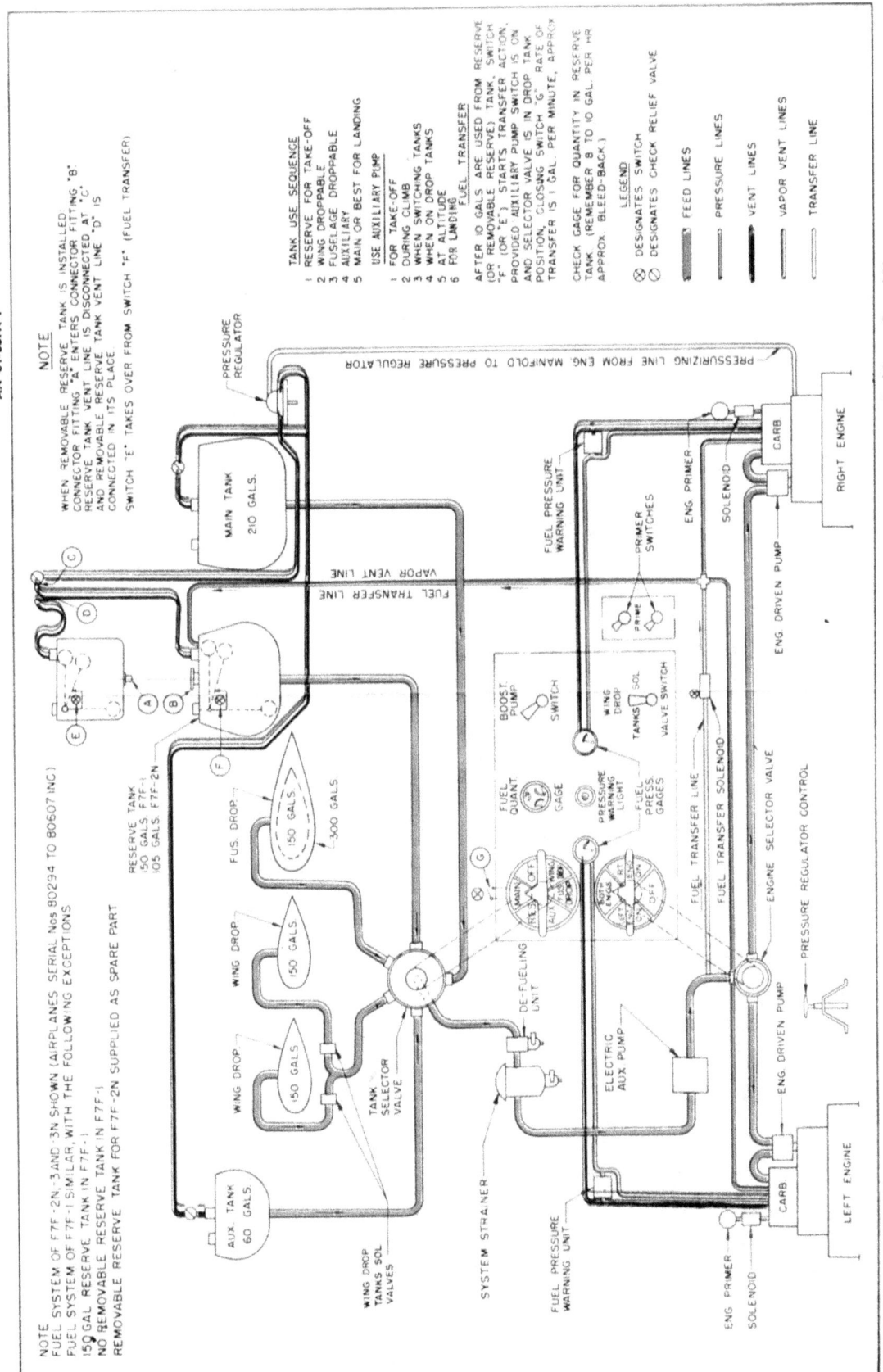

Figure 12—Fuel System Control Diagram

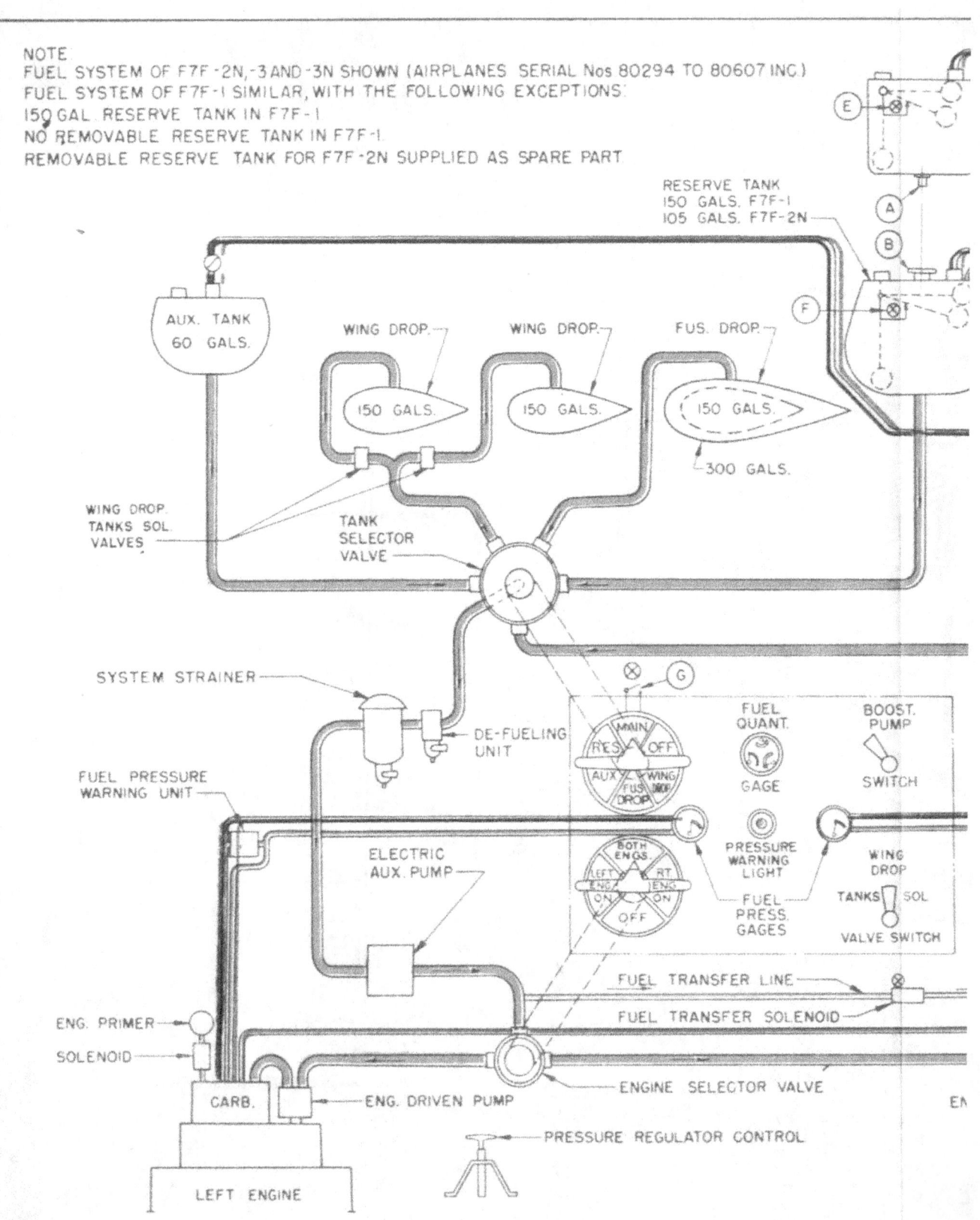

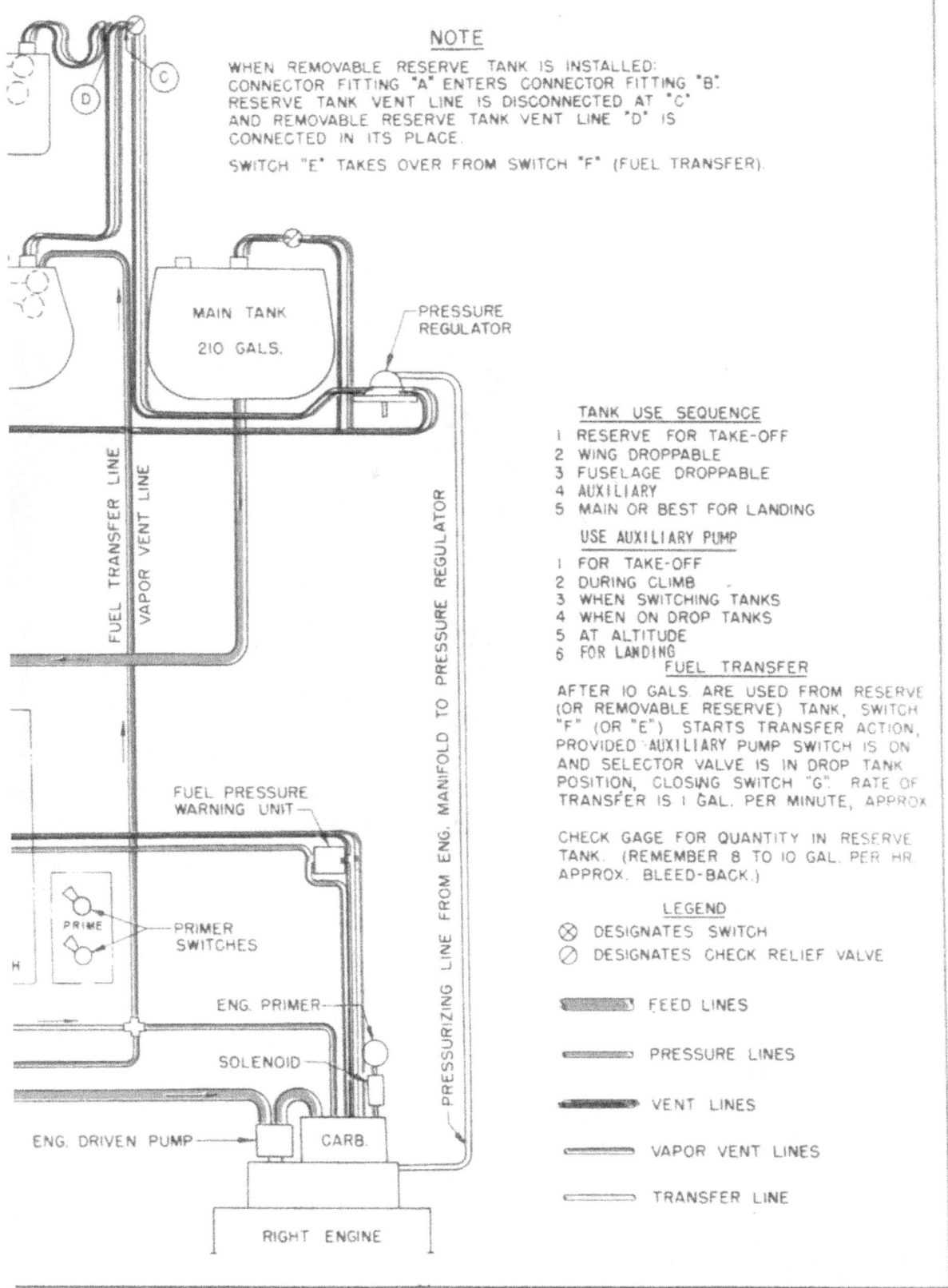

automatic switch on the selector valve, an automatic switch on the liquid level indicator assembly on the reserve tank, a solenoid valve, and electric wiring. When the selector valve handle is set at FUSELAGE OR WING DROPPABLE (if WING DROPPABLE setting is used, WING DROP TANK selector switch must be set to LEFT OR RIGHT, as desired), and the auxiliary pump switch is set at ON, this solenoid valve opens, and fuel flows from the strainer to the reserve tank until the tank is filled, when the level indicator float actuates the switch to break the circuit. If there is no space in the reserve tank for additional fuel, the level indicator switch will keep the circuit open, and the solenoid will not operate.

Note

Stops are installed on the face of the tank selector valve when no droppable tanks are carried to prevent setting the valve in either of these positions.

(7) TANK PRESSURIZING SYSTEM.— The pressure dome for the standard pressurizing system is located in the fuselage. The system maintains a pressure differential above atmospheric pressure at altitudes above 9,000 feet, effected by a sylphon actuated by manifold pressure. Relief, regulator, and cut-off valves are installed in the system. The manual override or cut-off valve control is a "T" handle located on the cockpit bulkhead, to the left of the seat.

PULL "T" handle to "RELEASE."
PUSH "T" handle for "PRESSURE."

CAUTION

Pull "T" handle to "RELEASE" pressure if tank is damaged.

(8) DROPPABLE TANK RELEASE CONTROLS.—Fittings for the installation of one fuselage and two wing droppable tanks (600 gals. total capac-

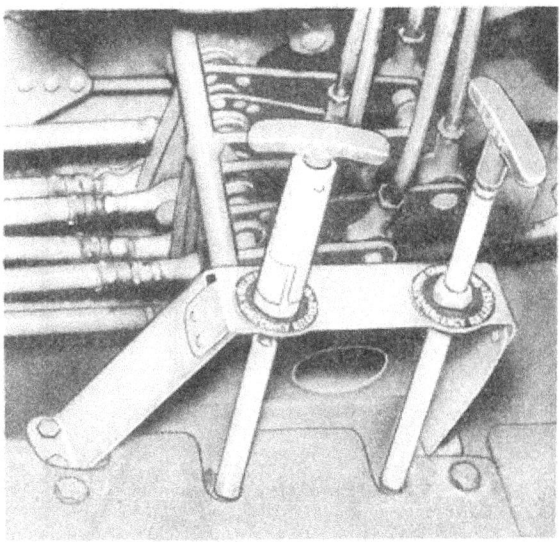

Figure 14—Droppable Tank Manual Release Handles

ity) are provided in both models.

(a) ELECTRICAL.—The tank release switches (left, right, center) and armament master switch (with safety cap) are located on the upper left hand corner of the main instrument panel; the thumb trigger is on the stick grip.

(b) TO RELEASE DROPPABLE TANKS ELECTRICALLY.

1. Fuel tank selector valve to MAIN, RESERVE, or AUXILIARY.

2. For fuselage tank only, pull manual release handle UP, until stopped, rotate ¼ turn clockwise.

3. Armament master switch to ON.

4. Switch for tank (or tanks) to be dropped—DOWN to RELEASE.

5. Press thumb trigger switch on top of stick grip.

(c) TO RELEASE FUSELAGE TANK (ONLY) MANUALLY.—Aft release "T" handle located on cockpit floor below engine control quadrant.

1. Fuel tank selector valve to MAIN, RESERVE, AUXILIARY or WING DROPPABLE.

2. Pull handle UP, until stopped by stud. ROTATE CLOCKWISE ¼ turn approximately, then PULL UP sharply.

Note

The manual release may be used after the electrical release, to insure release of the fuselage tank.

(d) TO RELEASE WING TANKS MANUALLY (JETTISON).—Forward release "T" handle located on cockpit floor below engine control quadrant.

1. Fuel tank selector valve to MAIN, RESERVE, AUXILIARY or FUSELAGE DROPPABLE.

2. Pull handle UP sharply.

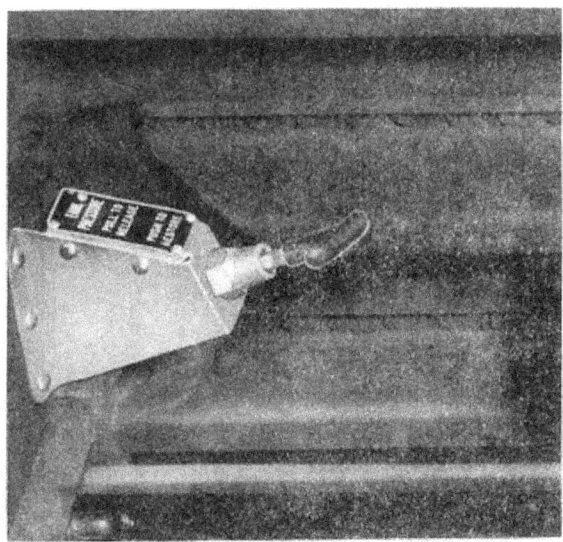

Figure 13—Tank Pressurizing Release Handle

Section I
AN 01-85FA-1

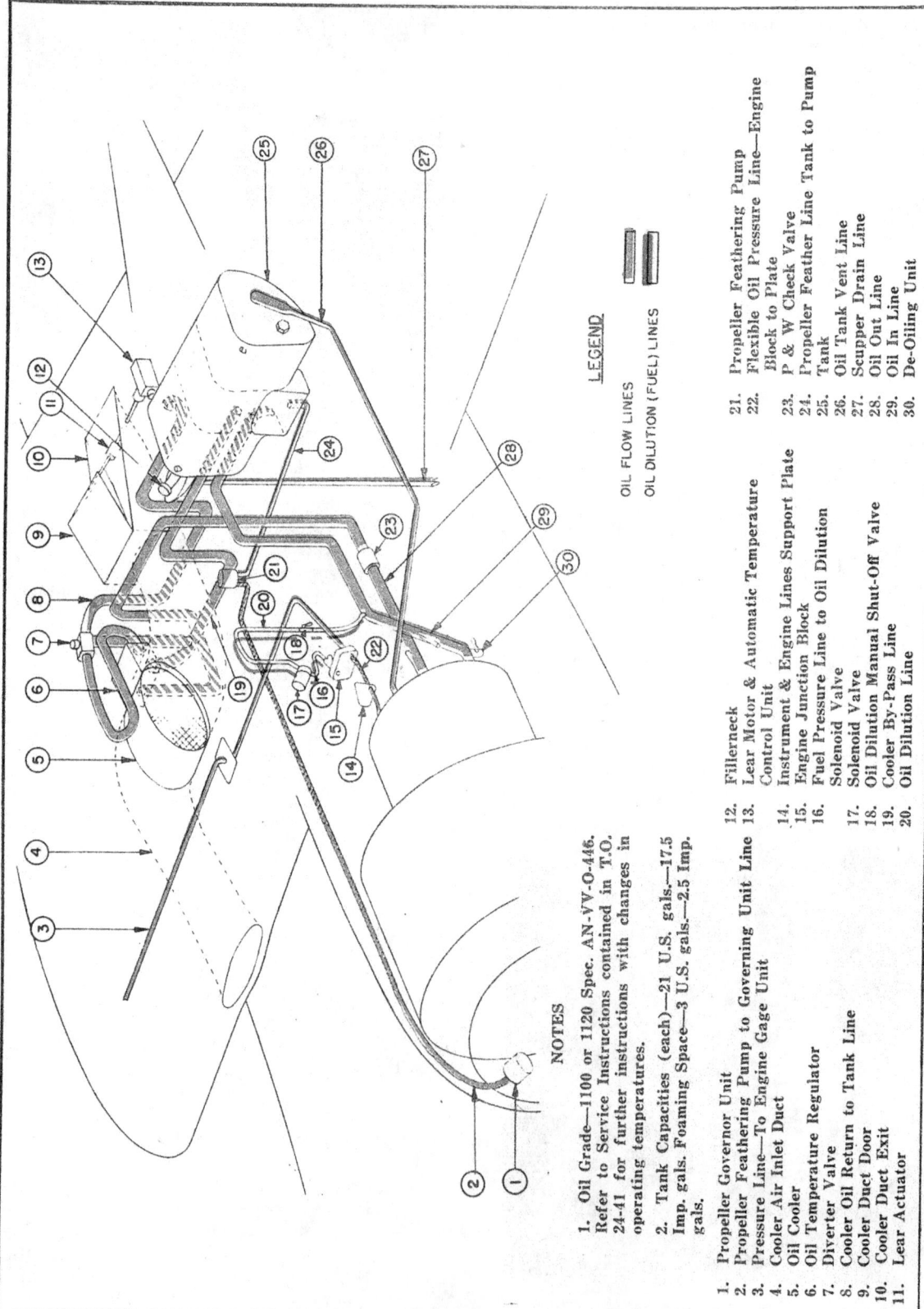

NOTES

1. Oil Grade—1100 or 1120 Spec. AN-VV-O-446. Refer to Service Instructions contained in T.O. 24-41 for further instructions with changes in operating temperatures.
2. Tank Capacities (each)—21 U.S. gals.—17.5 Imp. gals. Foaming Space—3 U.S. gals.—2.5 Imp. gals.

1. Propeller Governor Unit
2. Propeller Feathering Pump to Governing Unit Line
3. Pressure Line—To Engine Gage Unit
4. Cooler Air Inlet Duct
5. Oil Cooler
6. Oil Temperature Regulator
7. Diverter Valve
8. Cooler Oil Return to Tank Line
9. Cooler Duct Door
10. Cooler Duct Exit
11. Lear Actuator
12. Fillerneck
13. Lear Motor & Automatic Temperature Control Unit
14. Instrument & Engine Lines Support Plate
15. Engine Junction Block
16. Fuel Pressure Line to Oil Dilution Solenoid Valve
17. Solenoid Valve
18. Oil Dilution Manual Shut-Off Valve
19. Cooler By-Pass Line
20. Oil Dilution Line
21. Propeller Feathering Pump
22. Flexible Oil Pressure Line—Engine Block to Plate
23. P & W Check Valve
24. Propeller Feather Line Tank to Pump
25. Tank
26. Oil Tank Vent Line
27. Scupper Drain Line
28. Oil Out Line
29. Oil In Line
30. De-Oiling Unit

LEGEND
OIL FLOW LINES
OIL DILUTION (FUEL) LINES

Figure 15—Oil System Diagram

4. OIL SYSTEM.

a. OIL SPECIFICATION—AN-O-8.

b. Identical oil systems are installed in the two engine nacelles. Each system is supplied by a welded aluminum alloy tank of 21 gals. capacity with three gallons foaming space, equipped with a sump and a drain plug.

Cooling air is carried from openings in the leading edges through curved ducts across the coolers and off through openings in the upper wing surfaces. The amount of outlet opening is controlled by an electrically operated door. (See paragraph *c.*) The coolers are equipped with thermostatic by-pass valves.

The oil dilution system consists of a line led from the fuel pressure line to the oil-in line. The system is controlled by a solenoid operated by the switch in the pilot's cockpit and manual shut-off valves are installed to isolate the system.

c. OIL SYSTEM CONTROLS.

(1) OIL COOLER EXIT DUCT DOORS CONTROL.

(a) GENERAL. — The oil cooler exit duct doors control switches (one each engine) are located on the upper left side of the lower control panel, to the left of the cowl flaps switch.

(b) OPERATION.

1. Switch UP—OPEN.

2. Switch to CENTER—OFF.

3. Switch DOWN—CLOSED.

The oil cooler duct outlets are located in the upper wing surfaces and the doors are a part of the surface. The duct outlets are always open—the doors control the amount of opening. They are operated by electric motors and screw jacks. The OFF position of the switches is used only in case of malfunctioning of the system, damage, or when the engines are stopped on the ground.

Note

To obtain intermediate settings—switch to OPEN or CLOSED, as desired, then switch to OFF position when desired door position is reached.

(2) OIL DILUTION CONTROL.

(a) A toggle switch is located on the outboard side of the pilot's switch panel to control the oil dilution solenoids.

(b) OPERATION.

1. Move switch OUTBOARD—ON (DILUTE OIL).

2. Move switch INBOARD—OFF.

When the switch is set at ON fuel flows from the fuel pressure line at the carburetor to the oil-in line. Refer to Section II for Operating Instructions.

5. FLIGHT CONTROLS.

a. AILERON AND ELEVATOR CONTROLS.— The control stick is equipped with gun trigger and bomb release switch buttons on the grip. Dual elevator control cables are installed to reduce the possibility of elevator control being lost through single bullet impact. The right hand elevator is equipped with a spring tab, to aid control. The left hand elevator carries the adjustable trim tab. On all F7F-3 and -3N airplanes, both elevator tabs also serve as balance tabs. The ailerons are operated by a linkage of push-pull rods and idler arms actuated by a lever arm mounted on the torque tube attached to the stick. Spring tabs are installed on both ailerons, to assist control. The tab on the left aileron also serves as an adjustable trim tab.

b. RUDDER AND BRAKE CONTROL PEDALS.

(1) ADJUSTMENT.—The standard underhung pedals are adjustable to four positions. The outer pedal arms carry adjustment levers. To adjust the pedals, press the levers down, and push the pedals full forward with the toes; then put the toes under the pedals and pull aft one notch at a time until the pedals are in the desired position. Check that each pedal has ratcheted past the same number of notches.

(2) RUDDER CONTROL.—The rudder is operated by cables running from sectors attached to the pedals aft to a sector and bellcrank linked by push-pull tubes to the rudder horn. A hydraulic booster unit, consisting of an actuating cylinder and an automatically operated selector valve, actuated by movement of the rudder sector, is installed to assist the direct mechanical rudder operation; i.e., to relieve the pilot of heavy rudder pedal loads. The action of the rudder controls is positive at all times; i.e., if

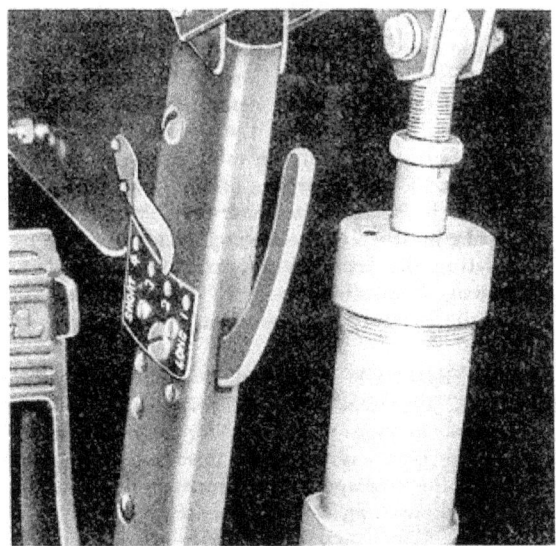

Figure 16—Pedal Adjustment Ratchet

Figure 17—Tabs Controls Unit

the booster unit should fail to operate, because of hydraulic system failure, the direct cable control would continue to operate the rudder. A by-pass valve, to cut out the booster, in case of hydraulic line block, is installed in the unit, and is controlled by a lever installed on the right hand cockpit shelf, adjacent to the hydraulic hand pump control panel. The rudder tab serves both as trim and balance tab.

Note

For additional rudder and brake control information, refer to Hydraulic System Controls, paragraph 6.

c. ELEVATOR, AILERON AND RUDDER TRIM TABS CONTROLS.

(1) CONTROL UNIT.—The three tab controls are incorporated in a unit located on the left hand side of the cockpit.

Note

The black and white neutral position index on the inboard side of the box is for the elevator tab only. The red and green neutral position index on the forward side of the box serves for both the aileron and rudder tabs.

The operation of the controls is standard.

(a) Elevator Tab Control (wheel on inboard side of unit). Rotate forward—nose down.

(b) Rudder Tab Control (knob on top of unit). Rotate clockwise—nose right.

(c) Aileron Tab Control (knob on forward end of unit). Rotate right side down—right wing down.

The tab installed on the left aileron serves both as a trim and an automatic spring control tab.

The two controls function independently and do not affect each other.

6. HYDRAULIC SYSTEM CONTROLS.

a. GENERAL.—Pressure for the hydraulic system, operating the extension and retraction of the landing gear, arresting hook, wing flaps, wing folding, gun charging, rudder booster and brake action, is normally supplied by two engine-driven pumps. A hand pump system is installed for auxiliary operation, when the engine-driven pumps are not operating. An engine-driven pump is installed on each engine and the fluid reservoir (4.22 U.S. gals., 3.51 Imp. gals. capacity), strainer and drain, system accumulator, unloader valve and system relief valve are located in the right engine nacelle, on the inboard side. Pressure and return lines run from the nacelle to the hydraulic controls (selector valves) and to the hand pump and hand pump selector valve panel, in the cockpit, and out to the various actuating cylinders. The normal hydraulic system operating pressure is 1500 psi. The normal pump pressure is zero, until some circuit is operating when pump pressure becomes 1500 psi. The system pressure gage is located on the hand pump selector valve panel on the right hand side of the cockpit. Hydraulic fluid specification AN-VV-O-366 (red color).

Note

1.

When the hand pump selector valve control is set at "SYSTEM" and the engine driven pumps are operating, if the pressure gage indicator falls below approx. 1250 psi, malfuncing of the pumps is indicated. Any circuit may be checked for malfunctioning by observing the gage while moving the selector valve control from one setting to another. When this control is not being used for operating one of the units, keep it at SYSTEM.

2.

In the event of hydraulic system failure, due to a leak or break in a line or unit, the location of the leak can be determined by using the hand pump to test the various systems. After setting the selector valve, approximately 8 to 10 double strokes of the hand pump should be sufficient to determine if pressure can be built up in the selected system. After locating the leak, do not use the damaged system, if possible, so as to retain the hydraulic pressure for operation of other systems.

b. EMERGENCY CONTROL FOR LANDING GEAR EXTENSION AND BRAKE SYSTEM.—Air bottles (one for nose wheel, one for main wheels and one for the brake system) are installed in the nose section of the fuselage. For information concerning emergency operation, refer to Section IV.

c. LANDING GEAR CONTROL.

(1) GENERAL.—The main and nose wheels are

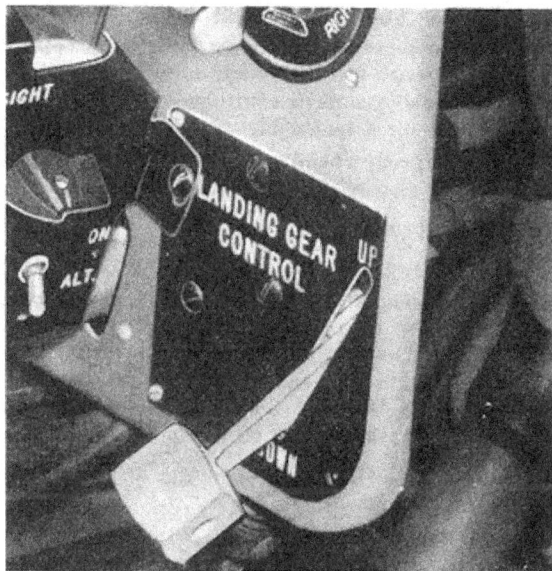

Figure 18—Landing Gear Control

raised and lowered by operating a lever with a square knob handle, located on the left side of the cockpit outboard of the left rudder pedal and below the ignition switch.

To lower the wheels—move lever DOWN.

To raise the wheels—move lever UP.

To prevent inadvertent retraction of the wheels when the airplane is on the ground, an automatic lock, to stop movement of the control lever, is installed. It is operated by the torque scissors on the left main wheel through a flexible control shaft. When the weight of the airplane is on the wheels, the scissors is partially closed and in such a position that the lock is set in place. When the airplane leaves the ground, the wheels drop down to open the scissors, pull down the control shaft, and disengage the lock.

CAUTION

When making sharp left hand turns, or taxiing over rough ground, the control lock may not be effective.

For emergency (hand pump or air bottle) operation of landing gear, refer to Section IV.

(2) LANDING GEAR POSITION INDICATOR.—A standard landing gear and flaps position indicator is located on the right side of the main instrument panel. The position of each main wheel and the nose wheel is shown separately; also whether the wheels are down and locked. The indicator is operated by micro-switches installed on each landing gear assembly. In case of landing gear indicator malfunctioning, the main wheels can be observed for locked position and the nose wheel can be felt locking by a thump as it reaches full extension. A section of the left engine cowl is buffed clear of paint to serve as a mirror in which the nose wheel position can be observed.

d. ARRESTING HOOK CONTROL.—The arresting hook is operated by a two-way control lever located on the right hand side of the cockpit forward of the hydraulic control panel. When the lever is moved aft, the hook lock is released and the hook drops down. When the lever is moved forward, the cylinder piston retracts to draw the hook up, and the lock snaps into the locked position. The approach light is turned on when the hook is lowered.

(1) To lower (extend) hook for carrier landings—move lever full aft.

(2) To raise (retract) hook—move lever full forward.

CAUTION

The pilot shall insure that the lever is in the HOOK LOWERED POSITION prior to landing aboard a carrier.

e. BRAKE CONTROL.—The brake control system, two power brake control valves mounted on the pedals, a separate brake system accumulator and lines to the disc type brakes, is a branch of the airplane hydraulic system; toe pressure on the upper sections of the rudder pedals applies the brakes.

In the event that the hydraulic system is shot up or otherwise damaged it is still possible that the brake system may operate approx. 12 times because of the fluid and pre-load of air in the accumulator. To ascertain whether or not the brake system is in operating condition before landing, deflect the brake pedals ONCE—if normal pressure is required it indicates that the system will function for a normal landing and a reasonable amount of taxiing.

Figure 19—Arresting Hook Control

Figure 20—Wing Flaps Control

Since the fluid and air load of the accumulator will be reduced each time brake pressure is applied and then relieved, test the pedals only ONCE and endeavor to make a smooth controlled stop after landing to allow for a reasonable amount of taxiing.

For emergency (hand pump or air bottle) operation of brake system, refer to Section IV.

f. WING FLAPS CONTROL.

(1) GENERAL.—The flaps control lever is installed on a quadrant on the left side of the cockpit, forward of and above the engine control quadrant. There are four settings on the quadrant—forward setting for FLAPS UP, and aft to 15°, 30°, and 40° (MAX. FLAPS DOWN). The settings are marked adjacent to the four notches on the quadrant.

(2) OPERATION.—Press button on handle and move lever as follows:

(a) FLAPS UP.

Lever in FULL FORWARD POSITION.

(b) FLAPS DOWN.

KEY TO FIGURE 21
HYDRAULIC SYSTEM DIAGRAM

1. Engine Driven Pump (R.H.)
1A Engine Driven Pump (L.H.)
2. Timer Check Valve—
   Main Wheels Down Line (2)
3. Shuttle Valve (2)
4. Unloader Valve
5. Vent Line Filter
6. Reservoir
7. System Accumulator
8. System Relief Valve
9. System Filter
10. Nacelle Door Actuating Cylinder (2)
11. Main Wheel Actuating Cylinder (2)
12. Timer Check Valve (2)
13. Wing Locking Cylinder (4)
14. Timer Check Valve (4)
15. Wing Folding Cylinder (4)
16. Shuttle Valve
17. Strainer (4)
18. Timer Check Valve—
    Nacelle Door Open Line (2)
19. Shuttle Valve—Main Wheels (2)
20. Wing Flap Actuating Cylinder (4)
21. Restrictors (8)
22. Cannon Charging Cylinder (4)
23. Wing Flaps Selector Valve
24. Wing Folding Selector Valve
25. Hand Pump Selector Valve
26. Arresting Hook Selector Valve
27. System Pressure Gage
28. Hand Pump
29. Hand Pump Pressure Line Filter
30. Pressure and Thermal Relief Manifold
31. Power Brake Valve (2)
32. Gun and Cannon Charging Valve (4)
33. Landing Gear Selector Valve
34. Brake Air Bottle Pressure Gage
35. Air Vent Valve
36. Landing Gear Dump Valve
37. Landing Gear Air Bottle Dump Valve (2)
38. Main Wheels Emergency Air Bottle
39. Nose Wheel Emergency Air Bottle
40. Main Wheels Emergency Air Bottle Gage
41. Nose Wheel Emergency Air Bottle Gage
42. Nose Wheel Actuating Cylinder
43. Shuttle Valve—Nose Wheel
44. Brake Emergency Air Bottle
45. Hydraulic Brake System Accumulator
46. Gun and Cannon Thermal Relief Manifold
47. Fuselage Guns Charging Cylinder (4)
48. Arresting Hook Actuating Cylinder
49. Rudder Booster By-Pass Valve
50. Rudder Booster Actuating Cylinder
51. Rudder Booster Selector Valve

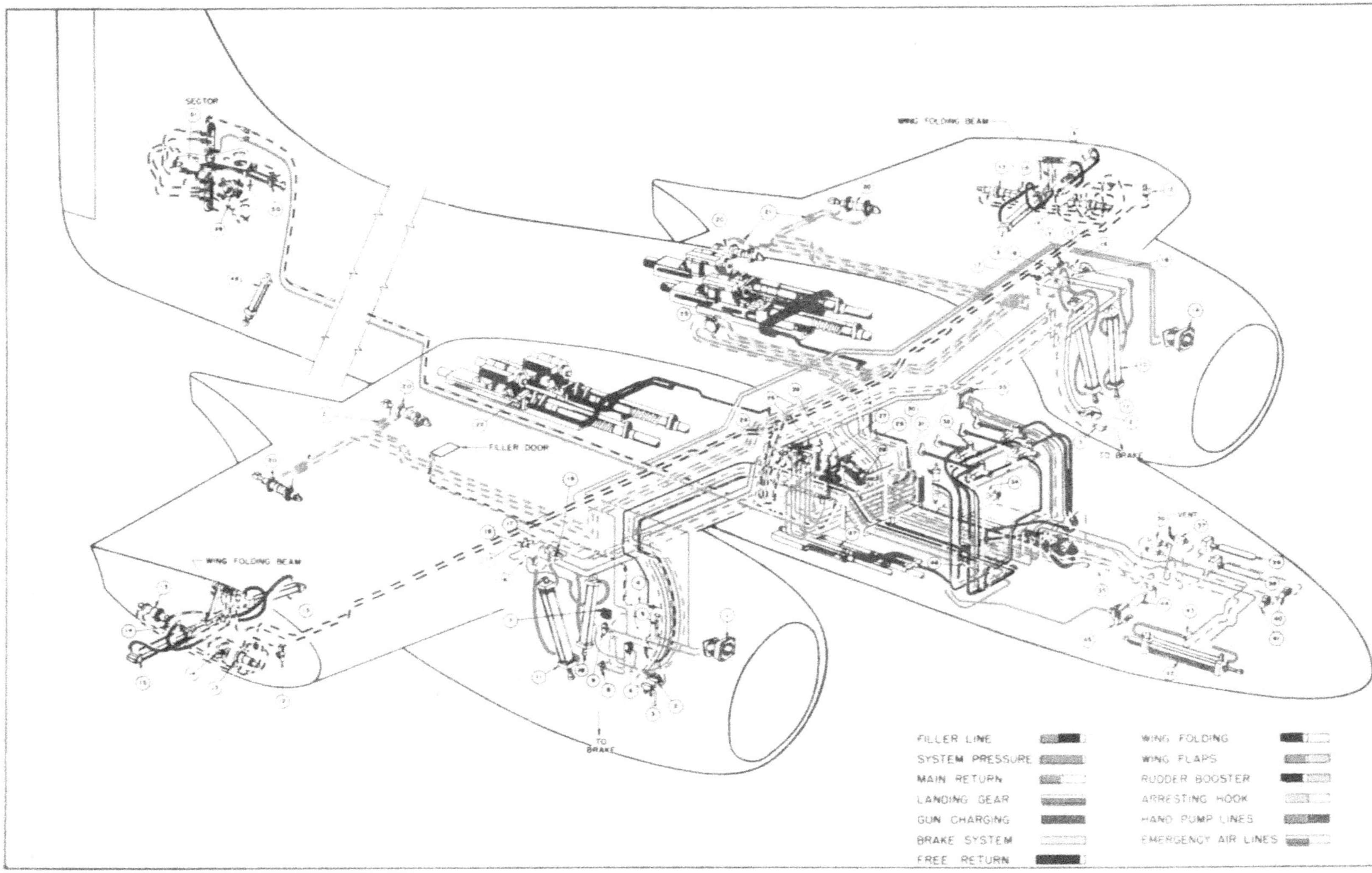

Figure 21 — Hydraulic System Diagram

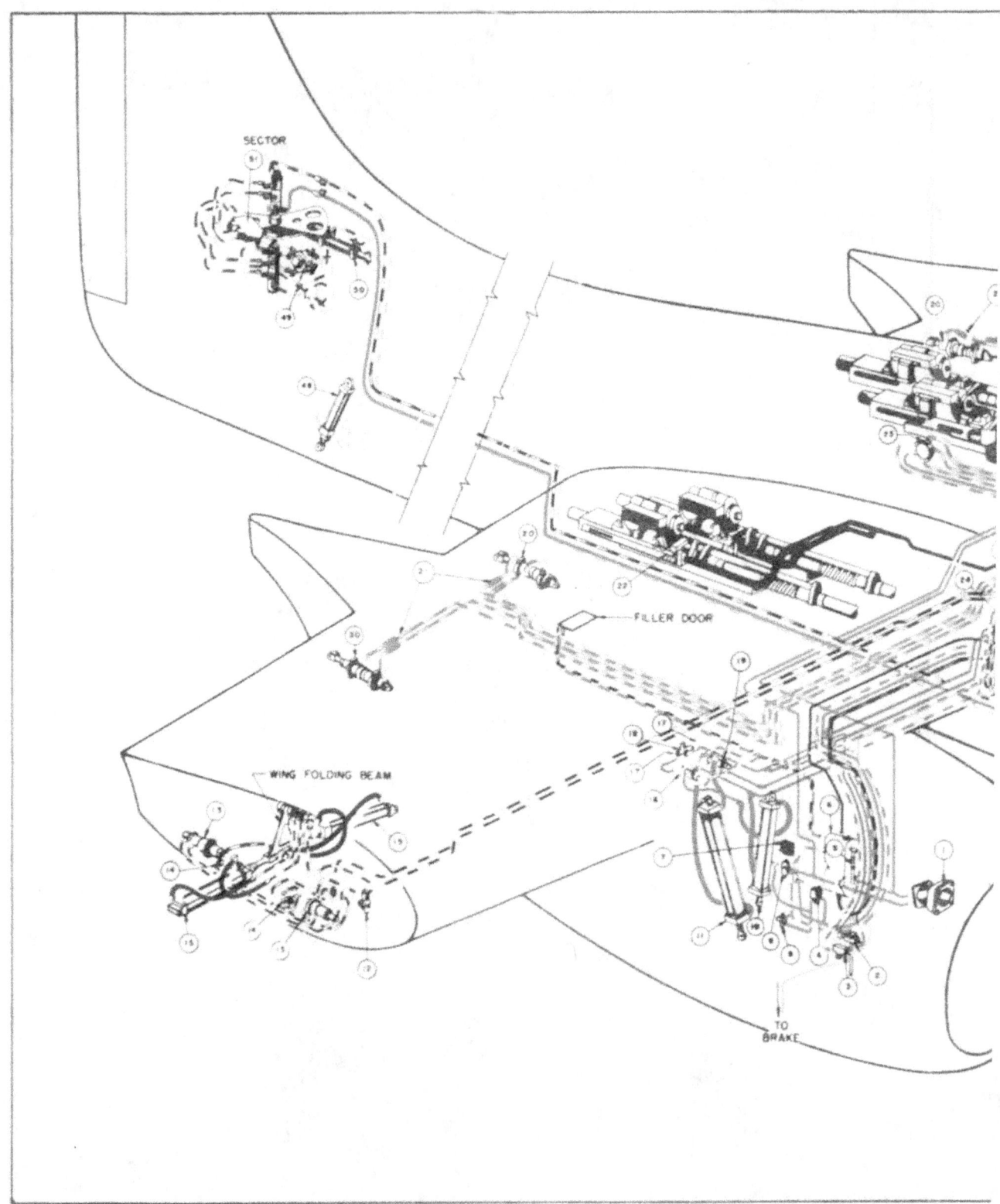

Figure 21—Hydraulic System Diagram

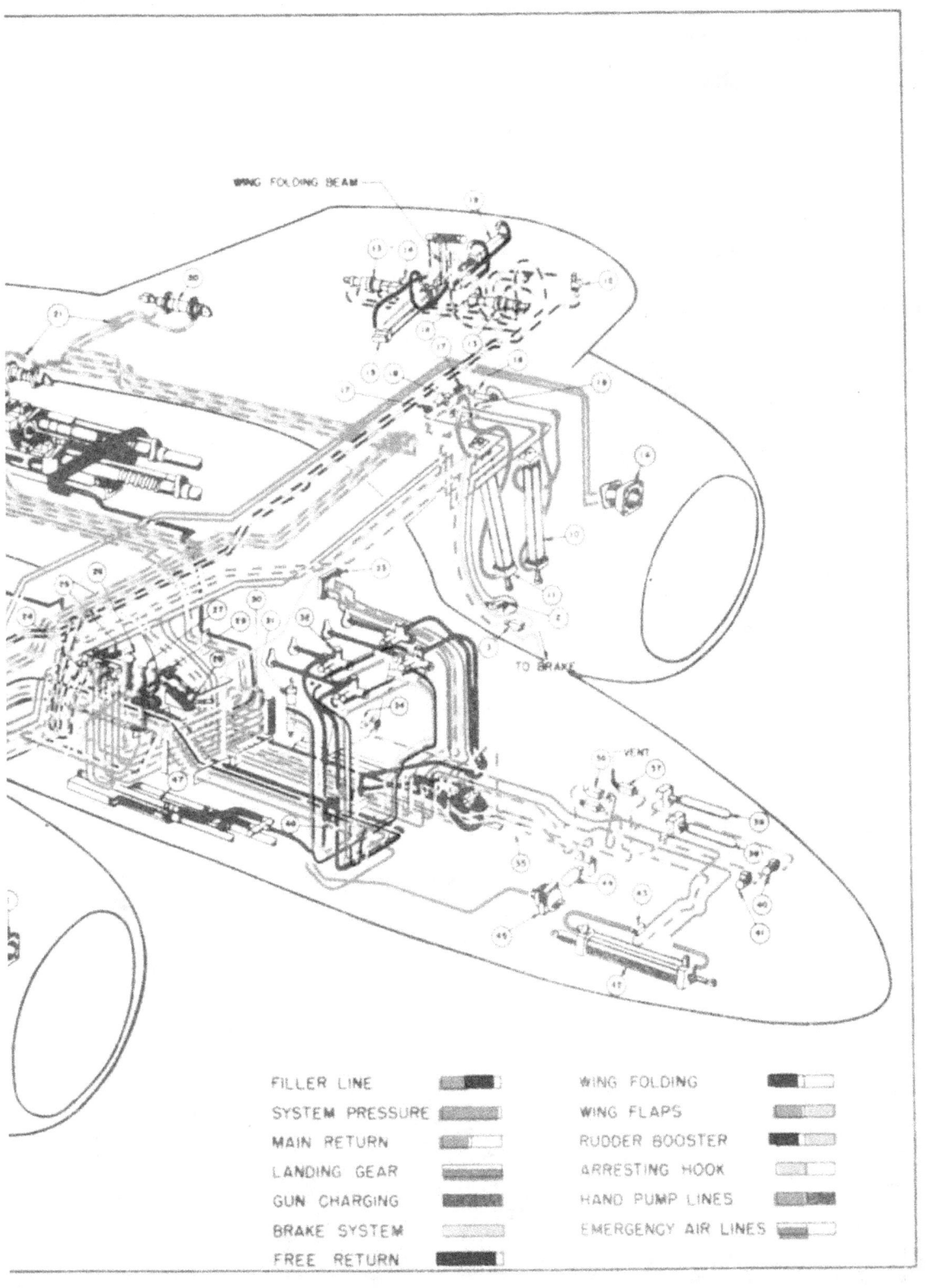

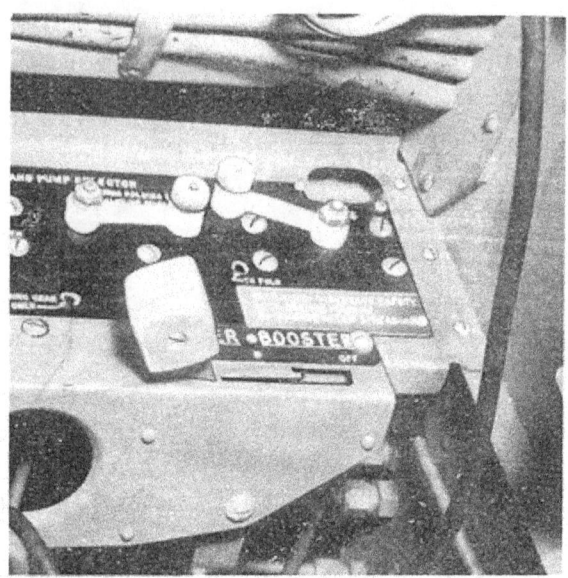

Figure 22—Wing Folding Control

15°—Lever in FIRST NOTCH AFT.
30°—Lever in SECOND NOTCH AFT.
40°—(Max. DOWN)—Lever is FULL AFT.

WARNING

For flaps UP, return lever to FULL FORWARD position.

(3) FLAPS POSITION INDICATOR. — The standard electrical landing gear and flaps position indicator is located on the right side of the main instrument panel.

CAUTION

When operating control, check position of flaps on indicator. On a new or overhauled airplane, operate flaps several times before take-off, as dirt may lodge in the lines or restrictors, (installed to insure simultaneous action) and may cause uneven flap action.

g. WING FOLDING CONTROLS.

(1) GENERAL.—The wings are folded vertically and spread, and locked in the spread position, by the action of the hydraulic wing folding (2L-2R) and locking (2L-2R) cylinders. A mechanical safety lock is installed to lock the hydraulically operated lockpins in place after the wings are spread. Jury struts are provided to hold the wings in place in the folded position. The folding control is a standard hydraulic selector valve control lever located on the hydraulic control panel to the right of the seat.

(2) TO SPREAD THE OUTER WING PANELS.

(a) Check that the wing jury struts are removed.

(b) Move the wing folding control handle outboard—TO SPREAD.

(c) When fully spread, push DOWN and LOCK the handle located at the upper right side of the lower instrument and control panel—to lock the wing lockpins in the spread position.

(3) TO FOLD THE OUTER WING PANELS.

(a) Pull UP the handle to UNLOCK the safety locks.

(b) Move the wing folding control handle inboard—TO FOLD.

(c) Set wing jury struts in place (the struts hook into fittings at inner panel Station #103 and outer panel Station #243 and are adjustable for length.)

(4) Lock Position Indicators, red painted flags, operated by the mechanical lock through bellcrank and pushrod linkages, are installed in the inner panels, at the folding axis. When the handle is pulled up, the indicators are raised above the wing surface; when the handle is pushed down, the indicators disappear into the wings to show that the wings are locked in spread position.

(5) A warning horn, or howler, is installed on the aft side of the headrest and is operated by microswitches installed at the folding axis. When the wings are spread the horn sounds as the outer panels leave the folded position and continues to sound until the handle is pushed down, to lock the lockpins in place. When the wings are folded, the horn sounds as the handle is pulled to unlock the lockpins and continues to sound until the outer panel reaches the full folded position.

Note

The horn will also sound when the wheels are lowered if the Master Armament Switch is set to "ON".

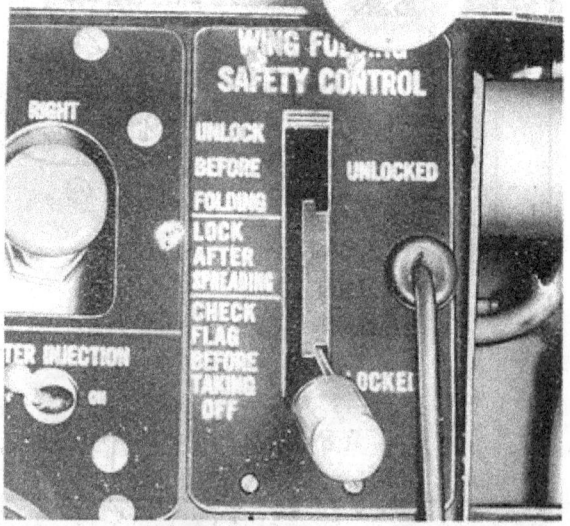

Figure 23—Wing Fold Safety Lock Control

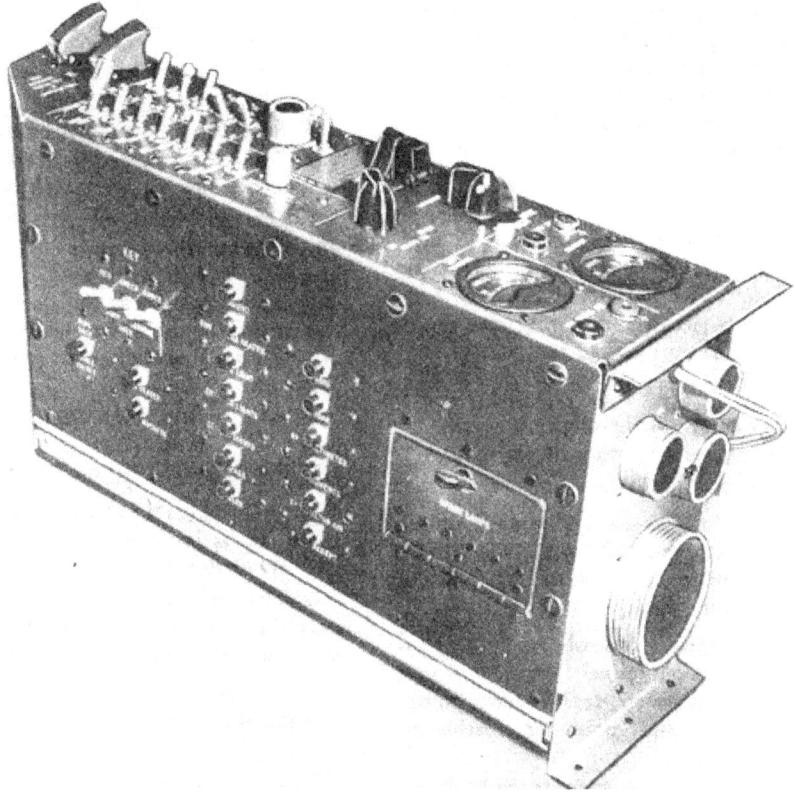

Figure 24—Pilot's Switch Box

If it is difficult to operate the handle, to lock or unlock the pins, in the folding or spreading operation, operate the hand pump system for several strokes, to move the lockpins fully into place—the pins must be fully extended or retracted before the "lock-lock" can be operated.

For emergency operation of wing folding control, refer to Section IV.

h. RUDDER BOOSTER BY-PASS CONTROL.— For information concerning operation of rudder booster by-pass control, refer to Section IV.

i. GUN CHARGING CONTROLS.—For information concerning operation of gun charging controls, refer to Section V.

7. ELECTRICAL SYSTEM CONTROLS.

a. Power for the 28 volt electrical system is provided by two generators, one on each engine. The system includes two cut-out relays, one for each generator. When the generators are not operating, power is supplied by a 24 volt battery installed in the aft end of the right hand nacelle.

b. In addition to the engine ignition, the following units are electrically operated: lights, propeller feathering controls, instruments, cowl flaps, water injection system, fuel transfer system, gun camera, oil cooler doors, gun heaters, carburetor air doors, cockpit heater, engine priming, oil dilution, starter, warning howler, fuel booster pump, radio and radar, gun and bomb release solenoids, wing drop tank selector and bomb-rocket selector.

c. The main junction box is located in the fuselage aft of the pilot's cockpit, and junction boxes are located at distribution points in various sections of the airplane.

d. The following controls are located on the distribution panel and switch box on the right hand side of the pilot's cockpit; directions for their operation are given on adjacent nameplates:

(1) Landing, wing running, tail running, formation, section, formation and section, exterior lights master, recognition and recognition keying lights switches.

CAUTION

Do not lower the landing light at speeds above 120 knots. Check position of light during engine warm-up.

(2) Instrument panel and cockpit lights rheostats.

(3) Generator (right and left), battery, pitot heater, cabin heater, oil dilution, radio master, engine primer, and engine starter (with safety cap) control switches.

(4) Circuit breaker re-set buttons for the following circuits are installed on the inboard side of the box: gunsight, gun camera heater, landing light, exterior lights, cockpit lights, compass, heater, radio, radar, radio altimeter, instruments, carburetor air, and radar, radio altimeter, instruments, carburetor air, panel receptacle, automatic pilot, wing bomb arming and wing drop tank selector.

e. A panel receptacle, for the attachment of electrically operated pilot equipment is installed in the center of the panel. Two voltmeters, one for each engine, equipped with jacks for attaching test equipment, are installed on the aft end of the panel.

CAUTION

A voltage range of 27.5—28.5 should show on the meters for proper operation of electrical equipment.

f. The gunsight light rheostat and toggle switch (with two settings—ON and ON—ALTERNATE) are located below the pilot's left cockpit rail, forward, adjacent to the ignition switch.

g. The following electrical controls are located on the pilot's lower instrument panel: oil cooler exit doors, cowl flaps, carburetor air, fuel booster pump, water injection system, and propeller feathering switches and circuit breaker.

h. A red jewel fuel pressure warning light is located on the pilot's lower panel, adjacent to the fuel booster pump control switch.

i. Micro-switches, operating the landing gear and flaps position indicator are installed in the nacelles and fuselage. Micro-switches for the wing folding warning howler are installed at the folding axes.

j. The cockpit, instrument panel and gunsight light rheostats shut off the lights when turned full counter-clockwise.

A separate cockpit lights rheostat is installed in the radar operator's cockpit.

k. Spare instrument panel bulbs are stowed in containers on the upper left hand side of the main instrument panels in both cockpits.

l. The radio master switch must be ON to operate any of the radio equipment. A two-way toggle switch equipped with a safety cap, is installed for use when an external AC power source is connected for ground testing radar—the switch is located on the right side of the pilot's cockpit above the electric switch box and control panel.

Move switch FORWARD for INTERNAL AC power.

Move switch AFT for EXTERNAL AC power.

m. THE IFF DESTRUCT switch, equipped with a safety cap is just outboard of the arresting hook control, aft of the electrical control box.

n. The battery switch must be ON to prime and start the engines. The following circuits are not affected by the position of the battery switch.

(1) Recognition lights.
(2) IFF "DESTRUCTOR".

Note

If any of the electrical equipment fails to operate, push the circuit breaker re-set button for the defective circuit.

o. The following armament switches are located on the upper left hand corner of the main instrument panel: armament master, wing bomb safetying and arming, guns selector, bomb and tank release, bomb and tank or rocket selector and rocket arming nose-tail.

Figure 25—Radar Operator's Cockpit Hood

Figure 26—Pilot's Cockpit Hood

8. MISCELLANEOUS CONTROLS AND EQUIPMENT.

a. COCKPIT HOODS.

(1) PILOT'S COCKPIT.—The cockpit hood consists of a fixed forward section, a sliding middle section, and the aft section, formed by the headrest bulkhead and headrest fairing. The sliding section is moved forward and aft by a handcrank, operating a chain and sprocket assembly, located on the forward right hand side of the cockpit.

(a) OPERATION.—The hood may be set at any desired position from full open to closed by rotating the handcrank.

Models F7F-1N and -2N—The hood may be locked in any position by allowing the spring loaded detent to engage in one of a series of holes drilled in the back plate. (Lock lever in outboard position.)

Models F7F-3 and -3N—An improved type handcrank moves the hood to the desired position. The handle of crank is equipped with a friction device which locks the hood in the desired position. The friction device is engaged when the "T" handle (formerly the lock handle) is in the outboard position.

1. To CLOSE the hood, ROTATE THE HANDCRANK COUNTERCLOCKWISE.

2. To OPEN the hood, ROTATE THE HANDCRANK CLOCKWISE.

(b) LOCK (F7F-1N AND -2N ONLY).—A yellow lock lever is installed below the crank. To LOCK the hood in position from inside PUSH YELLOW LEVER OUTBOARD. To UNLOCK, PULL YELLOW LEVER INBOARD.

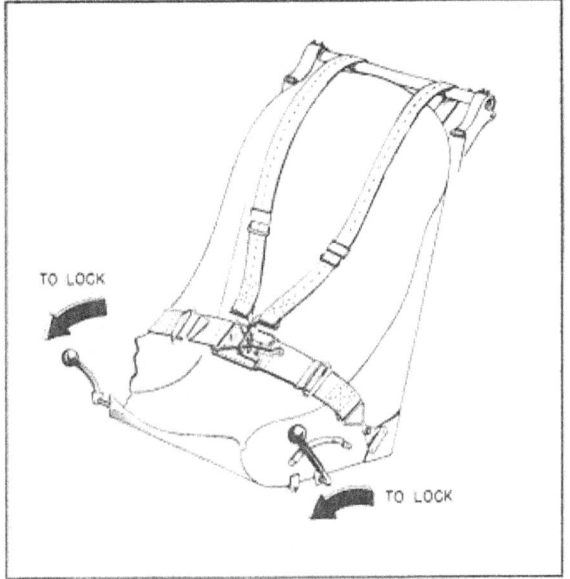

Figure 28—Pilot's Seat and Harness

Note

On F7F-1N and -2N airplanes, Serial No. 80259-80358 inclusive a red release button on fuselage skin unlocks the hood from outside. On airplanes Serial No. 80359 and subsequent the outside release button is removed. The hood is not locked and may be pulled open.

(2) RADAR OPERATOR'S COCKPIT.—The radar operator's hood, hinged on the left cockpit rail and opening on the right consists of a single molded plexiglas panel.

To open hood, lift finger latch on right side and raise hood to OPEN.

To lock hood closed, push red handle on right side full forward.

b. PILOT'S SEAT AND HARNESS.—The standard pilot's seat may be adjusted vertically to any one of four positions (total adjustment three inches). The adjustment lever is located on the right hand side of the seat. The adjusting mechanism is spring loaded; to adjust the seat position, pull the lever up, JOGGLE the seat to the height desired, and release lever to lock seat in position. The pilot's weight will bring the seat down to a lower position when the lever is pulled up to unlock. To operate properly, the standard type shoulder harness must be passed over the horizontal tube at the back of the seat and then fastened to the safety belt. It may be loosened to enable the pilot to lean forward, by pulling up the lever on the left hand side of seat. MAKE CERTAIN THAT THE LEVER IS RETURNED TO THE FORWARD (LOCKED) POSITION FOR TAKE-OFF AND LANDING.

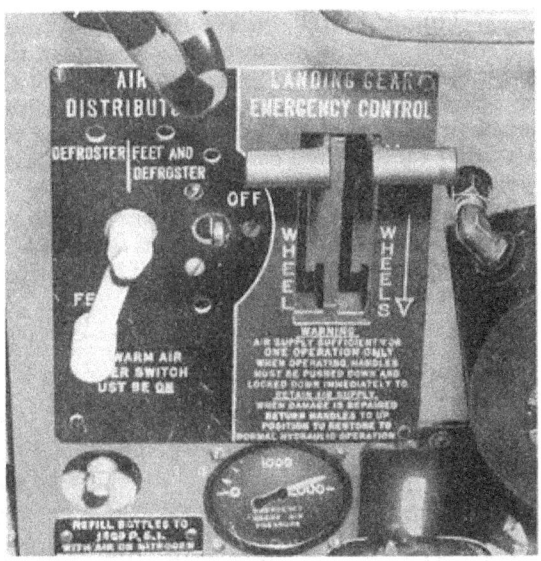

Figure 27—Pilot's Heater and Defroster Control

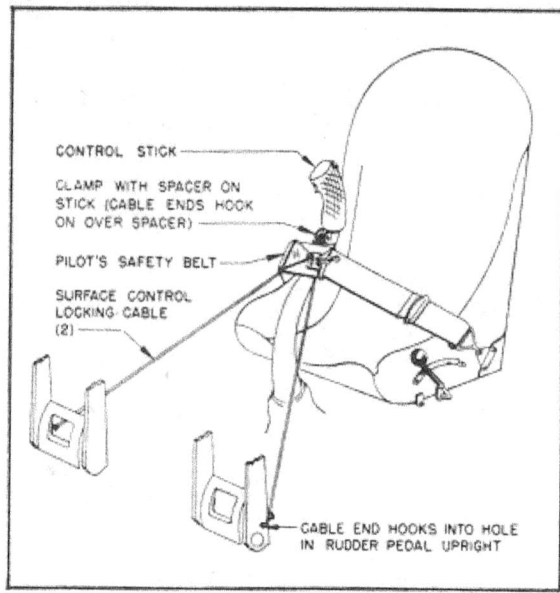

Figure 29—Controls Lock

c. EQUIPMENT CONTROLS.

(1) COCKPIT HEATER AND DEFROSTER.—The cockpit heater control switch is located on the outboard side of the electric distribution panel; the selector lever for the pilot's cockpit is located on the lower part of the lower control panel.

(a) Move switch OUTBOARD—ON.
INBOARD—OFF.

(b) Set control lever (pilot's) at desired position.

1. UP to LEFT—WINDSHIELD DEFROSTER.

2. UP to RIGHT — WINDSHIELD DEFROSTER and OUTLET AT FEET. (Two settings).

3. DOWN — OUTLET AT FEET ONLY. (Two settings.)

4. To RIGHT—OFF.

Note

Pilot's control switch and lever must be ON for heat to the radar operator's cockpit.

The standard hot air combustion type heater operates on fuel drawn from the fuel pressure gage line. The toggle switch controls the metering valve and ignitor, and the control lever controls valves in the distribution ducts. A spring loaded safety switch is controlled automatically by setting the lever —when lever is set at OFF the heater circuit is broken. A heater circuit breaker re-set button is located on the side of the electric distribution panel and a switch operated by the landing gear is installed in the circuit—the heater is automatically shut off when the gear is extended.

The heater controls may be used for cold air by setting the control switch at OFF and setting the lever as desired.

WARNING

Do not operate heater during take-off, landing, full power operation or armed combat.

d. CONTROLS LOCK.—The controls lock or parking harness, supplied with the airplane, consists of two steel cables equipped with hooks at the ends, a clamp, equipped with a bolt and spacer assembly, installed on the control stick below the grip, and the pilot's safety belt. To lock the controls, hook each cable to a rudder pedal arm and the spacer on the clamp and draw the safety belt tight over the stick above cables until the cables are taut, and lock belt.

e. CHARTBOARDS. — The pilot's chartboard is supported on rails located forward of the main instrument panel. The radar operator's chartboard is stowed below his instrument panel. To use, rotate the securing clip to free the board, and pull out (board slides out on rails). The clip must be set in position to lock the board in place when landing or taking off.

f. MAP CASES.—The pilot's case is installed on the left side of the cockpit below the rail, adjacent to the seat. The radar operator's case is installed on the right side, forward.

g. RELIEF TUBES.—The relief tubes are stowed in clips beneath the seats.

h. ANTI-BLACKOUT PROVISIONS. — An automatic control valve is mounted on a bracket on the cockpit floor at the left forward corner of the pilot's seat. Three lines run to this valve; one vents to the atmosphere, one to a quick disconnect (mounted on pilot's seat) and the third connects with the left hand engine vacuum system at the oil separator.

When the pilot's personal equipment is attached to the quick disconnect the operation of the system is entirely automatic. For more detailed information refer to applicable Service Publications.

Note

For information on Oxygen, Armament and Radio Equipment Controls, refer to Section V.

RESTRICTED
AN 01-85FA-1

Section I

1. Armament Switch Panel
2. Gunsight Cut-out
3. Compass Correction Card
4. Spare Light Bulb Containers
5. Chartboard Rails
6. Compass Indicator
7. Clock
8. Airspeed Indicator
9. Gyro Horizon
10. Radio Altimeter Indicator (Night Fighters Only)
11. Landing Gear and Flap Position Indicator
12. Sensitive Altimeter
13. Cutout for Radar Indicator
14. Manifold Pressure Gage
15. Tachometer
16. Rate of Climb Indicator
17. Directional Gyro
18. Check-Off Placard
19. Turn and Bank Indicator
20. Cylinder Head Temperature Gage
21. Left Engine Gage Unit
22. Right Engine Gage Unit
23. Radio Altimeter Indicator Lights Cut-out

Figure 30—Pilot's Main Instrument Panel

Section I

RESTRICTED
AN 01-85FA-1

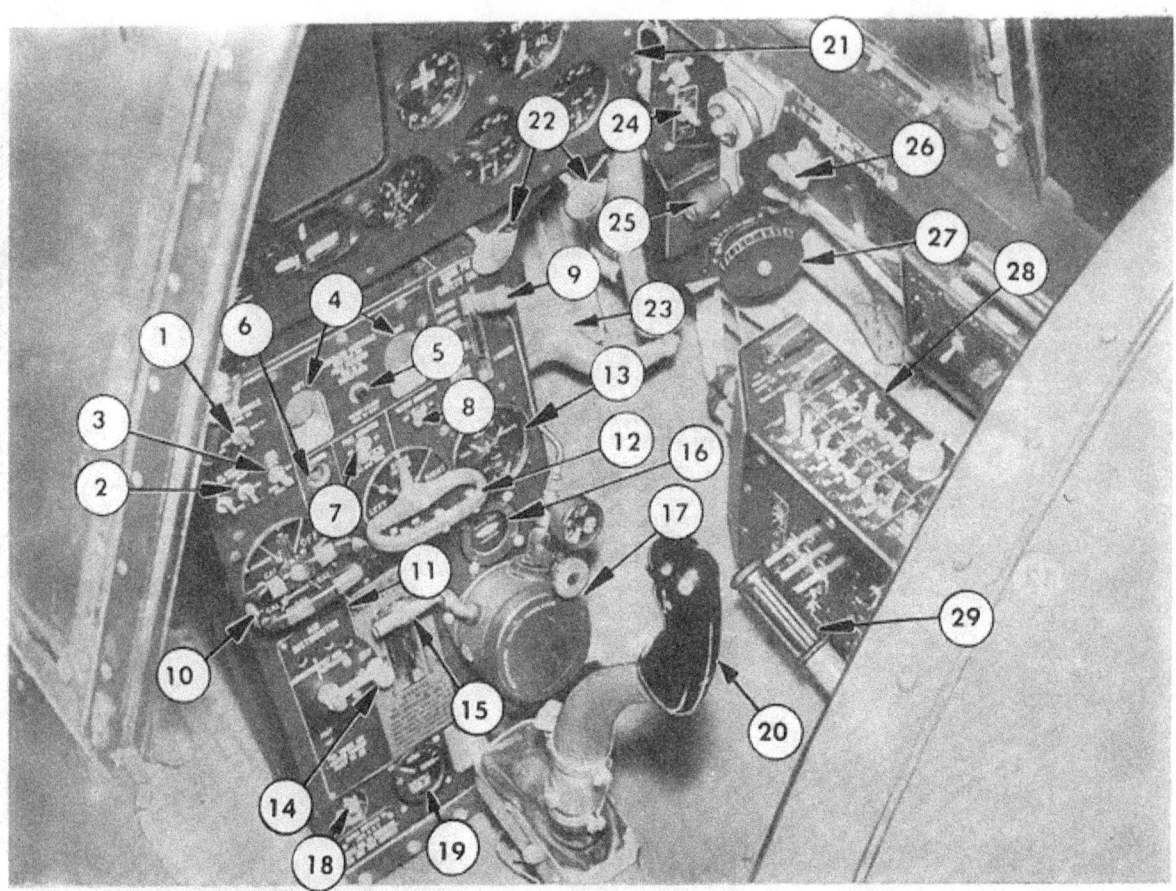

1. Carburetor Air Control Switch
2. Oil Cooler Exit Duct Door Switches
3. Cowl Flaps Control Switch
4. Propeller Feathering Controls
5. Propeller Feathering Circuit Breaker Reset Button
6. Fuel Pressure Warning Light
7. Auxiliary Fuel Pump Control
8. Water Injection Control
9. Wing Fold Safety Lock Control
10. Fuel Tank Selector Valve Control
11. Wing Drop. Tanks Solenoid Valve Control Switch
12. Engine Selector Valve
13. Fuel Quantity Gage
14. Cockpit Heater Selector
15. L.G. (Nose and Main) Emergency Dump Controls
16. Oxygen Flow Blinker
17. Oxygen Regulator
18. Emergency Brake Air Bottle Filler Plug
19. Emergency Brake Air Bottle Gage
20. Control Stick Grip
21. Main Instrument Panel
22. Gun Charger Controls
23. Rudder and Brake Pedal
24. IFF Control Switch (Replaced by Radio Altimeter Control on Night Fighters)
25. Cockpit Hood Control
26. Cockpit Hood Control Release
27. Oxygen Cylinder Control
28. Pilot's Switch Box
29. Hydraulic Hand Pump

Figure 31—Pilot's Lower and Right Side Instrument Panels

RESTRICTED

1. Fuel Tank Pressurizing Release Control
2. Map Case
3. Emergency Brake Control
4. Rudder Trim Tab Control
5. Aileron Trim Tab Control
6. Elevator Trim Tab Control
7. Engine Control Quadrant
8. Supercharger Control
9. Propeller Controls
10. Friction Adjustment
11. Mixture Controls
12. Throttle Controls
13. Flap Control Push-Pull Rod
14. Rocket Selector Switch
15. Wing Tank or Bomb Manual Release (Jettison)
16. Fuselage Tank or Bomb Manual Release

Figure 32—Pilot's Cockpit—L.H. Side

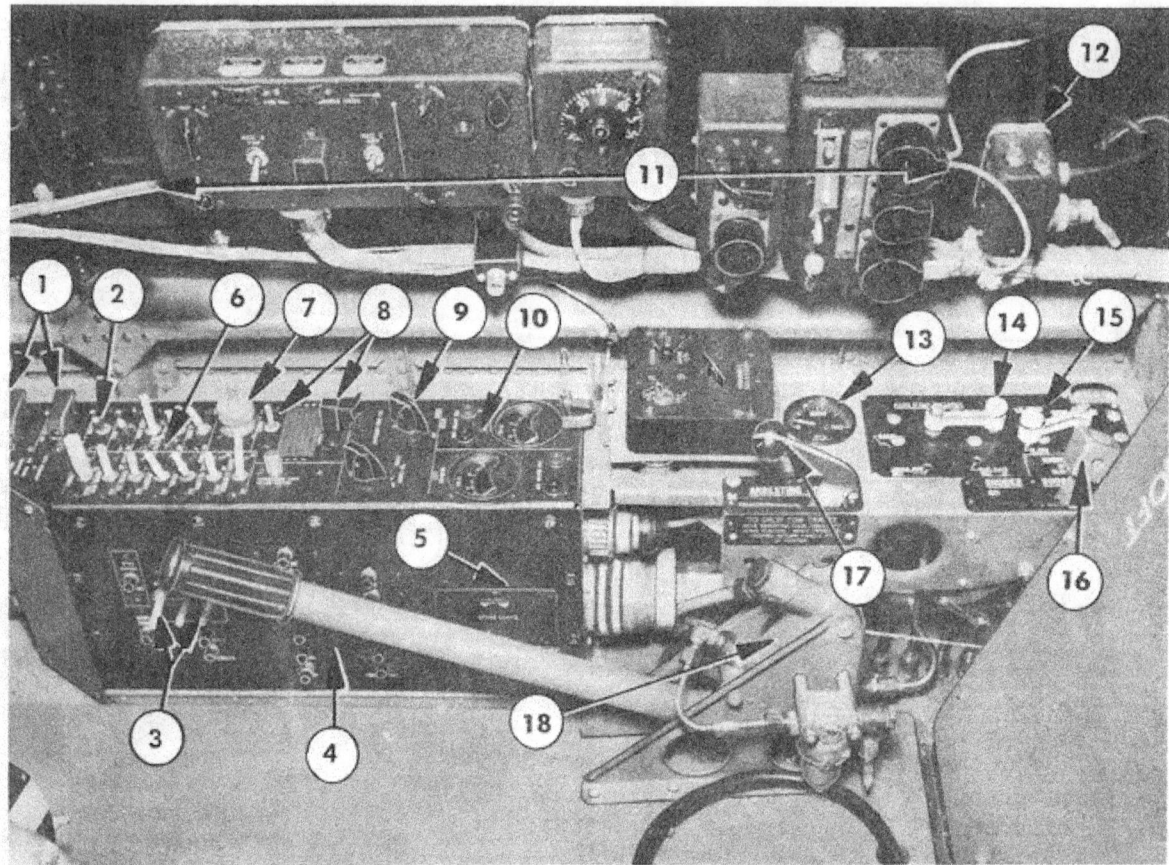

1. Generator Switches
2. Main Battery Switch
3. Recognition Lights Switches
4. Circuit Breaker Reset Buttons
5. Spare Lamp Container
6. Miscellaneous Light and Control Switches
7. Panel Receptacle
8. Primer and Starter Switches
9. Cockpit and Panel Lights Rheostat
10. Volt-Ammeter and Test Pin Jacks
11. Communicating Controls
12. Radio Jack Box
13. Hydraulic Pressure Gage
14. Hydraulic Hand Pump Selector Valve Control
15. Wing Folding Selector Valve Control
16. Rudder Booster By-pass Valve Control
17. Arresting Hook Selector Valve Control
18. Hydraulic Hand Pump

Figure 33—Pilot's Cockpit—R.H. Side

RESTRICTED
AN 01-85FA-1

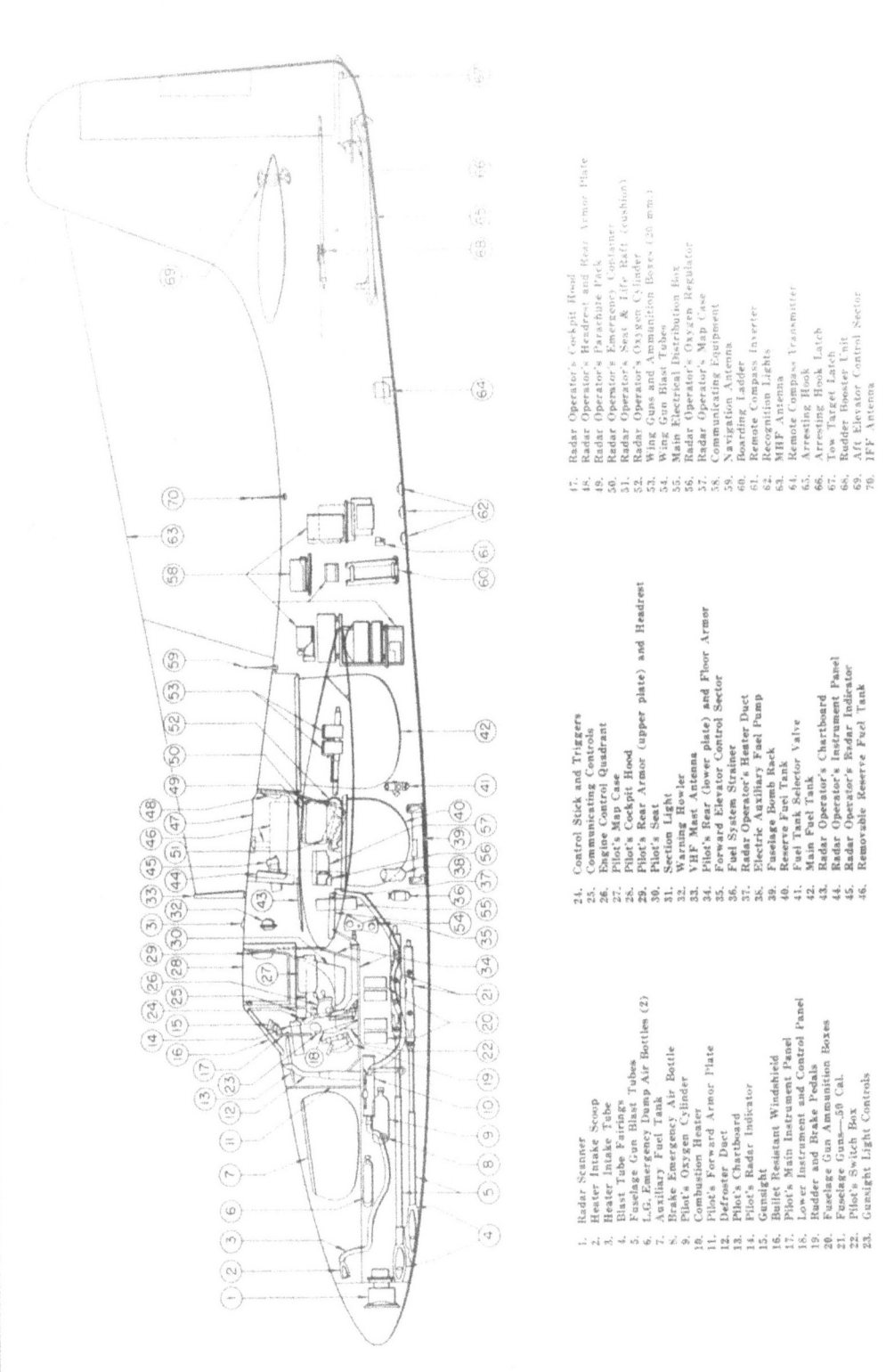

1. Radar Scanner
2. Heater Intake Scoop
3. Heater Intake Tube
4. Blast Tube Fairings
5. Fuselage Gun Blast Tubes
6. L.G. Emergency Dump Air Bottles (2)
7. Auxiliary Fuel Tank
8. Brake Emergency Air Bottle
9. Pilot's Oxygen Cylinder
10. Combustion Heater
11. Pilot's Forward Armor Plate
12. Defroster Duct
13. Pilot's Chartboard
14. Pilot's Radar Indicator
15. Gunsight
16. Bullet Resistant Windshield
17. Pilot's Main Instrument Panel
18. Lower Instrument and Control Panel
19. Rudder and Brake Pedals
20. Fuselage Gun Ammunition Boxes
21. Fuselage Guns—.50 Cal.
22. Pilot's Switch Box
23. Gunsight Light Controls
24. Control Stick and Triggers
25. Communicating Controls
26. Engine Control Quadrant
27. Pilot's Map Case
28. Pilot's Cockpit Hood
29. Pilot's Rear Armor (upper plate) and Headrest
30. Pilot's Seat
31. Section Light
32. Warning Howler
33. VHF Mast Antenna
34. Pilot's Rear (lower plate) and Floor Armor
35. Forward Elevator Control Sector
36. Fuel System Strainer
37. Radar Operator's Heater Duct
38. Electric Auxiliary Fuel Pump
39. Fuselage Bomb Rack
40. Reserve Fuel Tank
41. Fuel Tank Selector Valve
42. Main Fuel Tank
43. Radar Operator's Chartboard
44. Radar Operator's Instrument Panel
45. Radar Operator's Radar Indicator
46. Removable Reserve Fuel Tank
47. Radar Operator's Cockpit Hood
48. Radar Operator's Headrest and Rear Armor Plate
49. Radar Operator's Parachute Pack
50. Radar Operator's Emergency Container
51. Radar Operator's Seat & Life Raft (cushion)
52. Radar Operator's Oxygen Cylinder
53. Wing Guns and Ammunition Boxes (20 mm)
54. Wing Gun Blast Tubes
55. Main Electrical Distribution Box
56. Radar Operator's Oxygen Regulator
57. Radar Operator's Map Case
58. Communicating Equipment
59. Navigation Antenna
60. Boarding Ladder
61. Remote Compass Inverter
62. Recognition Lights
63. MHF Antenna
64. Remote Compass Transmitter
65. Arresting Hook
66. Arresting Hook Latch
67. Tow Target Latch
68. Rudder Booster Unit
69. Aft Elevator Control Sector
70. IFF Antenna

Figure 34—Interior Arrangement Diagram

RESTRICTED

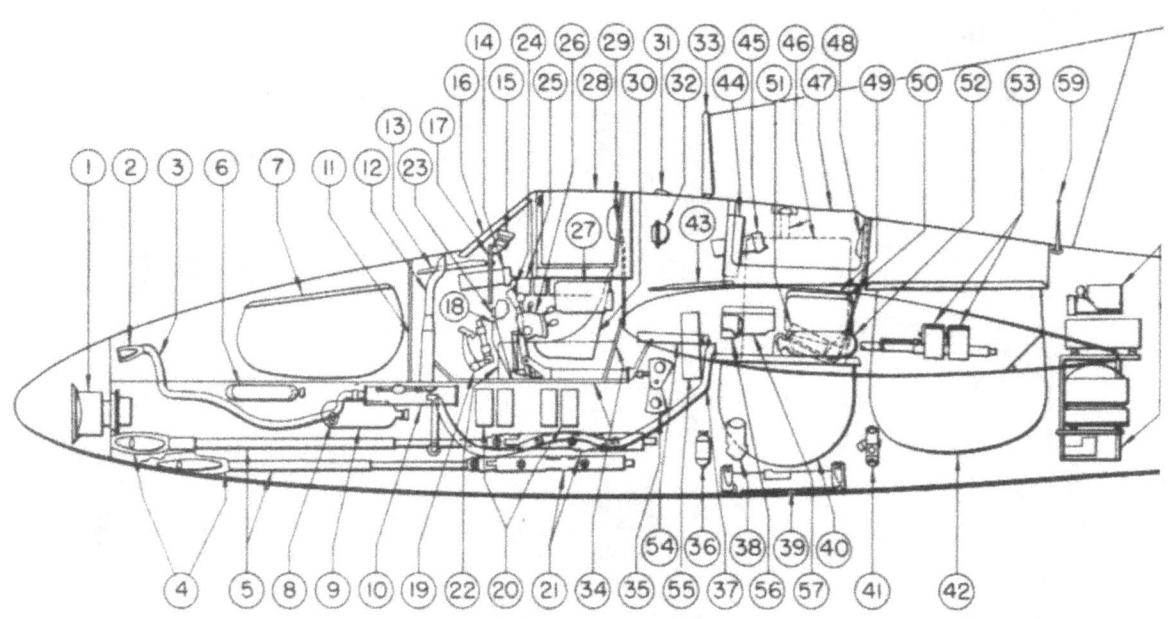

1. Radar Scanner
2. Heater Intake Scoop
3. Heater Intake Tube
4. Blast Tube Fairings
5. Fuselage Gun Blast Tubes
6. L.G. Emergency Dump Air Bottles (2)
7. Auxiliary Fuel Tank
8. Brake Emergency Air Bottle
9. Pilot's Oxygen Cylinder
10. Combustion Heater
11. Pilot's Forward Armor Plate
12. Defroster Duct
13. Pilot's Chartboard
14. Pilot's Radar Indicator
15. Gunsight
16. Bullet Resistant Windshield
17. Pilot's Main Instrument Panel
18. Lower Instrument and Control Panel
19. Rudder and Brake Pedals
20. Fuselage Gun Ammunition Boxes
21. Fuselage Guns—.50 Cal.
22. Pilot's Switch Box
23. Gunsight Light Controls
24. Control Stick and Triggers
25. Communicating Controls
26. Engine Control Quadrant
27. Pilot's Map Case
28. Pilot's Cockpit Hood
29. Pilot's Rear Armor (upper plate) and Headr
30. Pilot's Seat
31. Section Light
32. Warning Howler
33. VHF Mast Antenna
34. Pilot's Rear (lower plate) and Floor Armor
35. Forward Elevator Control Sector
36. Fuel System Strainer
37. Radar Operator's Heater Duct
38. Electric Auxiliary Fuel Pump
39. Fuselage Bomb Rack
40. Reserve Fuel Tank
41. Fuel Tank Selector Valve
42. Main Fuel Tank
43. Radar Operator's Chartboard
44. Radar Operator's Instrument Panel
45. Radar Operator's Radar Indicator
46. Removable Reserve Fuel Tank

Figure 34—Interior Arrangement Diagram

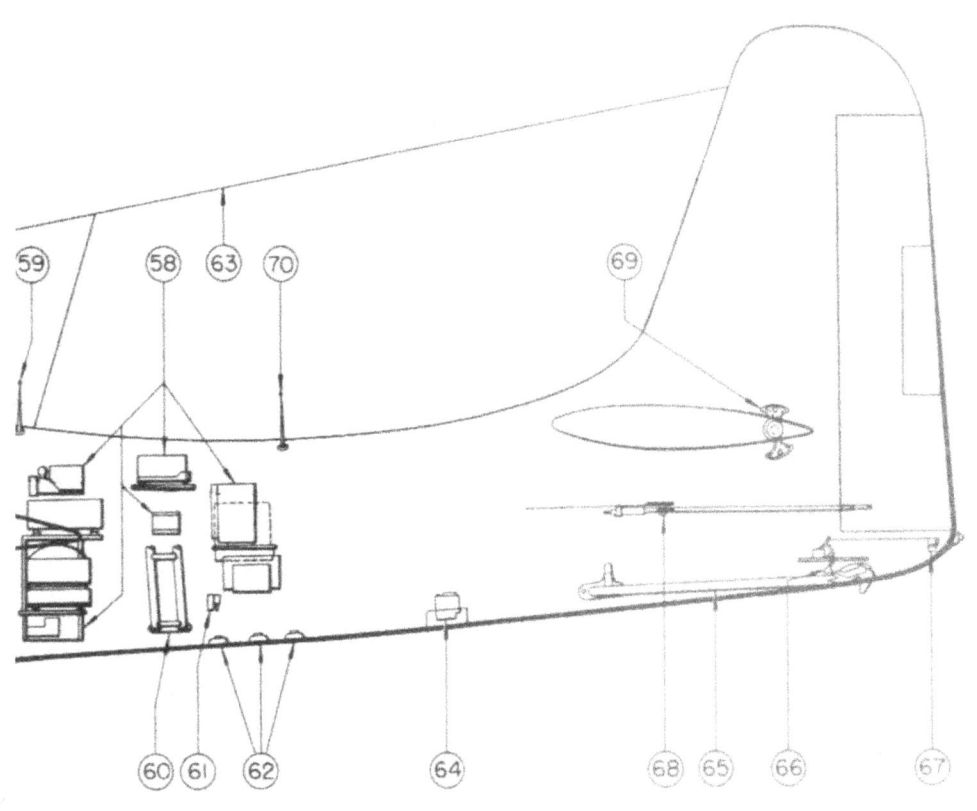

and Headrest

oor Armor

el
r

47. Radar Operator's Cockpit Hood
48. Radar Operator's Headrest and Rear Armor Plate
49. Radar Operator's Parachute Pack
50. Radar Operator's Emergency Container
51. Radar Operator's Seat & Life Raft (cushion)
52. Radar Operator's Oxygen Cylinder
53. Wing Guns and Ammunition Boxes (20 mm.)
54. Wing Gun Blast Tubes
55. Main Electrical Distribution Box
56. Radar Operator's Oxygen Regulator
57. Radar Operator's Map Case
58. Communicating Equipment
59. Navigation Antenna
60. Boarding Ladder
61. Remote Compass Inverter
62. Recognition Lights
63. MHF Antenna
64. Remote Compass Transmitter
65. Arresting Hook
66. Arresting Hook Latch
67. Tow Target Latch
68. Rudder Booster Unit
69. Aft Elevator Control Sector
70. IFF Antenna

Section I

RESTRICTED
AN 01-85FA-1

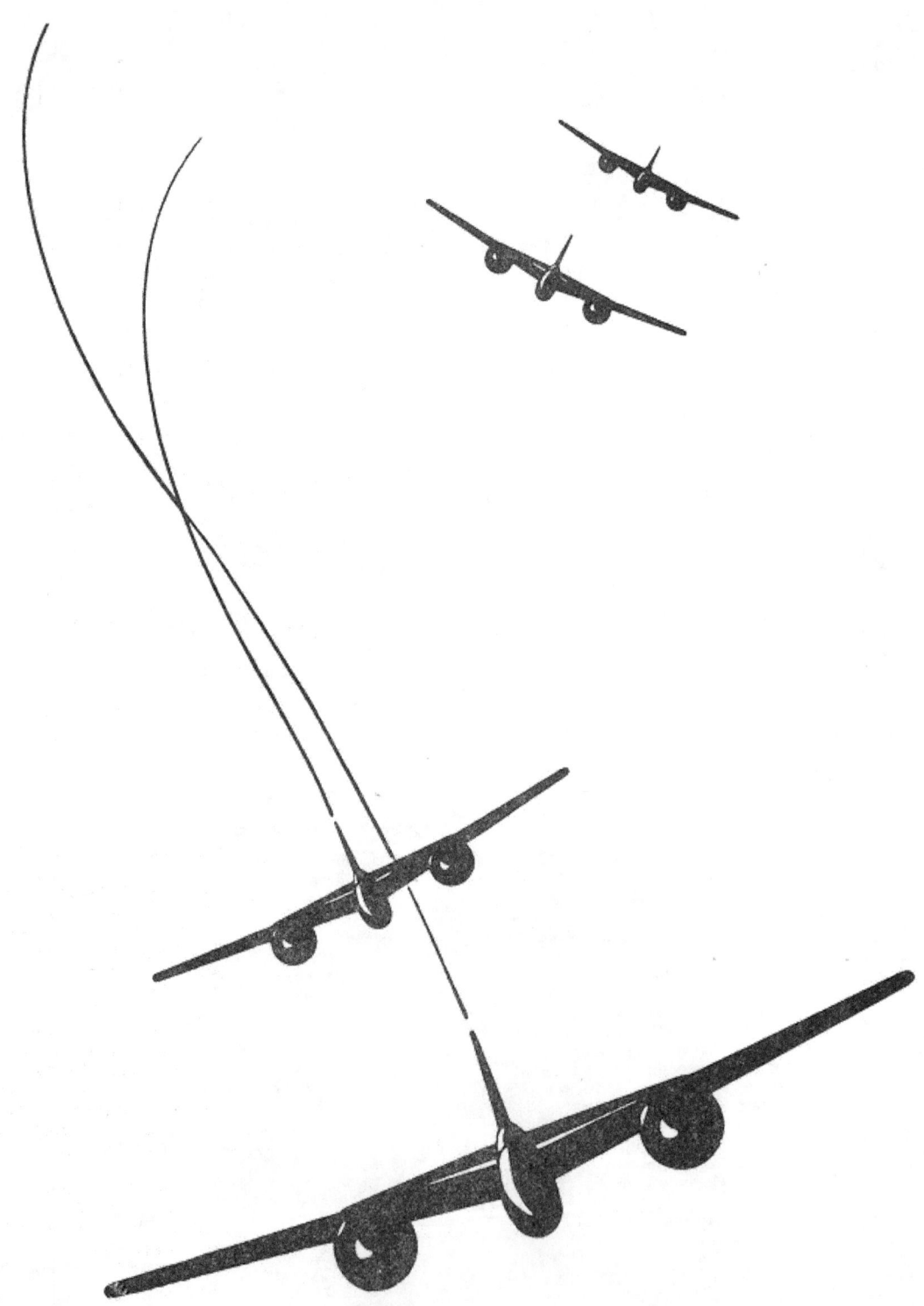

26

RESTRICTED
AN 01-85FA-1

Section II
Paragraph 1

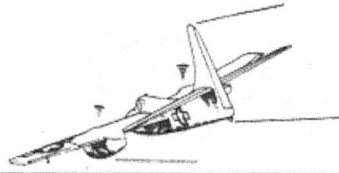

SECTION II
NORMAL OPERATING INSTRUCTIONS

1. **BEFORE ENTERING THE COCKPIT.**

    a. Note the following flight limitations and restrictions:

    MANEUVERS.
      Prohibited—Intentional spins, snap rolls and inverted flight
      Permissible (with no external loading—tanks, bombs, etc.)
        Loop   Chandelle   Wing-over
        Aileron roll   Immelman turn   Vertical turn
      Permissible (with external loading—tanks, bombs, etc.)
        Wing-over   Aileron roll (only for entering dive)
        Vertical turn

    MAXIMUM SPEEDS

Diving Speeds	Knots IAS
0-10000	435
10000-15000	400
15000-20000	365
20000-25000	330
25000-30000	303

    MAXIMUM ACCELERATIONS (Normal fighter load approximately 21000 lbs.)
      refer to Fig. 66.

0-10000	6.2g
10000-20000	4.4g

Gross Wt. lbs.	Acceleration
19000 or less	6.8g
20000	6.5g
21000	6.2g
22000	5.9g
23000	5.5g
24000	5.1g
25000	4.8g

    WARNING

    Maximum accelerations must not be imposed at maximum speeds.

    See Fig. 66

    AIRSPEED LIMITATIONS (Normal fighter load 21700 lbs.)

For control—one engine operation	120 knots IAS Min.
Straight flight—one propeller feathered	113 knots IAS Min.

    MAXIMUM SPEEDS (IAS) for various operations

Full flaps down	130 knots
30° flaps down	150 knots
15° flaps down	225 knots
Extending landing gear and flight with gear down	250 knots
Emergency extension of landing gear	110 knots
Extension of landing light	120 knots
Unlimited use of ailerons	300 knots
Maximum acceleration (at 21000 lbs. gross wt.) to be combined with unlimited use of ailerons	5.0g
Approach speed (desired)	110 knots
Stalling speeds (power OFF)	65 knots

    Maximum Recommended gross wt.—various operations

Landing—ordinary fields	17500 lbs.
—prepared runways	21700 lbs.

For more detailed information refer to the latest BuAer technical on restrictions.
These limitations may be supplemented or superseded by instructions included in Service Publications.

RESTRICTED

b. The pilot shall obtain the initial gross weight and loading condition before entering the airplane.

c. ENTRANCE TO AIRPLANE.—A boarding ladder is installed in the right hand side of the fuselage, just aft of wing trailing edge between Station #347 and Station #362. When the step, directly above the ladder opening, is pushed in, the ladder is automatically released to slide down from the fuselage. To reach the cockpits, mount the ladder (left foot first), and using the step and handgrips, proceed forward over the wing. The ladder must be pushed back into the fuselage by the ground crew before take-off.

To open the pilot's cockpit, push the red release button on the fuselage skin below the hood and pull the hood aft.

To open the radar operator's cockpit, release the finger latch on the hood frame and lift hood, hinged on left side.

Figure 35—Ladder and Steps

2. ON ENTERING PILOT'S COCKPIT.

a. STANDARD CHECK FOR ALL FLIGHTS.

(1) Controls lock device—OFF.

(2) Ignition switch—OFF.

(3) Mixture controls—IDLE CUT-OFF.

(4) Wheels chocked (main wheels only).

(5) Check stick and pedals for free movement through full throw.

(6) Adjust seat.

(7) Battery switch—ON.

(8) Check fuel and oil supplies.

(9) Check communicating equipment.

(10) Check gun sight light.

(11) Check oxygen equipment.

(12) All armament switches—OFF.

(13) Gun charging handles to—SAFE.

(14) Check ammunition loading.

(15) Set sensitive altimeter.

(16) Gyro-horizon—uncaged.

(17) Directional gyro—uncaged.

(18) Check propellers for clearance.

b. SPECIAL CHECK FOR NIGHT FLIGHTS.

(1) Battery switch—ON.

(2) Instrument panel and cockpit lights—turn on and adjust to best light.

(3) Test operation of following switches and lights:

(a) Approach (operate hook).

(b) Landing.

(c) Wing running.

(d) Tail running.

(e) Formation.

(f) Section.

(g) Formation and section.

(h) Recognition (operate keying switch).

(4) Check radar equipment. (Refer to section V).

3. FUEL AND OIL SYSTEM MANAGEMENT.

a. OPERATION OF FUEL SYSTEM.

(1) Set engine selector valve on BOTH—since this system is not a cross-feed type the valve should be on BOTH, for operation, at all times except in the case of damage or fire when the valve should be set on the operating engine.

(2) Set tank selector valve on RESERVE—the carburetor bleed-back (vapor vent) lines return 8-10 gallons per hour to the reserve tank. Also when the fuel transfer system is in operation, fuel at the rate of 60 gallons per hour is fed to this tank. Therefore, as space must be made to accomodate this return fuel, use this tank first to avoid waste by overflow.

After warm-up, take-off, climb and leveling off, switch tank selector valve to WING DROPPABLE, FUSELAGE DROPPABLE, AUXILIARY, then MAIN tank as necessary.

CAUTION

This sequence of use of tanks is suggested but may be altered as required. Since the bleed-back and fuel transfer system direct flow to the reserve tank, its use for warm-up and take-off makes space available. When operating on droppable tanks, check quantity gage frequently for reserve tank load. If gage shows tank near full (185 gals. with and 105 gals. without removable tank) set selector valve to RESERVE and operate for sufficient time to provide space for further bleed-back and transfer.

(3) Turn fuel booster pump—ON (refer to Section I, paragraph 3, Fuel System).

(4) Primer switch — flick ON intermittently. This switch operates primer solenoid when booster pump is ON.

(5) Changing tanks in flight—
  (a) Fuel booster pump switch—ON.
  (b) Tank selector valve—TO TANK DESIRED.

Note
Be sure detent clicks into place (control definitely in place). When using Wing Drop Tanks—set toggle selector as desired before setting tank selector valve to WING DROP TANK.

(6) Fuel pressurizing—operation of this system is fully automatic at all times. Pull "T" handle to cut-off system only in armed combat or in the event of cell damage.

Note
The pressure warning light on the pilot's lower control panel glows when the pressure drops below 17 ± 1 psi.

Refer to Section I, paragraph 3, Fuel System, for further information.

b. OPERATION OF OIL SYSTEM.—The operation of these independent systems is entirely automatic except for the oil dilution and the setting of the cooler exit duct doors. The duct doors are controlled by switches on the pilot's lower control panel. Refer to Section I, paragraph 4, Oil System, and paragraphs below for settings.

The oil dilution system (when installed) is controlled by a switch on the pilot's electrical control panel. Refer to Section I, paragraph 4, Oil System, and paragraph 18.*j.*, this section.

HOLD STARTER SWITCH ON UNTIL ENGINE TURNS UNDER ITS OWN POWER

4. STARTING ENGINES.

a. With ignition and battery switches OFF, manually rotate propellers four or five times.

Note
If engines have been idle for an hour or more, it may be necessary to remove plugs from the lower cylinders to expel accumulated oil.

b. BATTERY SWITCH—ON.

c. MIXTURE—IDLE CUT-OFF.

d. FUEL TANK SELECTOR—RESERVE TANK.

e. ENGINE SELECTOR—BOTH ENGINES.

f. SUPERCHARGER—LOW.

g. CARBURETOR AIR—NORMAL.

h. COWL FLAPS—FULL OPEN.

i. OIL COOLER EXIT DOORS—OPEN.

j. GENERATORS—ON.

k. PROPELLERS — FULL INCREASE (take-off RPM).

l. THROTTLES—ONE INCH OPEN (approx.).

m. FUEL BOOSTER PUMP—ON.

Note
When starting engines see that fuel pressure gage indicates 22 ± 1 psi. Do not leave fuel booster pump switch on any longer than necessary for priming the engine that is being started. Prolonged running of the booster pump will flood the carburetor of the dead engine.

n. RIGHT ENGINE.

(1) PRIMER SWITCH—to LEFT to ON.

DON'T FLOOD DEAD ENGINE

CAUTION

Flick intermittently when using fuel booster pump.

(2) IGNITION SWITCH—ON—BOTH magnetos (right engine).

(3) STARTER SWITCH—to RIGHT to ON.

(4) MIXTURE CONTROL, RIGHT ENGINE ONLY—advance to AUTO-RICH as engine fires. If engine fails to continue running, return to IDLE CUT-OFF.

o. LEFT ENGINE.

(1) PRIMER SWITCH—to LEFT to ON.

(2) IGNITION SWITCH—ON—BOTH magnetos (left engine).

(3) STARTER SWITCH—to LEFT to ON.

(4) MIXTURE CONTROL, LEFT ENGINE ONLY—advance to AUTO-RICH as engine fires—if engine fails to continue running, return to IDLE CUT-OFF.

p. IDLE BOTH ENGINES—at 1000 r.p.m.

CAUTION

Never run engine oil pressure over 200 p.s.i. during warm-up.

If the oil pressure gage indicators do not show pressure within 30 seconds stop engines and investigate. In cold weather, due to the long oil pressure gage lines, full oil pressure may not read for several minutes. If the oil dilution system has been used, prior to shutting down, warm up engine sufficiently before take-off so that oil system is operating efficiently, except in cases of extreme emergency. As the oil operating the hydromatic propellers has not been diluted, take care to see that the propeller pitch changing mechanism is operating properly.

5. WARM-UP AND GROUND TEST.

a. Open throttles to 1200 r.p.m. until oil-in-temperature reaches 40°C (104°F). A drop in oil pressure when the throttle is opened indicates that further warm-up is required.

b. CHECK MAGNETOS.

(1) When oil-in temperature is in 50°-60°C (122-140°F) range, run engine at 32" Hg. M.P.

(2) Operate on each magneto for shortest possible time. If r.p.m. drop exceeds 75-100 stop engines and investigate.

CAUTION

Return switch to BOTH between checks to clear engines.

c. SUPERCHARGER CHECK AND DESLUDGING PROCEDURE.—The supercharger check should never be made nor the clutches desludged until the oil temperature has reached 40°C (104°F), and it is preferable to wait until the oil temperature has reached 60°C (140°F). If there is not enough time to complete a regular supercharger check, desludge the clutches twice as directed in paragraph (4) below.

(1) Adjust the throttle to obtain 1400 r.p.m.; then move the supercharger control rapidly into the "HIGH" position. Never stop movement of the control between the "LOW" and "HIGH" positions.

(2) Advance the throttle to obtain 30 in. Hg. and note the tachometer reading as soon as the manifold pressure has stabilized. Remain in high blower for a minimum of 30 seconds.

(3) Move the supercharger control from "HIGH" to "LOW," and readjust the throttle to obtain 30 in. Hg. Note the tachometer reading as soon as the manifold pressure has stabilized. If the supercharger is operating correctly, the r.p.m. in low blower will be higher than the r.p.m. in high blower for the same manifold pressure.

(4) To complete the desludging of the clutches, readjust the throttle to obtain 1400 r.p.m., and move the supercharger control into the "HIGH" position. After 30 seconds in "HIGH," return the supercharger control to "LOW."

d. CHECK PROPELLER CONTROLS. — With engine speed at 1800 r.p.m. move propeller controls up to DECREASE R.P.M. until a 300 drop in r.p.m. is shown, then return control to INCREASE R.P.M. The constant speed range of the governor is between 1200 and 2800 r.p.m.

e. CHECK PROPELLER FEATHERING CONTROLS.

(1) Run one engine at 1000 r.p.m. for high amperage drawn for feathering pumps.

(2) Run engine to be feathered at 1500 r.p.m.

(3) Push feathering button and release to feather propeller.

(4) As propeller feathers, advance throttle slightly, to prevent engine from stopping completely.

(5) When button pops out, immediately push in and hold to unfeather propeller—hold in until r.p.m. returns to idling.

f. CHECK CARBURETOR IDLE MIXTURE. — With the throttle closed and the propeller governor control in full "INCREASE RPM" the engine should idle at 600 r.p.m. Move the mixture control lever momentarily, but with a smooth steady pull, to the idle cut-off position and observe tachometer for any change in r.p.m. A momentary rise above 10 r.p.m. indicates too rich a mixture; no change indicates too lean a mixture. A 5-10 r.p.m. rise is desired.

g. CHECK INSTRUMENTS, RUNNING ENGINES AT 2000 R.P.M. IN LOW PITCH.

(1) Oil temperature 60°-85°C.

(2) Oil pressure 85-90 psi.

(3) Fuel pressure 22 ±1 psi.

(4) Cylinder head temperature 232°C (450°F max.

(5) Note MP as reference for future checks.

Note

Fuel pressure (22 ±1 psi) is relative to carburetor air pressure. It may drop to 12 psi at low r.p.m. This is normal, if pressure rises when r.p.m. is increased to 800 or 1000.

h. CHECK FUEL PUMPS.—Set fuel booster pump switch to OFF, and see that gage indicates 22 ±1 psi.

i. CHECK HYDRAULIC PRESSURE GAGE.—1250-1500 psi.

j. RUDDER BOOST SHUT-OFF CONTROL.—ON.

k. WING SPREADING. — (Jury struts removed.)

(1) Set control to SPREAD.

(2) Safety lock to LOCKED.

(3) Check position of red signal (retracted).

CHECK WING FOLDING SIGNALS BEFORE TAKE-OFF

l. FLAPS.—Operate flaps control—check to see that flaps operate properly (4 flaps move simultaneously). Check position on cockpit indicator.

CAUTION

The flaps are not interconnected mechanically but are actuated by individual hydraulic cylinders operated by a single control—it is possible that dirt may lodge in parts of the installation on a new or overhauled airplane and prevent one of the flaps from extending or retracting. Therefore, check for proper operation before take-off and lower in the air at a safe speed and altitude.

m. CHECK EMERGENCY AIR BRAKE PRESSURE.—1800 psi (gage on lower control panel).

n. CHECK GENERATOR SYSTEM.

(1) Disconnect external power, if used.

(2) With engines idling turn on cockpit lights or some other system load.

(3) Turn ON one generator switch.

(4) Slowly increase speed of engine and watch corresponding voltmeter. Reading should increase to 26.5 (approx.) volts when a slight dip will be noted indicating the closing of the reverse current cut-out. As speed is further increased voltage should reach 28.0 volts and remain constant regardless of further increase in engine r.p.m.

(5) Check other generator by reversing switch settings and repeating the operation.

(6) Defective operation is indicated (which should be corrected before take-off) if:

(a) Voltage dip at 26.5 (approx.) is not noted for either generator, indicating reverse current cut-out has not closed.

(b) Either voltmeter reading is above 28.5 or below 27.5.

o. CHECK RADIO EQUIPMENT CONTROLS.—Refer to Section V.

p. PITOT HEAD HEATER.—ON if icing conditions prevail.

q. COCKPIT HOOD.—Open.

r. LANDING LIGHT.—Check position (OFF).

s. BOARDING LADDER.—Stowed.

6. SCRAMBLE TAKEOFF.

An emergency take-off may be made in accordance with the regular take-off procedure provided that;

a Oil pressure is steady.

b. Oil temperature—at least 40°C (104°F).

c. Throttle may be advanced without causing engine to cough or cut out.

7. TAXIING INSTRUCTIONS.

The nose wheel swivels through 360°, but is equipped with a centering device which acts to return it to the trailing position. Motion of the airplane is necessary before the nose wheel casters. Apply even power to the engines to begin rolling and control the rolling speed by throttling the engines and applying the brakes. Steer the airplane by differential braking and use of engines. Abrupt and sharp turns will cause uneven tire wear and should be avoided. Once the airplane has begun to roll, it can be stopped only by braking and retarding both engines, as the thrust of one idling propeller is sufficient to overcome rolling friction. The pilot should familiarize himself with brake operation and should thoroughly understand the hydraulic system and emergency air system in case of line or pump failure. Taxi slowly over rough ground—sinking of the nose wheel causes the C.G. to move forward and impose undue loads on the nose wheel. If possible avoid rocks, ditches, etc. Forward loads may be minimized by using full up elevator and minimum braking. As speed increases, the nose wheel action stabilizes, (ground looping is impossible) and normal control is attained, by using the rudder, differential engine, and brakes, or all three together. Use the first two whenever possible to minimize brake wear.

To stop rolling, retard throttles, apply the brakes evenly, and reduce braking gradually to lessen pitching. Taxi to take-off position, allowing airplane to roll a few feet in the direction of take-off to straighten nose wheel. When taxiing across wind, control the airplane by carrying less power on the lee engine.

CAUTION

Do not taxi with wings folded without jury struts in place.

8. TAKE-OFF.

a. Refer to TAKE-OFF, CLIMB AND LANDING CHART, Appendix I.

b. Check-off list.

(1) Traffic clearance.

(2) Shoulder harness—SECURED and LOCKED.

(3) Wings—SPREAD and LOCKED.

DON'T TAXI THROUGH ANYTHING!

(4) Landing light—OFF.

(5) Pitot head—ON (if icing).

(6) Cockpit hood — OPEN (close before 140 knots).

(7) Boarding ladder—STOWED.

(8) Rudder booster—ON.

(9) Cowl flaps—AUTOMATIC (open).

(10) Oil cooler exit duct doors—OPEN.

(11) Carburetor air—NORMAL.

(12) Propellers—INCREASE.

(13) Mixture—AUTO-RICH.

(14) Supercharger—LOW.

(15) Engine selector—BOTH.

(16) Tank selector—RESERVE.

(17) Fuel booster pump—ON.

(18) Tabs control settings—ALL NEUTRAL.

(19) Flaps setting—AS REQUIRED.

Note

Flaps may be set in any one of the four positions. Airplane can become airborne in 500 feet (approx.) with zero wind and flaps FULL DOWN (40°).

c. Hold airplane with brakes until 30-40" Hg. M.P. is indicated on both engines, then release. Before 20 to 30 knots speed is reached, directional control can be maintained easily with brakes or engines; at approximately this speed, rudder control and castering become effective. During the first part of the roll, it is desirable to lift the nose wheel slightly clear of the ground in order to obtain better directional control with the rudder. If a short take-off must be made, the airplane may be dragged off at low speed. However, for normal field operation it is recommended that the airplane be flown off at high speed to insure better control in the event of engine failure. Minimum speed for take-off is 57-70 knots approximately—normal speed is 75-80 knots. For shortest ground run, and for safe clearance of obstacles, use full flaps. Since the C.G. is only slightly forward of the main wheels, smaller elevator stick forces are necessary, as the wheel load changes to wing load. Allow the airplane to accelerate to 140 knots I.A.S. before starting climb to insure control if one engine should fail. Minimum indicated airspeed of 120 knots is necessary for rudder control if one engine fails.

d. Open throttles to 53.5" Hg. M.P. for five minutes only.

e. Immediately after leaving the ground RAISE LANDING GEAR.

f. RAISE FLAPS.

g. Adjust power plant according to the POWER PLANT CHART, Section III.

9. ENGINE FAILURE DURING TAKE-OFF.

a. If one or both engines fail before airplane is airborne close both throttles and apply brakes.

b. If one or both engines fail after take-off but before 120 knots I.A.S. is reached:

(1) Close both throttles.

(2) Land straight ahead.

(3) Retract landing gear if landing must be made beyond field limits, on soft or rough ground, or in water.

c. If one engine fails, and 140 knots I.A.S. is reached or sufficient altitude has been attained:

(1) Nose down to pick up flying speed (120 knots is minimum for control with one engine).

(2) Rudder into running engine.

(3) Drop wing as fast as possible on side toward runing engine.

(4) Close throttle of dead engine and feather the propeller.

(5) Check that landing gear is up, or coming up.

(6) Set rudder tab to hold straight course.

(7) Engine selector valve to good engine only.

(8) Mixture control (dead engine) IDLE CUT-OFF.

(9) Ignition switch of dead engine to OFF.

(10) Lower landing gear during final approach.

(11) Circle field, turning toward good engine, maintaining speed and make engine assisted approach at 120 knots I.A.S. minimum.

(12) To avoid excessive rudder force, reduce rudder tab as speed falls off in final approach. The tricycle landing gear makes it possible for this airplane to be flown in at a higher speed than an airplane equipped with the two-wheeled landing gear.

CAUTION

Do not lower wheels until final approach.
Do not lower flaps until certain the field can be reached.

If engine failure is due to fuel pressure loss as indicated by the gage (and the booster fuel pump is ON) a break in the fuel line is probable. Make certain that the engine selector valve is set to cut off the bad engine.

With the left engine dead (the critical condition), and windmilling at 2400 r.p.m., and the right engine operating at 75% power, the minimum speed necessary for straight flight and landing is 120 knots. At this speed, little aileron is necessary to oppose rolling tendencies.

With the left propeller feathered, and the minimum speed for straight flight 113 knots approximately, 1/3 aileron deflection is necessary to maintain straight and wing level flight. All rudder forces can be held easily with the rudder booster on, and fairly easily with the booster off.

At 151 knots approximately all forces can be trimmed out with tabs, for cruising, and a fair rate of climb can be maintained.

10. CLIMB.

a. Reduce manifold pressure to 41" Hg. approximately and r.p.m. to 2600 as soon as practicable.

b. Check that oil cooler duct doors are open and cowl flap control switch is in AUTOMATIC.

Refer to Section III, power plant chart and Appendix I—take-off, climb and landing chart, and flight operation instruction chart for best climbing speed, power settings, range, etc.

Maximum permissible cylinder head temperature 260°C (502°F).

Maximum permissible oil temperature 95°C (203°F).

Note

Full military power is permissible for five minutes but it is not good practice unless absolutely necessary.

11. GENERAL FLYING CHARACTERISTICS.

a. GENERAL.—Refer to Appendix I—flight operation instruction chart, for cruising speed, fuel consumption, etc. Cruising operations may be conducted at any engine power below normal rated power but if minimum fuel consumption is important, and, if it is tactically feasible, cruising operations should be conducted in a range not exceeding the maximum cruise settings given in the Power Plant Chart.

The engines should be operated in AUTO-LEAN for cruising power operation as shown on the power plant chart. If 232°C (450°F) cylinder head temperature is exceeded, the mixture should be enriched.

Do not exceed the cruising M.P.—r.p.m. relationships specified in the chart.

Set tabs controls for best trim.

If droppable tanks are carried, fuel from them should be used up before the MAIN, RESERVE, and AUXILIARY tanks. Remember that the bleed-back from the carburetor vapor vent lines returns 8-10 gallons per hour to the RESERVE tank. Refer to Section II, paragraph 3, fuel management.

General flight characteristics of this airplane are good. Stick forces in most flight maneuvers are light and controllability is good. Very little change in trim is apparent with changes of speed and power. The excellent visibility adds materially to the ease of flying the airplane.

Note

Throttles are synchronized at cruising settings. At take-off settings they are approximately 1/2" apart.

b. SUPERCHARGER OPERATION.

These engines are equipped with two-speed superchargers and should be operated in the blower ratios specified on the power plant chart, Section III. High blower ratio should only be used as indicated on the chart to obtain maximum speed and rate of climb. High blower should not be used at cruising altitudes when cruising power is available in low blower, as fuel economy is inferior and there is greater tendency for the engine to detonate.

Do not shift the supercharger control more often than at five minute intervals, except in an emergency, to allow dissipation of heat from the blower clutches. The control must be either fully up or fully down, to prevent clutch slippage and to insure availability of rated power at all times. If practicable, at the end of five hours operation in either blower ratio, shift to the other ratio for five minutes to eliminate sludge accumulation in the clutches.

Although it is possible to make clutch shifts at Military and War Emergency Power, it should not be done except in an emergency; and, in general, clutch shifting should be confined to engine speeds between 1200 r.p.m. and 2400 r.p.m. If "AUTO LEAN" mixture is being used before shifting from "LOW" to "HIGH" it is not necessary to move the mixture control to "AUTO RICH" before making the shift. However, if the engine tends to cut out during a shift while operating in "AUTO LEAN," this tendency will be reduced if the mixture control is moved to "AUTO RICH" before making the shift.

(1) SHIFT FROM "LOW" TO "HIGH".

(a) Move supercharger control to the "HIGH" position. Then immediately retard the throttle to reduce the manifold pressure 3 or 4 in. Hg. before the high ratio clutches can engage.

(b) As soon as the high ratio clutches have engaged and the manifold pressure has stabilized, adjust the propeller control and the throttle control to obtain the desired power.

(2) To change from HIGH to LOW:

(a) Mixture control—AUTO RICH.

(b) Shift control rapidly from HIGH to LOW.

(c) Readjust rpm throttle setting and mixture control to obtain desired power.

c. WATER INJECTION SYSTEM OPERATION.—The system supply provides fluid for approximately five minutes operation therefore it must be conserved for emergency use only.

(1) Set water pump switch on lower control panel to ON. This switch starts the A.D.I. pumps to deliver fluid under pressure to the regulators.

(2) Mixture—AUTO RICH.

(3) Propellers—FULL INCREASE R.P.M.

(4) Throttles—FULL FORWARD (last ¼ inch travel closes switch to operate regulators and admit fluid to blowers).

12. STALLS.

The airplane will shake and mush slowly, losing altitude until the stick is pushed forward—flying speed will be re-attained quickly with the forward movement of the stick. Stalling characteristics are similar in both clean and landing conditions, and, therefore, can be reduced to two classifications, power-on and power-off.

The stalling speeds for the airplane in the landing condition are:

Power OFF—69-70 knots.

Power ON —59-60 knots.

Minimum power for level flight is used in power stalls. Speed is reduced by slowly bringing the nose above the horizon. About 10 knots above the stalling speed the entire airplane begins to tremble with increasing amplitude until the airspeed becomes constant.

No clean breakaway is ever felt. The airplane shakes and mushes slowly, losing altitude until the stick is pushed forward. With this movement the stall shake disappears immediately and flying speed is regained.

Power off stalls are approximately the same except the stall breaks clean without either wing "falling off". Flying speed is quickly resumed with forward movement of the stick. Slow speed control is good. Lateral control in a prolonged stall could be maintained with rudder. Elevator forces to stall are fairly high but not uncomfortable. This force immediately lightens with stall recovery. Most stall recoveries could be made with only 300 to 400 feet loss of altitude.

13. SPINS.

INTENTIONAL SPINS ARE PROHIBITED. Refer to paragraph 1a, this section. To recover from an inadvertant spin (which will be very violent and oscillating):

a. Simultaneously REVERSE RUDDER and NEUTRAL STICK for ½ turn (approx.).

b. Move stick FORWARD. The airplane will not recover until the stick is pushed FORWARD—then it will come out sharply. During recovery the nose will drop 30° (approx.) and the airplane will come out in the direction of rotation of the spin.

CAUTION
DO NOT PULL OUT OF DIVE UNTIL FLYING SPEED IS REGAINED, especially in a heavy loading condition.

14. PERMISSIBLE ACROBATICS.

All acrobatics, with the exception of those listed in paragraph 1a., this section, may be performed with this airplane. However, before starting any acrobatics or violent maneuvers:

a. Cage—gyro horizon.

b. Cage—directional gyro.

15. DIVING.

a. For ordinary short dives in maneuvers the engine nose sections will not load up nor will the engines cool off to any extent.

(1) Set propellers to 1900-2200 r.p.m.

(2) Close cowl flaps (manual).

(3) Set supercharger—low blower.

(4) Set trim tabs control.

(a) Rudder—0.

(b) Elevator—0.

(c) Aileron—0.

b. For prolonged dives to avoid loading up the engine nose sections or cooling the engines excessively:

(1) Set propeller controls to max. cruising r.p.m. (2250 ±100).

(2) Set throttles to 15" Hg. M.P.

c. MAX. DIVING R.P.M. — 3120 FOR 30 SECONDS.

d. In the event that overspeeding beyond the overspeed limit of the engines occurs the following procedure is recommended:

(1) Throttles to CLOSE.

(2) Propellers to DECREASE.

(3) Reduce air speed to minimum speed for safe glide.

CAUTION

When diving from a high altitude, manifold pressure will build up rapidly at a constant throttle setting. At completion of dive, advance throttles very slowly so that partly cooled engine will not cut-out.

e. HIGH SPEED DIVES.—Since it may become difficult for the pilot, during operations, to remember the restricted speed and "g" for the airplane at various altitudes when making high speed dives and consequently making it difficult to fly the airplane to its maximum performance, the following dive characteristics are given:

(1) DIVE ENTRY.—Dives of from 0° to 25° angle can be started from high speed level flight and full power from almost any altitude without running into any aerodynamic or compressibility troubles. Dives of from 25° to 30° at full power extended below 10000 feet might exceed the ultimate restricted speed of the airplane. Therefore, when prolonged dives are extended below 10000 feet, careful engine control should be maintained in order not to exceed the restricted speed of 430 k. at any time.

In dives of over 30° extreme care must be given to the method of entry. Half rolls and half loops may be done in the F7F, starting from an altitude of 20000 feet at approximately 200 k. The half roll and the half loop at this altitude cannot be extended over 1000 or 2000 feet in an absolute vertical dive path before recovery must be made prior to running into compressibility troubles therefore, overhead gunnery approaches from over 20000 feet should be carefully planned in order to execute the entry into a vertical dive from as slow a speed as possible.

WARNING

Steep dive entries from altitudes above 20000 feet should always be started from as slow a speed as possible.

(2) CONTINUED DIVING.—In prolonged dives up to 30°, the dive angle can be maintained by the use of the stick or the elevator tab control. Care should be exercised (in the F7F-1) that the restricted manifold pressure limits of the engine are not exceeded. It is very easy (in the F7F-1) to pick up a large increase in manifold pressure in only a few thousand feet of diving because of the excellent ram effect in this airplane and the fact that manifold pressure regulators have not been installed on all production airplanes. A similar increase in manifold pressure will occur even though a manifold pressure regulator is installed, if a dive is entered above critical altitude.

In dives of over 30° the airspeed will increase quickly and will place the airplane in the compressibility range in a very short time. The first evidences of the compressibility effects are loss of elevator tab effectiveness and a spongy elevator control feeling until the stick is pulled back far enough to bottom the elevator spring tab. The airplane then tends to nose over into a steeper dive angle and finally the elevator becomes immovable. After the first nose-down tendencies of the airplane are felt, a large pull force on the elevator control will enable the pilot to make his dive path shallower. In cases of very steep dives these first tendencies will give the pilot only a very short time to appreciate the situation, and unless very quick realization is felt for his predicament, the elevator stick forces will be in the frozen condition before the pilot will have time to make use of the first symptoms of compressibility. When the airplane is in the compressibility range and after the elevator control tab has lost its effectiveness, it will be of no avail to use the elevator tab control because after the elevator tab control is set in some other position than the position it was when the compressibility range was entered, excessive loads may be imposed on the airplane when the airplane again comes out of compressibility range.

Note

Do not use the elevator tab for control after the compressibility range has been entered.

(3) DIVE RECOVERY.—Starting from 16000 feet at approximately 100 to 110 k, vertical dives have been made up to 6000 feet in length. Using a constant 5 g acceleration for recovery, the pull-out was begun at 340 k. Before the airplane had approached level flight in the pull-out, the airspeed increased to 410 k IAS. This will serve as an example to show that steep dives must be recovered with a large margin of speed prior to reaching the restricted speed of the airplane.

WARNING

Do not wait until compressibility effects are felt in steep angle dives and especially at high altitudes. If recoveries are withheld until the compressibility effects are felt, there will be insufficient control for proper recovery.

If all of the symptoms mentioned are carefully considered and the pilot is careful to look-out for such effects during the early part of his training, no difficulty should be experienced in flying this airplane to its maximum performance.

16. NIGHT FLYING.

a. Wear red goggles for ½ hour before each flight.

b. Avoid all light (searchlights, flares, etc.) as much as possible, except red light.

c. Do not look at lighted instruments longer than necessary even though light is red.

d. Practice "blindfold drills" until all controls can be operated with ease in the dark.

e. Scan the sky systematically, moving the eyes over small areas at a time. Do not stare. Learn to look for night targets out of the corners of the eyes.

f. Use oxygen for all night flights.

g. Learn to look for and identify objects solely by contrast (light and shadow).

17. APPROACH AND LANDING.

a. Check-off list:

(1) TANK SELECTOR—MAIN or best tank.

(2) FUEL BOOST PUMP—ON.

(3) MIXTURE—AUTO-RICH.

(4) SUPERCHARGER—low blower.

(5) CARBURETOR AIR — NORMAL or as needed.

(6) PROPELLERS — 2400 r.p.m. (on the approach).

Note

If more power is necessary, in landing, move throttle slowly and smoothly, to prevent overspeeding of the engine.

(7) Reduce speed below 120 knots and lower landing gear.

(8) ARRESTING HOOK — DOWN (if carrier landing).

(9) Depress brake pedals and check hydraulic pressure.

(10) ARMAMENT MASTER SWITCH—OFF.

(11) LANDING GEAR—DOWN.

(12) FLAPS CONTROL—DOWN.

SAFETY YOUR GUNS BEFORE COMING IN

CAUTION

Do not operate flaps at—
15° in excess of 225 knots I.A.S.
30° in excess of 150 knots I.A.S.
40° in excess of 130 knots I.A.S.

Reasonable control may be maintained with any one flap not synchronized. The loss of hydraulic pressure cannot cause flaps to become unsynchronized.

(13) Check positions on landing gear and flap indicator and check visually main wheels and nose wheel (mirror on L.H. nacelle).

(14) COCKPIT HOOD—locked open.

(15) Refer to Appendix I, Take-off, Climb and Landing Chart, for landing run distances.

b. NORMAL LANDING PROCEDURE.

(1) The feeling of controllability during the approach may be deceiving to pilots accustomed to airplanes not equipped with spring controls. Stick forces are light and effective. There is no change in trim with extension of the landing gear only—extension of the landing gear and flaps makes the airplane slightly nose heavy.

(2) The position of the cowl flaps and oil cooler exit duct doors affects neither landing speed, trim or feel, and landings can be made with these flaps closed —OPEN FLAPS IMMEDIATELY UPON LANDING.

(3) For best approach and landing, with the landing gear and flaps extended, with 15-20" Hg. M.P. approximately and at about 100 knots, close the throttle at approximately 100 ft. altitude, before reaching the end of the runway—this will give the airplane considerable float after leveling off.

(4) Minimum approach speed, with landing gear and flaps extended, is 87 knots approximately. Stick forces in leveling off are fairly light and controllability is good. As soon as the airplane is leveled out above the runway, the elevator stick forces increase considerably.

(5) With the C.G. normal (at about 24.5% M.A.C.) a landing can be made easily with one hand, but when the C.G. is 22.5-23% M.A.C., stick forces become critical for one handed landing.

(6) The best procedure for normal landings is to hold the nose wheel off until the main wheels contact, then let the nose wheel touch the runway of its own accord and apply the brakes. When the airplane is rolling on the main wheels, excellent control can be maintained with rudder alone, until the nose wheel touches; then either the brakes or engines may be used for directional control.

(7) A carrier wave-off can be made with this airplane with little difficulty. There is little torque effect from power even with full tail heavy tab; the stick forces are not excessive when full power is applied.

(8) Apply brakes evenly; if brakes are applied

LAND ON MAIN WHEELS FIRST - HOLD NOSE WHEEL OFF

with the nose wheel off the ground, undue bouncing of the nose wheel may occur. On slippery runways, for more effective braking, hold the nose wheel off and apply up elevator; more load will be put upon the main wheels, off-setting the pitching movement as the brakes are applied. If one brake should lock, due to uneven pressure application, or uneven surface friction on a slippery runway, the airplane will swing toward the locked wheel. Release the brakes, and re-apply evenly.

c. CROSS WIND LANDING.—The airplane may be landed in 90° cross winds up to 30 MPH with no difficulty. As long as the flight path is concurrent with the runway, the airplane will turn itself into a straight path along the runway upon contact without the necessity of the pilot kicking the airplane straight before touching. To overcome cross winds in taxiing reduce power on the lee engine.

d. MINIMUM RUN LANDING.

THIS INFORMATION WILL BE SUPPLIED WHEN AVAILABLE

e TAKE-OFF IF LANDING IS NOT COMPLETED:
 (1) Open both throttles slowly and smoothly.
 (2) Move governor controls to full INCREASE R.P.M. if propellers were not previously set to 2800 r.p.m.
 (3) Raise landing gear.
 (4) Raise flaps after minimum safe altitude has been attained.
 (5) Reduce power.

f. AT COMPLETION OF LANDING:
 (1) FLAPS—UP.
 (2) COWL FLAPS—OPEN (manual).
 (3) OIL COOLER EXIT DUCT DOORS—OPEN (manual).
 (4) ELECTRIC BOOSTER FUEL PUMP—OFF.
 (5) Taxi clear of runway. Avoid taxiing through tall grass, mud, etc., to avoid damage to nose wheel or propellers.

18. STOPPING ENGINES.

a. PROPELLERS—Full "INCREASE RPM" position.
b. SUPERCHARGER CONTROL.—Run each engine at 1200 to 1400 rpm and make several shifts through HIGH and LOW remaining in each position for about 30 seconds.
c. MIXTURE CONTROLS—IDLE CUT-OFF.
d. IGNITION SWITCH (BOTH)—OFF (when engine stops).
e. BATTERY SWITCH—OFF.
f. RADIO CONTROLS AND SWITCHES—OFF.
g. ENGINE SELECTOR VALVE—OFF.
h. TANK SELECTOR VALVE—OFF.
i. OIL DILUTION PROCEDURE—If cold weather starting temperature below −5°C (−23°F)—is anticipated the oil dilution system should be operated as follows:

Note

Applicable only if oil dilution parts have been installed.

 (1) OIL DILUTION SHUT-OFF COCK—open.
 (2) ENGINE SPEED—1000 r.p.m.
 (3) OIL DILUTION SWITCH—ON for two minutes approximately.

Note

When the solenoid valve is opened by the switch action, there will be a sharp drop in indicated fuel pressure. Fuel pressure should return to normal immediately after closing the valve. If not, stop the engine at once and check for valve leakage

 (4) MIXTURE CONTROL—IDLE CUT-OFF (after two minutes—to stop engine).

(5) IGNITION SWITCH—OFF.

(6) OIL DILUTION SWITCH—OFF (after engine stops turning). If the oil pressure of a cold engine, started after oil dilution, fluctuates or drops, after running a short time, the oil dilution switch should be moved to ON, for intervals of a few seconds each, for about fifteen seconds. If oil pressure still does not steady out, stop the engine and wait five minutes before attempting another start.

19. BEFORE LEAVING THE PILOT'S COCKPIT.

a. ARMAMENT SWITCHES—OFF.

b. IGNITION SWITCH—OFF.

c. RADIO SWITCHES—OFF.

d. TANK SELECTOR VALVE—OFF.

e. ENGINE SELECTOR VALVE—OFF.

f. COWL FLAPS—OPEN.

g. OIL COOLER EXIT DUCT DOORS—CLOSED (if cool).

h. WING FLAPS—UP.

i. WINGS.—Folded, jury struts in place—or spread, if desired.

j. FLYING CONTROLS.—Controls lock in place.

k. MAIN BATTERY SWITCH—OFF.

l. GENERATOR SWITCHES—OFF.

m. COCKPIT HOOD(S)—CLOSED.

20. MOORING.

Mooring rings are provided on the bottoms of the main landing gear struts, at the axles.

SECTION III
OPERATING DATA

AIRSPEED INSTALLATION CORRECTION TABLE	
I.A.S. (KNOTS)	CORRECTION
FLAPS DOWN	
100	Add 7.0
110	Add 2.5
120	Deduct 1.5
130	Deduct 3.5
135	Deduct 2.0
FLAPS UP	
100	Add 11.0
120	Add 9.0
140	Add 7.0
160	Add 5.0
180	Add 3.0
200	— 0
220	Deduct 1.0
240	Deduct 3.5
270	Deduct 6.5
300	Deduct 9.5
350	Deduct 14.5
400	Deduct 20.0
430	Deduct 24.0

Figure 36—Airspeed Installation Correction Table

Section III
RESTRICTED
AN 01-85FA-1

POWER PLANT CHART

AIRCRAFT MODEL(S)	PROPELLER(S)	ENGINE MODEL(S)
F7F	Hamilton-Standard Hydromatic Full-Feathering	R2800-22W

GAUGE READING	FUEL PRESS.	OIL PRESS.	OIL TEMP.	COOLANT TEMP.	OIL CONS.		
DESIRED MAXIMUM	22 / 23	75-95 / 100	60-85 / 95			MAXIMUM PERMISSABLE DIVING RPM: MINIMUM RECOMMENDED CRUISE RPM: MAXIMUM RECOMMENDED TURBO RPM:	
MINIMUM IDLING	21 / 18	60 / 25	40(8)			OIL GRADE: (S) 1100 (W) Spec. AN-VV-O-446a FUEL GRADE: 100/130 Spec. AN-F-28	

WAR EMERGENCY (COMBAT EMERGENCY)			MILITARY POWER (NON-COMBAT EMERGENCY)			OPERATING CONDITION			NORMAL RATED (MAXIMUM CONTINUOUS)			MAXIMUM CRUISE (NORMAL OPERATION)		
MINUTES			Five MINUTES			TIME LIMIT			1 Hour Unlimited			Unlimited		
			260°C			MAX. CYL. HD. TEMP.			260°C 232°C			232°C		
			Auto Rich 2800			MIXTURE R.P.M.			Auto Lean (4) 2600			Auto Lean 2200		
MANIF. PRESS.	SUPER-CHARGER	FUEL Gal/Min	MANIF. PRESS.	SUPER-CHARGER	FUEL Gal/Min	STD. TEMP. °C	PRESSURE ALTITUDE	STD. TEMP. °F	MANIF. PRESS.	SUPER-CHARGER	FUEL GPH	MANIF. PRESS.	SUPER-CHARGER	FUEL GPH
						-55.0	40,000 FT.	-67.0						
						-55.0	38,000 FT.	-67.0						
						-55.0	36,000 FT.	-67.0						
						-52.4	34,000 FT.	-62.3						
						-48.1	32,000 FT.	-55.1						
			F.T.	High	1.9	-44.0	30,000 FT.	-48.0	F.T.	High	82	F.T.	High	55
			F.T.	High	2.2	-40.5	28,000 FT.	-40.9	F.T.	High	93	F.T.	High	59
			F.T.	High	2.4	-36.5	26,000 FT.	-33.7	F.T.	High	106	F.T.	High	63
			F.T.	High	2.6	-32.5	24,000 FT.	-26.5	F.T.	High	121	F.T.	High	68
			F.T.	High	2.9	-28.6	22,000 FT.	-19.6	F.T.	High	136	F.T.	High	73
			F.T.	High	3.2	-24.6	20,000 FT.	-12.3	F.T.	High	155	F.T.	High	78
			F.T.	High	3.5	-20.7	18,000 FT.	-5.2	41.5	High	172	F.T.	High	86
			48.5	High	3.7	-16.7	16,000 FT.	2.0	41.5	High	170	33	High	89
			48.5	High	3.7	-12.7	14,000 FT.	9.1	41.5	High	168	33	High	88
			48.5	High	3.7	-8.8	12,000 FT.	16.2	F.T.	Low	145	F.T.(7)	Low	83
			(5)F.T.	Low	3.5	-4.8	10,000 FT.	23.6	(6)F.T.	Low	164	32	Low	89
			F.T.	Low	3.9	-0.8	8,000 FT.	30.6	41	Low	172	32	Low	89
			F.T.	Low	4.2	3.1	6,000 FT.	37.4	41	Low	170	32	Low	87
			F.T.	Low	4.5	7.1	4,000 FT.	44.7	41	Low	168	32	Low	85
			53	Low	4.6	11.8	2,000 FT.	51.8	41	Low	166	32	Low	83
			53	Low	4.6	15.0	SEA LEVEL	59.0	41	Low	163	32	Low	78

(Left columns note: "This information will be supplied when available")

GENERAL NOTES

(1) OIL CONSUMPTION: MAXIMUM U.S. QUART PER HOUR PER ENGINE.
(2) Gal/Min: APPROXIMATE U.S. GALLON PER MINUTE PER ENGINE.
(3) GPH: APPROXIMATE U.S. GALLON PER HOUR PER ENGINE.
F.T.: MEANS FULL THROTTLE OPERATION.
VALUES ARE FOR LEVEL FLIGHT WITH RAM.

FOR COMPLETE CRUISING DATA SEE APPENDIX II
NOTE: TO DETERMINE CONSUMPTION IN BRITISH IMPERIAL UNITS, MULTIPLY BY 10 THEN DIVIDE BY 12. RED FIGURES ARE PRELIMINARY SUBJECT TO REVISION AFTER FLIGHT CHECK.

TAKE-OFF CONDITIONS:	2800 RPM	53.5" MP	CONDITIONS TO AVOID:
Low Blower Cyl. Hd. Temp.	Auto Rich 2600° Max.		

SPECIAL NOTES

(4) Use Auto Rich for all operation above 2600 RPM. Use Auto Lean for flight operation at 2600 RPM and below, provided cylinder head temperature limits are not exceeded.
(5) Shift to High Blower when MP drops to 40".
(6) Shift to High Blower when MP drops to 35".
(7) Shift to High Blower when MP drops to 29.5".
Blower-Shift Altitudes are approximate and vary with carburetor entrance conditions.
(8) Minimum oil temperature for normal Take-Off.

DATA AS OF 2-1-45 BASED ON R2800-22W Operating Limits Chart dated 2 Jan. 1945

Figure 37 (Sheet 1 of 2 Sheets)—Power Plant Chart

RESTRICTED
AN 01-85FA-1
Section III

POWER PLANT CHART

AIRCRAFT MODEL(S)	PROPELLER(S)	ENGINE MODEL(S)
F7F	Hamilton-Standard Hydromatic Full-Feathering	R-2800-34W

GAUGE READING	FUEL PRESS.	OIL PRESS.	OIL TEMP.	COOLANT TEMP.		OIL CONS.
DESIRED MAXIMUM	22	75-95	60-85			
	23	100	95			
MINIMUM IDLING	21	60	40(8)			
	18	25				

MAXIMUM PERMISSABLE DIVING RPM: 3120
MINIMUM RECOMMENDED CRUISE RPM:
MAXIMUM RECOMMENDED TURBO RPM:

OIL GRADE: (a) 1100 (w)Spec: AN-VV-O-446a
FUEL GRADE: 100/130 Spec. AN-F-28

OPERATING CONDITION	WAR EMERGENCY (COMBAT EMERGENCY)			MILITARY POWER (NON-COMBAT EMERGENCY)						NORMAL RATED (MAXIMUM CONTINUOUS)			MAXIMUM CRUISE (NORMAL OPERATION)		
TIME LIMIT	MINUTES			Five MINUTES						One hour Unlimited			Unlimited		
MAX. CYL. HD. TEMP.				260°C						260°C 232°C			232°C		
MIXTURE				Auto Rich						Auto Lean			Auto Lean		
R.P.M.				2800						2600			2200		
	MANIF. PRESS.	SUPER-CHARGER	FUEL GAL/HR	MANIF. PRESS.	SUPER-CHARGER	FUEL GAL/HR	STD. TEMP. °C	PRESSURE ALTITUDE	STD. TEMP. °F	MANIF. PRESS.	SUPER-CHARGER	FUEL GPH	MANIF. PRESS.	SUPER-CHARGER	FUEL GPH
							-56.0	40,000 FT.	-67.0						
							-56.0	38,000 FT.	-67.0						
							-56.0	36,000 FT.	-67.0						
							-52.4	34,000 FT.	-62.3						
							-48.4	32,000 FT.	-55.1						
				F.T.	High	1.9	-44.6	30,000 FT.	-48.0	F.T.	High	84	F.T.	High	57
				F.T.	High	2.2	-40.5	28,000 FT.	-40.9	F.T.	High	86	F.T.	High	61
				F.T.	High	2.5	-36.5	26,000 FT.	-33.7	F.T.	High	95	F.T.	High	66
				F.T.	High	2.8	-32.5	24,000 FT.	-26.5	F.T.	High	115	F.T.	High	70
				F.T.	High	3.1	-28.6	22,000 FT.	-19.4	F.T.	High	134	F.T.	High	76
				F.T.	High	3.5	-24.6	20,000 FT.	-12.3	F.T.	High	149	F.T.	High	81
				F.T.	High	3.8	-20.7	18,000 FT.	-5.2	42	High	165	33	High	88
				49.5	High	4.0	-16.7	16,000 FT.	2.0	42	High	164	33	High	87
				49.5	High	4.0	-12.7	14,000 FT.	9.1	42	High	163	33	High	86
				49.5	High	3.9	-8.8	12,000 FT.	16.2	(6)F.T.	Low	145	(7)F.T.	Low	83
				(5)F.T.	Low	3.5	-4.8	10,000 FT.	23.4	F.T.	Low	164	32	Low	89
				F.T.	Low	3.9	-0.8	8,000 FT.	30.5	41	Low	172	32	Low	89
				F.T.	Low	4.2	3.1	6,000 FT.	37.6	41	Low	170	32	Low	87
				F.T.	Low	4.5	7.1	4,000 FT.	44.7	41	Low	168	32	Low	85
				53	Low	4.6	11.0	2,000 FT.	51.8	41	Low	166	32	Low	83
				53	Low	4.6	15.0	SEA LEVEL	58.0	41	Low	163	32	Low	78

This information will be supplied at a later date

GENERAL NOTES

(1) OIL CONSUMPTION: MAXIMUM U.S. QUART PER HOUR PER ENGINE.
(2) Gal/Hr: APPROXIMATE U.S. GALLON PER MINUTE PER ENGINE.
(3) GPH: APPROXIMATE U.S. GALLON PER HOUR PER ENGINE.
F.T.: MEANS FULL THROTTLE OPERATION.
VALUES ARE FOR LEVEL FLIGHT WITH RAM.

FOR COMPLETE CRUISING DATA SEE APPENDIX II
NOTE: TO DETERMINE CONSUMPTION IN BRITISH IMPERIAL UNITS, MULTIPLY BY 10 THEN DIVIDE BY 12. RED FIGURES ARE PRELIMINARY SUBJECT TO REVISION AFTER FLIGHT CHECK.

TAKE-OFF CONDITIONS:	2800 RPM	53.5" MP	CONDITIONS TO AVOID:
Low Blower	Auto Rich		
Cyl. Hd. Temp.	260°C Max.		

SPECIAL NOTES

(4) Use Auto Rich for all operation above 2600 RPM. Use Auto Lean for flight operation at 2600 RPM and below, provided cylinder head temperature limits are not exceeded.
(5) Shift to High Blower when manifold pressure drops to 41".
(6) Shift to High Blower when manifold pressure drops to 36".
(7) Shift to High Blower when manifold pressure drops to 30".
Blower-Shift Altitudes are approximate and vary with carburetor entrance conditions.
(8) Minimum oil temperature for Normal Take-Off.

DATA AS OF 2-1-45 BASED ON R2800-34W Operating Limits Chart, dated 8 Jan. 1945

Figure 37 (Sheet 2 of 2 Sheets)—Power Plant Chart

SECTION IV
EMERGENCY OPERATING INSTRUCTIONS

1. FIRE.

a. Engine selector valve to cut off engine afire.

b. Cowl flaps—OPEN.

c. Oil cooler exit duct doors—OPEN.

d. Throttle (engine afire)—OPEN to blow out fire.

2. ENGINE FAILURE.

a. On take-off before leaving ground (one or both engines).

(1) Close throttles.

(2) Apply brakes.

b. On take-off after leaving ground but before reaching 120 knots I.A.S. (Necessary for control) (one or both engines).

(1) Close throttles.

(2) Land straight ahead.

(3) Retract gear if landing must be made beyond field limits, on rough or soft ground or in water.

c. In flight after 120 knots I.A.S. has been reached.

(1) ONE ENGINE.

(*a*) Nose down to pick-up flying speed.

(*b*) Full feather propeller of dead engine.

(*c*) Rudder into running engine.

(*d*) Drop wing slightly below horizontal on side toward running engine.

(*e*) Close throttle of dead engine.

(*f*) Dead engine mixture—IDLE CUT-OFF.

(*g*) Ignition switch dead engine—OFF.

(*h*) Check that landing gear is UP or coming up.

(*i*) Set rudder to hold straight course.

(*j*) Set trim tabs as required.

(*k*) Save good engine by using only necessary power to maintain safe altitude.

(*l*) Single engine operation—refer to Appendix I, Flight Operation Instruction Chart.

(2) BOTH ENGINES.

(*a*) Nose down to pick up flying speed.

(*b*) Full feather both propellers.

(*c*) Check tank selector valve and fuel quantity gage—failure may be due to empty tank.

(*d*) If fuel is OK—set mixture at AUTO-RICH.

(*e*) Check both magnetos (each engine) individually.

d. To restart engine(s) during flight.

(1) Set dead engine controls as follows:

(*a*) Check engine selector valve for proper setting.

(*b*) Throttle—CLOSED.

(*c*) Propeller—decrease r.p.m.

(*d*) Mixture—IDLE CUT-OFF.

(*e*) Ignition—ON.

(*f*) Propeller feathering control—hold IN to unfeather and until r.p.m. reaches 1200 (or propeller will feather again) when governor will take over.

(*g*) Move mixture control to AUTO-RICH

(*h*) Warm up engine and increase power as required.

CAUTION

The engine must not be run on full power until oil pressure is normal and temperature reaches 50°C (122°F).

3. FORCED LANDINGS.

a. ON GROUND.

(1) Maintain flying speed.

(2) Jettison droppable tanks or bombs (safed).

(3) If landing must be made on soft or rough ground retract landing gear.

If a wheels-down landing is to be made use emergency air system ("T" handles — air bottles) to lower gear. Refer to paragraph 4, this section.

(4) Flaps—DOWN.

(5) Lock shoulder harness.

(6) Advise radar operator (F7F-2N).

(7) Release cockpit hood(s).

(8) Make landing well above stalling speed into the wind.

(9) Immediately before contact—

(a) Battery, generator, ignition switches—OFF.

(b) Engine selector valve—OFF.

b. ON WATER.—The procedure for an emergency landing on water is essentially the same as that for on land except that the landing gear must always be UP.

(1) Smooth sea—land into the wind.

(2) Rough sea—land along trough of swell—across wind if necessary.

4. EMERGENCY LANDING GEAR OPERATION.

If the wheels fail to come down when the control lever is operated (using either engine driven or hand pump hydraulic pressure);—

a. Move square knob control lever to DOWN.

b. Pull DOWN and LOCK red "T" handles on lower instrument and control panel. To LOWER and LOCK wheels DOWN, handles may be operated independently (either or both). DO NOT OPERATE "T" HANDLES ABOVE 100-110 KNOTS I.A.S.

Main wheels control is outboard (to right).

Nose wheel control is inboard (to left)

Note

If handles are not LOCKED in the DOWN position the gear may not lock DOWN. Check visually and on L.G. indicator to see if wheels are DOWN and LOCKED.

These "T" handles control the valves on two (one for the main wheels, one for the nose wheel) compressed air bottles installed in the nose of the

SLOW DOWN FOR WHEELS DOWN

fuselage. There is no specific order in pulling the "T" handles for the emergency landing gear dump but because of the excellent control when landing on the main wheels alone it would seem advisable to extend the main wheels first and then nose wheel. The landing gear bottle gages are located on the left hand side of the nose wheel well. 1600-1900 lbs. pressure should show on the gages for proper operation.

CAUTION

Emergency system will only lower wheels once, therefore, use only if certain the hydraulic system will not function. Do not attempt to lower wheels with emergency dump bottles above 100-110 knots I.A.S. At higher speeds wheels will not extend completely, leakage might dissipate enough air to prevent full extension; therefore, fly at lowest possible speed until certain all wheels are down and locked. Once down, locks will hold wheels safely in down position, regardless of air or hydraulic pressure. Be sure handles are locked in down position—air will be lost if handles are allowed to return to up position.

On ground test, to restore the system to normal hydraulic operation, pressure may be relieved, and the gear made free for normal operation, by returning the emergency handles to the normal position. After returning the handles to the UP position, allow sufficient time for all the air to escape before retracting the landing gear.

Figure 38—Landing Gear Emergency Dump Control and Brake Air Gage

5. EMERGENCY BRAKE SYSTEM OPERATION.

a. If brakes do not hold—pull and hold red "T" handle on left side of cockpit until airplane stops.

An emergency air bottle, similar to those for the landing gear is installed in the nose section of the fuselage for the brakes. After using this air system the brakes can only be released by bleeding the system at the fitting adjacent to the pressure gage located on the lower instrument panel. 1800 p.s.i. pressure should show on the gage for proper braking operation.

6. EMERGENCY ESCAPE FROM AIRPLANE.

a. PILOT'S COCKPIT.

(1) Pull aft red levers at forward corners of hood simultaneously to prevent jamming.

(2) Push both edges of hood outboard to free studs at four corners from carriage fittings.

(3) Push hood up into air stream, which will carry it away.

b. RADAR OPERATOR'S COCKPIT.

(1) Push outboard and forward handle below rail on left side—and simultaneously pull inboard and aft control handle on right side rail.

(2) Push hood up into airstream.

7. EMERGENCY OPERATION OF ELECTRICAL SYSTEM.

If voltmeter readings exceed 28.5 volts a faulty voltage regulator is indicated. To prevent burning out the battery and other equipment determine which regulator is faulty as follows:

a. Set one generator switch to OFF; if its voltmeter reads high and the other reads normal—leave high reading generator switch OFF.

Figure 39—Emergency Brake Control

b. Repeat the operation with the other generator.

c. Operate only essential circuits to avoid overloading the remaining generator and the battery.

8. EMERGENCY OPERATION OF HYDRAULIC SYSTEM.

If there is insufficient hydraulic pressure to operate any of the various systems due to line failure, malfunctioning of the engine driven pumps, or engine failure, the hand pump (located on floor to right of seat) may be used to supply pressure to the respective systems as follows:

a. LANDING GEAR.

(1) Move landing gear control lever—UP or DOWN as desired.

(2) Move hand pump selector valve control (on hydraulic panel on right side of cockpit) to LANDING GEAR ONLY.

(3) Operate hand pump through:

184 cycles (double strokes) to RAISE WHEELS.
268 cycles (double strokes) to LOWER WHEELS.

CAUTION

The landing gear will not lock down at speeds above 120 knots.

b. WING FLAPS.

(1) Set flap control lever as desired—15° or 30° Down.

Note

The flap selector valve is shut off in these positions only—positive hydraulic lock is created. In FULL DOWN (40°) position valve remains open and air load on flaps will cause bleeding of pressure allowing flaps to come up.

(2) Move hand pump selector valve to FLAPS ONLY.

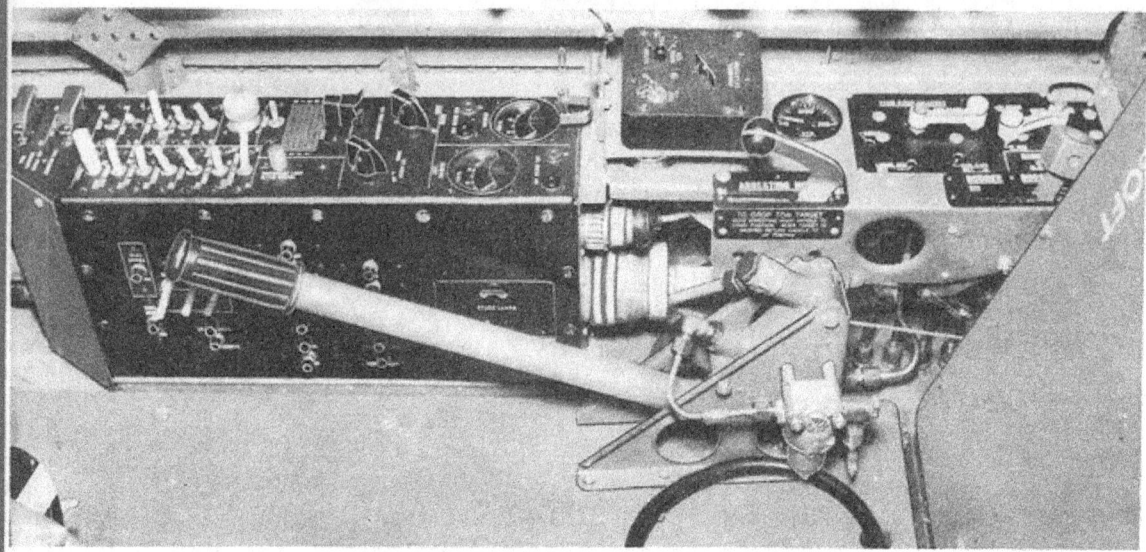

Figure 40—Hydraulic Hand Pump and Panel

(3) Operate hand pump through:

21 cycles (double strokes) to LOWER FLAPS.

15 cycles (double strokes) to RAISE FLAPS.

Refer to Section II, paragraph 1, for speed limitations relative to flap operation.

Note

The flaps are held down only by hydraulic pressure remaining constant—there is no mechanical lock. Therefore, in an emergency when loss of pressure or leaks in the system are indicated it is recommended that the landing gear be lowered before the flaps; if the flaps are lowered first, except to the 15° or 30° DOWN position the force of the air stream may cause a bleeding of pressure and spilling of fluid and there may not be sufficient fluid to lower the landing gear and then the flaps again.

c. BRAKE SYSTEM.—Brakes may be operated by hand pump pressure by setting the hand pump selector valve on SYSTEM and operating the pump and brake pedals. However, a special brake accumulator provides sufficient fluid and pressure for a normal landing with a reasonable run and taxiing. Refer to Section I, paragraph 6e.

d. GUN CHARGING.—Refer to Section V, paragraph 1a.

e. ARRESTING HOOK.—No hydraulic pressure is required to lower the hook. When the control is moved to DOWN a lock is released and the hook drops by gravity and the initial force of the dashpots. To raise the hook:

(1) Move arresting hook control (right side of cockpit) to UP.

(2) Move hand pump selector valve to WING FOLD.—GUNS—ARREST. HOOK.

(3) Operate the hand pump cycles, (double strokes) to raise hook.

f. WING FOLDING AND SPREADING.

(1) To fold the outer panels:

(a) Pull UP handle to UNLOCK the safety locks.

(b) Move wing folding control handle (aft of hand pump selector valve handle) inboard TO FOLD.

(c) Move hand pump selector valve handle to WING FOLD.—GUNS—ARREST. HOOK.

(d) Operate hand pump 146 cycles, (double strokes) to fold wings.

(2) To spread the outer panels:

(a) Move wing folding control handle outboard to SPREAD.

(b) Move hand pump selector valve handle to WING FOLD.—GUNS—ARREST. HOOK.

(c) Operate hand pump 128 cycles, (double strokes) to spread the wings.

(d) Push DOWN the handle to LOCK the safety locks.

(e) Check position of red indicator flags.

g. RUDDER BOOSTER BY-PASS.—In the event of lack of pressure or line failure in the rudder booster system, a hydraulic block will result. Since hand pump operation of this system is impractical, the only

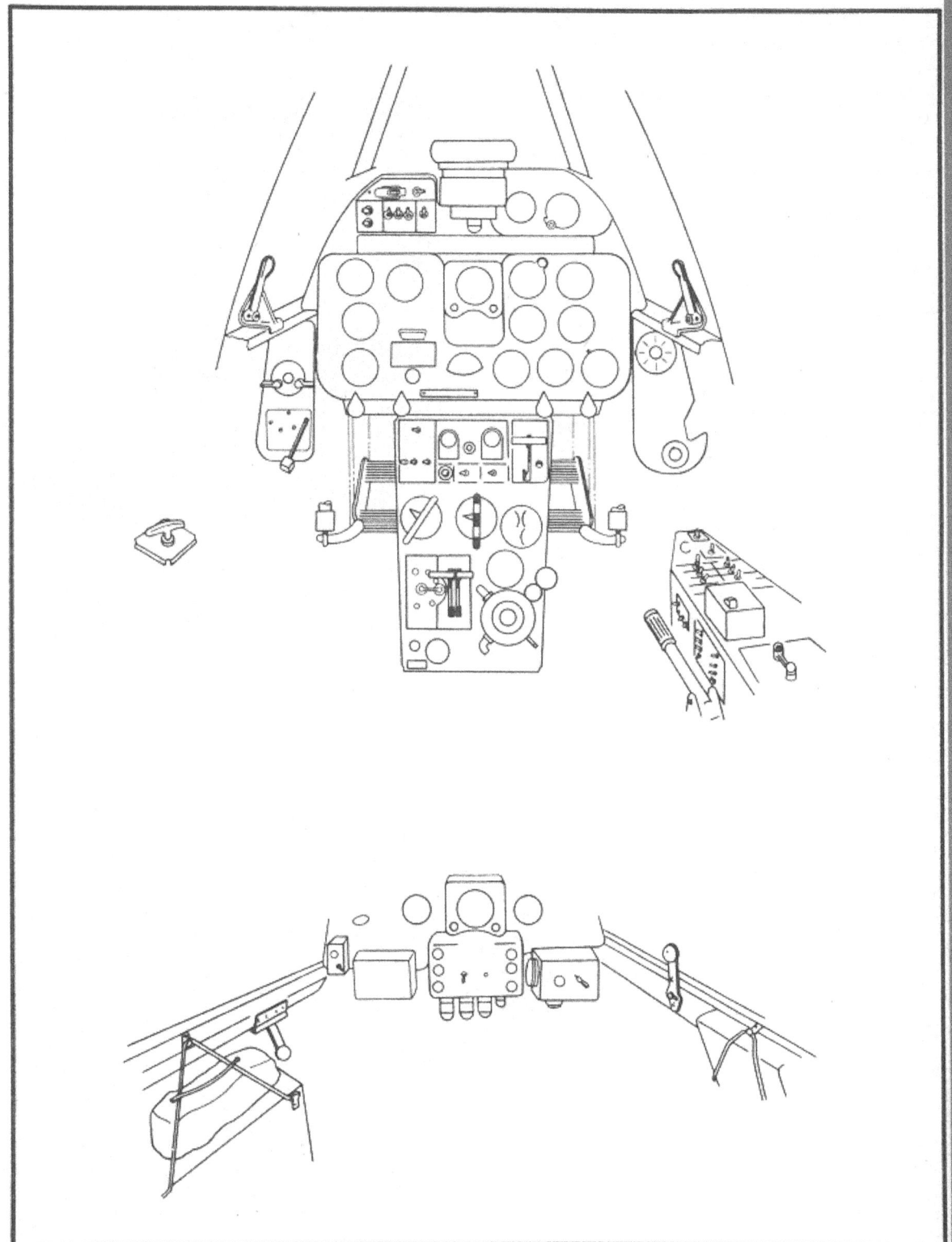

Figure 41—Emergency Controls

emergency operation is to by-pass pressure and break the hydraulic block. Refer to paragraph 10b, this section.

9. EMERGENCY OPERATION OF FUEL SYSTEM.

a. If the fuel pressure, indicated on the gage in the cockpit, drops below 22 ± 1 psi (warning light glows when pressure drops below 17 ± 1 psi):

(1) Check that fuel booster pump is ON.

(2) Check fuel gage for quantity in tank in use.

(3) Switch to another tank if gage indicates near empty.

b. If one engine is not operating set engine selector valve to the other engine ONLY—to cut off fuel to non-operating engine.

c. In the event of damage to any internal tank pull "T" handle to relieve tank pressurizing.

10. EMERGENCY OPERATION OF CONTROLS.

a. If flight controls are damaged, use trim tabs and endeavor to maintain normal control.

b. If damage to hydraulic system causes rudder booster to jam due to hydraulic block, move rudder booster by-pass control (square knob mounted on hydraulic hand pump panel on right side of cockpit) aft and lock to OFF. (Rudder control will become direct by cables from pedals).

Figure 42—Rudder Booster By-Pass Control

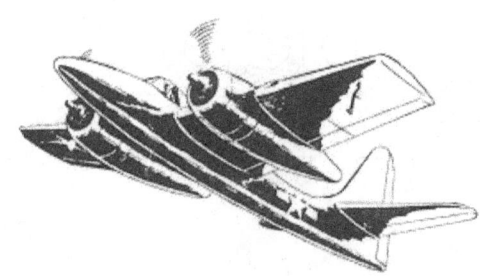

SECTION V
OPERATIONAL EQUIPMENT

1. ARMAMENT.

a. GUNNERY.

(1) GENERAL.—Four .50 cal. machine guns are installed in the lower forward section of the fuselage and four 20 mm aircraft cannon are installed in the wing inner panels (two left and two right).

Note

Model F7F-1 airplanes serial nos. 80259-80263 inclusive, and nos. 80265-80293 inclusive are equipped with four .50 cal. machine guns in the fuselage and four M-2 20 mm cannon in the wings.

Model F7F-1 airplane serial no. 80264 and Models F7F-2N and F7F-3 airplanes serial no. 80294 and subsequent are equipped with four .50 cal. machine guns in the fuselage and four M-3 (T-31) 20 mm cannon in the wings.

The four fuselage gun ammunition boxes are installed through hinged doors in the skin; the boxes for the left hand guns are installed from the left and those for the right hand guns from the right.

The four wing gun ammunition box assemblies are installed through large hinged access doors which are parts of the wing upper surface.

Ammunition box capacities:

Gun	Max. Rounds each gun	Total Rounds available
20 mm. wing (4)	200	800
.50 cal fuselage (4)	400	1600

The guns are charged hydraulically and fired electrically. Provision is made for the installation of automatic electric heaters on the gun breeches.

Note

The circuit is connected directly to the generators through circuit breakers, and the heaters will be energized whenever the generators are running. The battery will not energize the heaters. The plugs must be pulled to prevent the heaters from operating when the engines are running.

Firing restrictions:

Gun	Length of burst	Interval
.50 cal.	75 rounds—first (6 sec.)	1 Min.
	25 rounds—subsequent (2 sec.)	1 Min.
20 mm	Refer to applicable T.O.'s	

All guns are set to fire in a line parallel to the line of flight, in the horizontal plane. In the vertical

Figure 43—Gun Charging Controls

Figure 44—Armament Control Switches

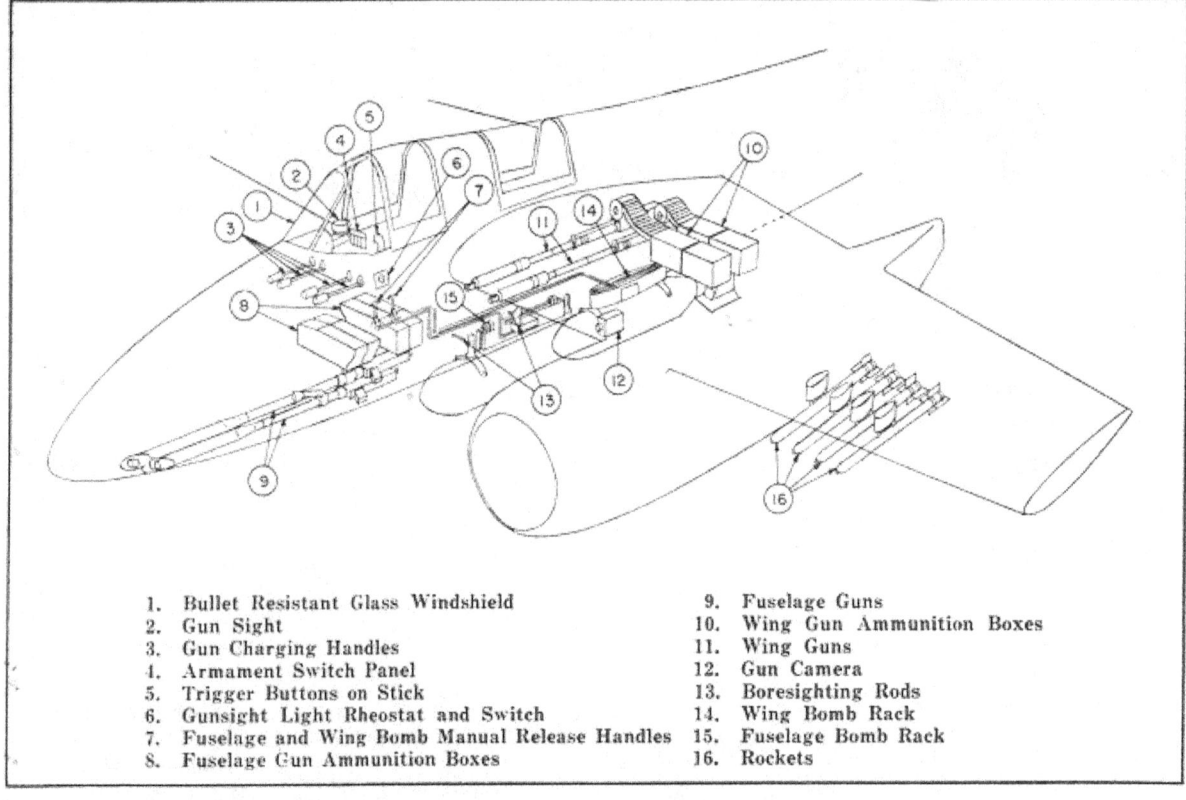

Figure 45—Armament Installation

1. Bullet Resistant Glass Windshield
2. Gun Sight
3. Gun Charging Handles
4. Armament Switch Panel
5. Trigger Buttons on Stick
6. Gunsight Light Rheostat and Switch
7. Fuselage and Wing Bomb Manual Release Handles
8. Fuselage Gun Ammunition Boxes
9. Fuselage Guns
10. Wing Gun Ammunition Boxes
11. Wing Guns
12. Gun Camera
13. Boresighting Rods
14. Wing Bomb Rack
15. Fuselage Bomb Rack
16. Rockets

plane, all wing guns are set to fire in a line parallel to the fuselage datum line. The fuselage guns' firing lines are parallel and the upper guns' firing lines converge with the gun sight line at 250 yards.

A Mark 8 illuminated gun sight is installed above the main instrument panel.

(2) GUN CONTROLS. — The four hydraulic charging controls are located along the bottom of the main instrument panel.

Left to right

Left wing guns
Left fuselage guns
Right fuselage guns
Right wing guns

(a) TO CHARGE GUNS.

1. Set handle pointers UP (to CHARGE).
2. Push handles FULL IN. Handles will automatically release, springing out when guns are charged.
3. Turn COUNTERCLOCKWISE 90° (pointer HORIZONTAL TO LEFT) to SAFETY position.

(b) TO SAFETY GUNS.

1. Set handle pointers to LEFT (90°) to SAFETY position.

2. Push handle FULL IN. Handle will remain in position.

(c) TO CHARGE FROM SAFETY POSITION.

1. Turn handles CLOCKWISE to UP — CHARGE position. The handles will then release automatically.
2. Push handles FULL IN. The handles will release automatically when guns are charged.

(d) AUXILIARY OPERATION. — If the engine driven hydraulic pump is not operating use the hand pump system as follows:

1. Set hand pump selector valve lever to WING FOLD.—GUNS—ARREST. HOOK.
2. Operate hand pump five strokes (approximately).
3. Set charging handle pointers UP — to CHARGE position.
4. Push handles FULL IN.
5. Operate hand pump until sufficient pressure is built up to charge guns, when handles will spring out automatically (800 p.s.i. approx.).
6. To safety guns.

 a. Set handle pointers to LEFT 90° to SAFETY position.

Figure 46—Gun Sight Light Controls

b. Push handles FULL IN.

c. Operate hand pump, etc. (See paragraph *(d)*5. above.)

(e) ARMAMENT MASTER SWITCH.

1. Set to RIGHT to ON.

2. Set to LEFT to OFF.

(f) GUN SELECTOR SWITCHES.

Wing guns—upper switch

Fuselage guns—lower switch

1. Set to RIGHT to ON.

2. Set to LEFT to OFF.

(g) GUN TRIGGER SWITCH. — Button on front of stick grip—PRESS to FIRE.

CAUTION

In the event of uncontrolled fire (runaway guns) set charging handles at SAFE position.

(3) GUN SIGHT LIGHT CONTROLS. — The toggle switch and rheostat are located on left side of cockpit, below rail, adjacent to ignition switch.

Set switch AFT to ON.

Set FORWARD to ON—ALTERNATE.

(Bulb has two filaments—alternate for reserve.)

Rotate the rheostat CLOCKWISE to ON and BRIGHT—COUNTERCLOCKWISE TO OFF.

WARNING

Safety guns before landing.

b. BOMBING EQUIPMENT.

(1) GENERAL.—A type D-6 bomb rack is installed in the fuselage to carry a 2000 lb. bomb, and a Mk 51 bomb rack is installed in each wing inner panel to carry either a 1600 or 1000 lb. bomb. A 500 lb. bomb may be carried in either rack.

Bomb control switches are installed on the upper left side of the main instrument panel and the bomb release button is installed on the control stick grip.

Manual bomb release handles for the fuselage and wing bombs are installed on the cockpit floor, left side forward.

(2) BOMB CONTROLS.

(a) ARMAMENT MASTER SWITCH.

1. Set to RIGHT to ON.

2. Set to LEFT to OFF.

(b) BOMB SELECTOR SWITCHES.

Left wing bomb—left

Right wing bomb—center

Belly (fuselage) bomb—right.

Set to DOWN to RELEASE.

(c) WING BOMB SAFE-ARM SWITCH.

1. Set to LEFT to SAFE.

2. Set to RIGHT to ARM.

(d) FUSELAGE (BELLY) BOMB MANUAL RELEASE.—Aft "T" handle on left side of cockpit floor below engine quadrant.

1. Handle pushed FULL DOWN and rotated FULL COUNTERCLOCKWISE — BOMB LOCKED against electrical release.

2. To cock release unit, to release bomb (ARMED) by electrical switches—PULL UP until slot hits stop, ROTATE ¼ turn CLOCKWISE.

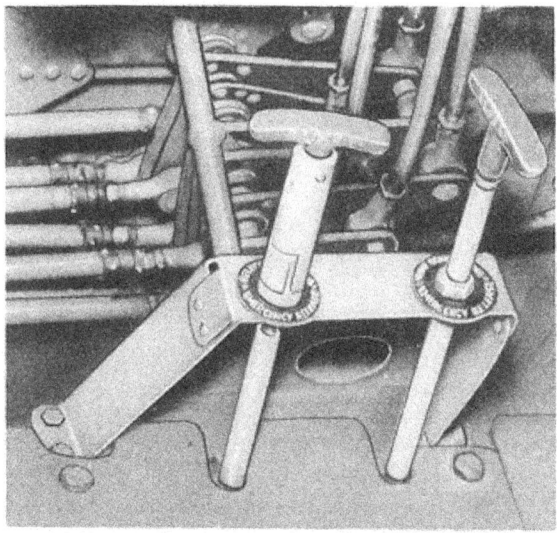

Figure 47—Manual Bomb Release Handles

3. To MANUALLY RELEASE THE BOMB SAFED, PULL UP QUICKLY after rotating as in *2.* above.

Note

1.

The fuselage bomb may only be released ARMED ELECTRICALLY, SAFED MANUALLY. The "T" handle safe release operates regardless of the toggle or trigger switches. For electrical armed release, the toggle and trigger switches must be operated.

2.

Wing bomb safe — arm switch and bomb sway brace provisions are not installed on airplanes serial nos. 80259 and 80260.

(e) WING BOMB MANUAL RELEASE (FOR EMERGENCY JETTISON).—"T" handle on left side of cockpit floor forward of fuselage bomb control.

1. To release bombs—pull UP forward "T" handle.

c. ROCKET PROJECTILE PROVISIONS.

(1) GENERAL.—Rocket projectile provisions are installed in model F7F airplanes, Serial No. 80294 and subsequent. The installation consists of a bomb-rocket selector, an arm nose-tail switch, a station distributor, wiring and pylons (launchers).

Note

Mk. 5 pylons are installed in airplanes Serial Nos. 80294-80507 inclusive. Mk. 9 pylons are installed in airplanes Serial No. 80508 and subsequent. The systems otherwise are identical.

(2) OPERATION.—To release rockets:

(a) Select rockets on Mk. 1 station selector—outboard, mid-outboard, mid-inboard or inboard.

(b) Set "Bomb or Rocket" selector to "ROCKET".

(c) Set arming switch to "ARM NOSE" or "ARM TAIL," as desired.

(d) Set Armament Master switch to "ON."

(e) Press bomb release switch button on stick grip.

d. MISCELLANEOUS EQUIPMENT.

(1) ARMOR PROTECTION.—The pilot and radar operator are protected from gun fire by face hardened steel armor and heavy aluminum alloy plates. Provision is made for the installation of wing gun ammunition box armor.

A section of $3/8$" face hardened armor bolted to the bulkhead forward of the cockpit extends up from cockpit floor to the cowl. The cowl deckplate on

Figure 48—Tow Target Control

which the bullet resistant windshield is mounted is made up of $1/4$" aluminum alloy.

An assembly of three $5/8$" aluminum alloy plates and one small $1/4$" face hardened steel plate is installed on the pilot's cockpit floor as protection against ground fire.

At the rear of the pilot's cockpit two plates of armor are installed; the lower, $3/8$" face hardened steel, and the head and body (upper), $1/2$" face hardened steel, give protection against gunfire from the rear.

In the F7F-2N airplanes two pieces of steel armor plate similar to those behind the pilot protect the radar operator from gunfire from the rear.

(2) TOW TARGET EQUIPMENT.

(a) A spring loaded latch is installed in the fuselage tail cone assembly for attaching a standard tow target. The target release is controlled by a cable operated by the arresting hook control lever on the right hand side of the cockpit. When the lever is moved aft the latch is pulled to allow the target to drop clear and the spring brings the latch back into position.

(b) To drop tow target—

1. Move control lever FULL AFT.

2. When target is clear, RETURN control lever to FULL FORWARD position.

Note

Remove access plate from tail cone assembly to attach target. In F7F-1 airplanes, serial nos. 80259-80264 inclusive, the tow target latch is installed on the tail skid assembly (this assembly not installed on airplanes Serial No. 80265 and subs.).

2. OXYGEN.

a. CYLINDER AND CONTROL.—A standard 514 cu. in. capacity shatterproof oxygen cylinder is installed in the fuselage nose, below the floor, on the right hand side.

The shut-off valve handwheel, rotating a shaft connected to the cylinder by a chain and sprocket (two right angle drive units and shaft on airplanes Serial No. 80359 and subs.) assembly, is mounted on the pilot's right side conrtol and instrument panel.

TO OPEN ROTATE—COUNTERCLOCKWISE.

A flow indicator is installed above the regulator on the pilot's lower instrument and control panel.

In the F7F-2N airplanes a separate cylinder with direct control is installed for the use of the radar operator. The cylinder is mounted in brackets on the left side of his cockpit: the regulator is mounted on the left side of the cockpit, forward, below the instrument panel and the flow indicator is mounted above it on the instrument panel.

b. REGULATOR. — The diluter-demand regulator is designed to meet the demands of the inhalation phase of the breathing cycle and deliver either a properly proportioned mixture of air and oxygen or 100% oxygen dependent upon the setting of the adjustable air-valve lever. With the air-valve set to the ON or NORMAL OXYGEN position, air is drawn into the breathing system and is automatically mixed with oxygen from the supply cylinder to give the total needed oxygen required up to approximately 30,000 ft., beyond which 100% oxygen is delivered. With the air-valve set to the OFF or 100% OXYGEN position, 100% oxygen is delivered at all altitudes. With the air-valve of the diluter-demand regulator set to the ON or NORMAL OXYGEN position, a relatively small inhalation suction (one inch of water suction)

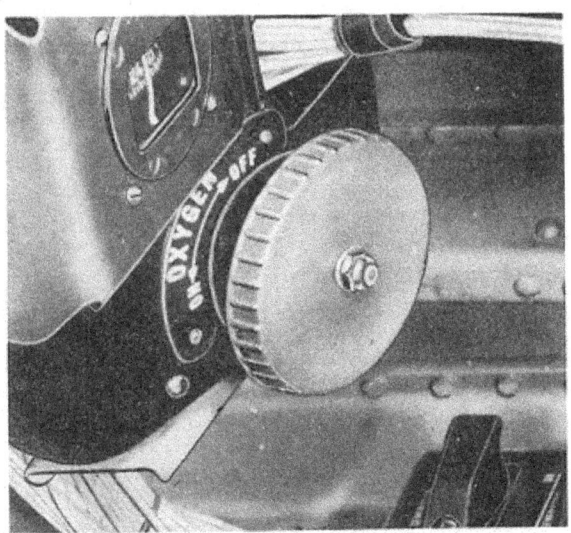

Figure 49—Pilot's Oxygen Cylinder Control

Figure 50—Oxygen Regulator

is sufficient to deliver a flow of 150 liters of oxygen per minute. This characteristic assures the user an adequate oxygen flow and ease of breathing.

The regulator is attached directly to the high pressure oxygen supply through 3/16 inch O.D. copper tubing connected to the cylinder; the pressure in the cylinder may decrease from 1800 or 2000 pounds per square inch to 50 pounds per square inch without effecting the normal operation of the regulator.

c. PREFLIGHT CHECK LIST. — The following items should be checked while the plane is on ground prior to flight in which oxygen is to be used, or is likely to be used, to assure proper functioning of the oxygen system.

(1) Emergency valve—closed.

(2) Open cylinder valve, allow at least ten seconds for pressure in line to equalize. Pressure gage should read 1800 ±50 p.s.i., if the cylinder is fully charged.

(3) Close cylinder valve. After a few minutes observe pressure gage and simultaneously open cylinder valve. If gage pointer jumps—leakage is indicated.

(a) If leakage was found by (3) above test further. Open cylinder valve, carefully noting pressure gage reading—then close cylinder valve. If gage pointer drops more than 100 p.s.i. in five minutes there is excessive leakage, and oxygen system must be repaired prior to use.

(4) Check mask fit by placing thumb over end of mask tube and inhale lightly. If there is no leakage, mask will adhere tightly to face due to suction created. If mask leaks — tighten mask suspension straps and/or adjust nose wire. DO NOT USE MASK THAT LEAKS.

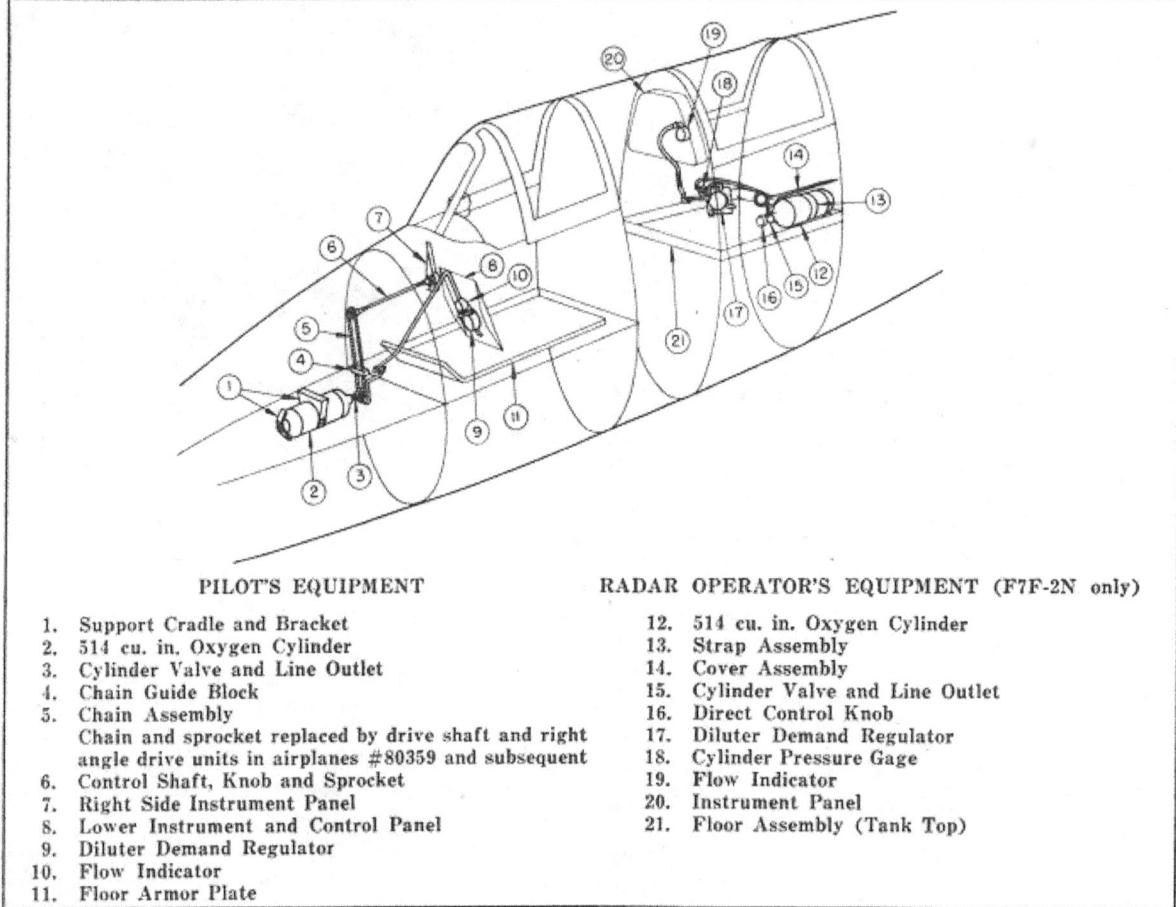

PILOT'S EQUIPMENT

1. Support Cradle and Bracket
2. 514 cu. in. Oxygen Cylinder
3. Cylinder Valve and Line Outlet
4. Chain Guide Block
5. Chain Assembly
   Chain and sprocket replaced by drive shaft and right angle drive units in airplanes #80359 and subsequent
6. Control Shaft, Knob and Sprocket
7. Right Side Instrument Panel
8. Lower Instrument and Control Panel
9. Diluter Demand Regulator
10. Flow Indicator
11. Floor Armor Plate

RADAR OPERATOR'S EQUIPMENT (F7F-2N only)

12. 514 cu. in. Oxygen Cylinder
13. Strap Assembly
14. Cover Assembly
15. Cylinder Valve and Line Outlet
16. Direct Control Knob
17. Diluter Demand Regulator
18. Cylinder Pressure Gage
19. Flow Indicator
20. Instrument Panel
21. Floor Assembly (Tank Top)

Figure 51—Oxygen Equipment Diagram

(5) Couple mask securely to breathing tube by means of quick disconnect coupling. IMPORTANT: Mating parts of coupling must not be "cocked" but be fully engaged.

(6) Open cylinder valve. Depress diaphragm knob through hole in center of regulator case, and feel flow of oxygen into the mask — then, release diaphragm knob. Breathe several times observing oxygen flow indicator (if installed) for "blink" verifying the positive flow of oxygen.

Note

Since the amount of added oxygen is very small at sea level the oxygen flow meter may not operate while the airplane is on the ground. In this case turn air-valve to OFF or 100% OXYGEN and test again. If oxygen flow indicator operation is now satisfactory, reset air-valve to ON or NORMAL OXYGEN in which setting adequate oxygen flow and "blinker" operation will be assured at oxygen use altitudes.

(7) Check emergency valve by turning counter-clockwise slowly until oxygen flows vigorously into mask—then close emergency valve.

(8) Upon completion of oxygen flight—close cylinder valve.

d. OPERATING INSTRUCTIONS.

(1) Open oxygen cylinder valve. Pressure gage should read 1800 ±50 p.s.i., if cylinder is fully charged.

(2) Set air-valve to ON or NORMAL OXYGEN position—except when the presence of excessive carbon-monoxide is suspected—then set to OFF or 100% OXYGEN position.

(3) Put on oxygen mask. Be sure that quick disconnect coupling is fully engaged.

(4) Check mask fit by squeezing mask tube and inhaling lightly. Mask will adhere tightly to face due to suction, if there is no leakage. If mask leaks tighten mask suspension straps.

CAUTION

Never check mask fit by squeezing mask tube while emergency valve is ON.

(5) Breathe normally and observe oxygen flow indicator for "blink," verifying positive flow of oxygen.

(6) Frequently check cylinder pressure gage for state of available oxygen supply, and oxygen flow indicator for flow of oxygen to mask.

(7) Upon completion of oxygen flight—close cylinder valve (rotate handle CLOCKWISE).

CAUTION

Keep oxygen equipment free from oil, grease and easily oxidized materials.

3. COMMUNICATION AND ELECTRONIC EQUIPMENT.

a. COMMUNICATION EQUIPMENT—MODEL F7F-1 AIRPLANE.

(1) COMMUNICATING RADIO. — AN/ARC-5 receiving and transmitting equipment is installed in the fuselage between Stations 318 and 362. The following controls are installed in the pilot's cockpit:

(*a*) RADIO MASTER SWITCH.—On top of electrical control panel.

(*b*) MASK MICROPHONE "PRESS-TO-TALK" SWITCH BUTTON.—On inboard (right engine) throttle handle.

(*c*) HAND MICROPHONE. — Microphone stowed in clip on right side of cockpit.

(*d*) C-38/ARC-5 RECEIVER CONTROL UNIT.—On right hand side of cockpit.

(*e*) C-30/ARC-5 VHF TRANSMITTER CONTROL UNIT.—On right hand side of cockpit.

(2) NAVIGATION RECEIVER.—An ARR-2 receiver is installed in the fuselage with the ARC-5 units; it is controlled by the communicating controls.

(3) FERRY RADIO.—An R-23/ARC-5 LF range receiver and associated tunable control C-26/ARC-5 is installed for ferrying use.

(4) TACTICAL RADIO.—In service, the tunable LF radio range receiver and associated control can be replaced by the lock tuned HF receiver. To put this HF receiver into operation, the plug in the middle position in the receiver rack must be removed and replaced by the plug stowed on the aft side of Station 318 bulkhead, directly in front of the receiver rack.

With this arrangement this receiver is controlled by the REC C switch on the pilot's C-38/ARC-5 control unit and the C-26/ARC-5 control and associated cables are not used.

(5) OPERATION.

(*a*) Plug in the microphone and headset in the jacks (aft of the control units) making sure that the plugs are completely engaged.

(*b*) Set radio master switch to ON.

(*c*) RECEPTION.

1. VHF RECEIVER. — To select the VHF channel desired, push one of the four top buttons on the transmitter control unit; the push button acts as an ON switch as well as a channel selector. Set switch "A" on the receiver control unit in the UP position, the toggle switch "C" in the OFF position, and the OUTPUT control knob in the minimum output position, and reception will be obtained only on the VHF channel selected. The sensitivity control above switch "A" should be set at maximum (position no. 11).

2. HF RECEIVER.—Set toggle switch "C" on the receiver control unit in the UP position and set the sensitivity control above switch "C" as desired. Make certain that the toggle switch "A" on the receiver control unit is in the OFF position, and that the OUTPUT control knob on the receiver control unit is in the minimum position while thus setting the level; however, unless sensitivity control is set for MAX. TOLERABLE NOISE, weak signals may not be heard.

3. NAVIGATION RECEIVER.—Operate the crank on the receiver control unit to bring the assigned channel number in the window. Set the NAV-VOICE selector switch to NAV. After making certain that the toggle switches for the VHF and HF (receivers "A" and "C") are in the OFF position, set the OUTPUT control to obtain a usable weak signal, or if the desired signal cannot be heard, to a fairly strong background hiss. The volume control should not be adjusted after once being set when navigating with the AN/ARR-2A Initially, the volume control of the C-38/ARC-5 should be set as high as can be tolerated and the OUTPUT control of the AN/ARR-2A operated as low as possible. Adjust the BEAT-NOTE control to produce a pleasing audible tone. If the signal is too strong, a clear cut indication of the course cannot be obtained.

4. SIMULTANEOUS OPERATION. — Normally all three receivers should be in operation with their outputs fed simultaneously into the headphones, unless specific orders to the contrary have been received. The volume control on the receiver control must necessarily be adjusted to obtain optimum output from the VHF receiver. To obtain the same output from the HF receiver, it is therefore necessary to adjust the sensitivity control above switch "C" on the receiver control unit. The volume of the navigation receiver should be adjusted only by its own OUTPUT control. In ferry operation, the range receiver output should be adjusted only by its own volume control, with the C-38/ARC-5 volume control in the full ON position.

(*d*) TRANSMISSION.—When the receiving equipment has been put in operation as described above, the transmitters may be put in operation as follows:

Section V
Paragraph 3

1. Test Power (Internal—External Switch
2. C-30/ARC-5 VHF Control Unit
3. C-38/ARC-4 Control Unit
4. C-26/ARC-5 LF Control Unit
5. J-22ARC-5 Jack Box
6. IFF Control Unit
7. "DESTRUCT" Switch
8. Hand Microphone
9. Location of Main Radar Control Unit
10. Radio Master Switch

Figure 52—Communicating Controls (F7F-1 Airplane)

1. VHF TRANSMITTER.—Select the desired VHF channel by pushing one of the top four buttons on the transmitter control unit. Make certain that the TONE-CW-VOICE switch is in the VOICE position. Wait four seconds after operating the push-button, then press the "press-to-talk" switch and commence transmission. To receive, release the "press-to-talk" switch.

2. HF TRANSMITTER.—Push button no. 2 on the transmitter control unit. Make certain that the TONE-CW-VOICE switch is in the VOICE position. It should be noted that pushing button no. 2 does not in any way disturb reception on the VHF channel. Button no. 3 must not be used in this installation.

(e) OPERATING NOTES AND PRECAUTIONS.

1. AFTER PUSHING ANY ONE OF THE TOP FOUR BUTTONS ON THE TRANSMITTER CONTROL UNIT, WAIT AT LEAST FOUR SECONDS BEFORE PUSHING BUTTON NO. 2. IF THIS CAUTION IS NOT OBSERVED, THE BAND SELECTOR MOTOR MAY CONTINUE TO RUN AND DANGEROUSLY OVERHEAT. IT MAY BE STOPPED BY PRESSING BUTTON "A", "B", "C" or "D". BUTTON no. 3 should not be pushed because RADIO TRANSMISSION WILL NOT TAKE PLACE in spite of the fact that sidetone will be heard. All buttons on the control unit, except the OFF button, turn the transmitters on in addition to selecting the proper channel. The various channels are selected in turn as desired. At the conclusion of the transmission the transmitters are shut down by pushing the OFF button.

2. Voice transmission, only, is provided by this installation although the selector switch on the transmitter control unit, is labeled TONE-CW-VOICE The selector should be set to VOICE at all times, preferably safety-wired.

(6) IFF EQUIPMENT.—The AN/APX-2 transmitter-receiver, RT-24/APX-2, is installed aft of Station 362. The pilot's control unit, C-57/APX-2 is located on the hydraulic control panel on the right side of the cockpit. The control unit, C-56/APX-2, is located adjacent to the transmitter receiver and is not accessible during flight.

(a) OPERATING INSTRUCTIONS.

1. TO START THE EQUIPMENT.—On the pilot control unit, C-57/APX-2 rotate the master control switch clockwise away from the OFF position and set it in the desired operating position.

2. TO CHANGE SELECTOR SWITCH POSITIONS.—On control unit, C-56/APX-2, rotate the Selector switch to the position designated by the Commanding Officer. Unless otherwise designated, this switch is set and left in position "1".

3. FOR G-BAND OPERATION.—On the pilot control unit throw the G-Band switch to the ON position or flip it to the TIME position.

4. FOR INT OPERATION.—On the pilot control unit throw the INT switch to the ON position or hold it momentarily in the PRESS position.

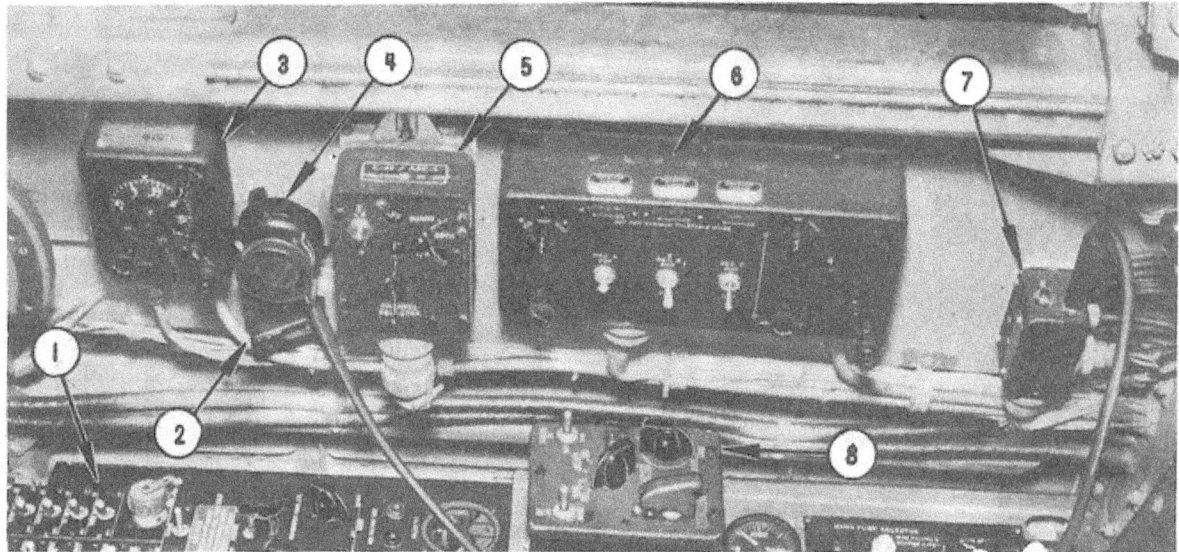

1. Radio Master Switch
2. Radar AC Test Power (Internal—External) Switch
3. Ferry Radio Tunable Control
4. Hand Microphone
5. VHF Transmitter Control (C-45/ARC-1)
6. Receiver Control (C-38/ARC-5)
7. Jack Box
8. IFF Control with DESTRUCT Switch

Figure 53—Pilot's Communicating Controls (F7F-2N Airplane)

5. FOR ROO OPERATION.—On the pilot control unit rotate the master control switch to the ROO position (only by specific direction of the Commanding Officer and only if a specified ROO adjustment has been made inside the receiver-transmitter unit by the maintenance crew).

6. FOR DISTRESS OPERATION.—On the pilot control unit push the guard latch to the right (tilting it up) and rotate the master control switch to the EMERGENCY (extreme clockwise) position.

7. TO DESTROY THE RECEIVER-TRANSMITTER UNIT.—If possible, warn operating personnel to stand clear of the receiver-transmitter unit. On the pilot control unit raise the red guard cover breaking the safety wire, and throw the DESTRUCT switch to the ON position. This will explode all Type AN/MI Destructors in the unit.

8. FURTHER OPERATING PROCEDURES.—Information on further operating procedures must be obtained from the Commanding Officer.

9. TO STOP THE EQUIPMENT.—On the pilot control unit rotate the master control switch to the extreme counterclockwise position, marked OFF.

(b) ALTERNATE EQUIPMENT. — Control, wiring and space provisions are made for the alternate installation of the ABA-1 IFF equipment.

(7) RADIO ALTIMETER.—The AN/APN-1 radio altimeter transmitter-receiver is installed in the fuselage radio compartment on the right side, aft of the ladder bracket. The antennae are installed on the underside of each wing inner panel. The indicator and the limit indicator lights are on the right side of the pilot's instrument panel. The limit switch is on the pilot's lower right instrument panel.

WARNING

The high ranges of the altimeter must never be used when flying at altitudes within the low range or when landing. The high range is not calibrated for such use and an accurate zero altitude indication would not be obtained.

(a) Turn the power switch, located on the indicator, to "ON".

(b) The limit switch SA-1/ARN-1 should be set at the desired altitude.

(c) True indication of altitude will be given by the indicator, 1D-14/APN-1, consecutively over the low and high ranges. (The effective high range starts at the upper limit of the low range.) Some fluctuation may be noticed in the indicator reading when flying over rough or uneven terrain or when flying through bumpy air. At an altitude considerably above the upper limit of each range the indicator needle may be expected to fall back from its full position.

(d) The limit indicator relieves the pilot of constant attention to the indicator scale. The indicator consists of three colored lamps, one for each of the three conditions of relay contact operation. The lamps are lighted as follows:

1. Red—indicates flight below the "pre-set altitude" (on Limit Switch).

Section V
Paragraph 3

1 Radar Auxiliary Control (C-47/APS-6)
2 Location of Radar Main Control
3 Radar Indicator
4 Hand Microphone
5 IFF Control Unit
6 Transmitter Control Unit (C-39/ARC-5)

Figure 54—Radar Operator's Communicating Controls (F7F-2N Airplane)

2. White—indicates flight at approximately the "pre-set altitude".

3. Green—indicates flight above the "pre-set altitude".

b. RADAR EQUIPMENT—MODEL F7F-1 AIRPLANE.—AN/APS-6 radar equipment is installed in the nose of the fuselage behind a radome, and in the fuselage aft of Station 318. The indicator is installed on the main instrument panel, on the centerline; the main control C-46/APS-6 is installed on the right side of the cockpit forward of the communication controls. The auxiliary control, C-47/APS-6 is located on the left side of the cockpit outboard of the throttle.

Note

For information on the operation of APX, APN and APS equipment refer to applicable manuals and T. O.'s.

c. COMMUNICATION EQUIPMENT—MODEL F7F-2N AIRPLANE.

(1) COMMUNICATING RADIO. — AN/ARC-5 and AN/ARC-1 receiving and transmitting equipment is installed in the fuselage between Stations 318 and 362.

The following controls are installed in the pilot's cockpit:

(*a*) RADIO MASTER SWITCH.—On top of electrical control panel.

(*b*) MASK MICROPHONE "PRESS-TO-TALK" SWITCH BUTTON.—On inboard (right engine) throttle handle.

(*c*) HAND MICROPHONE.—Stowed in clip on right side of cockpit.

(*d*) C-38/ARC-5 AND C-45/ARC-1 CONTROL UNITS.—On right side of cockpit.

The following controls are installed in the radar operator's cockpit:

(*a*) MASK MICROPHONE "PRESS-TO-TALK" SWITCH BUTTON.—On grip assembly mounted on left cockpit rail.

(*b*) HAND MICROPHONE.—Stowed in clip on main instrument panel.

(*c*) C-39/ARC-5 CONTROL UNIT.—On lower right side of main instrument panel.

(2) INTERPHONE.—An RL-7 ICS unit is installed in the bottom of the fuselage aft of Station 318. The control switches are on the ARC-5 control units.

(3) NAVIGATION RECEIVER.—An ARR-2A receiver is installed in the fuselage with the ARC-5 units; it is controlled by the communicating controls.

(4) FERRY RADIO.—An R-23/ARC-5 LF range receiver and associated tunable control C-26/ARC-5 is installed for ferrying use.

(5) TACTICAL RADIO.

(*a*) In service, the tunable LF radio range receiver and associated control can be replaced by a lock-tuned HF receiver. To put this HF receiver into operation, the plug in the middle position in the receiver rack must be removed and replaced by the plug stowed on the aft side of Station 318 bulkhead, directly in front of the receiver rack.

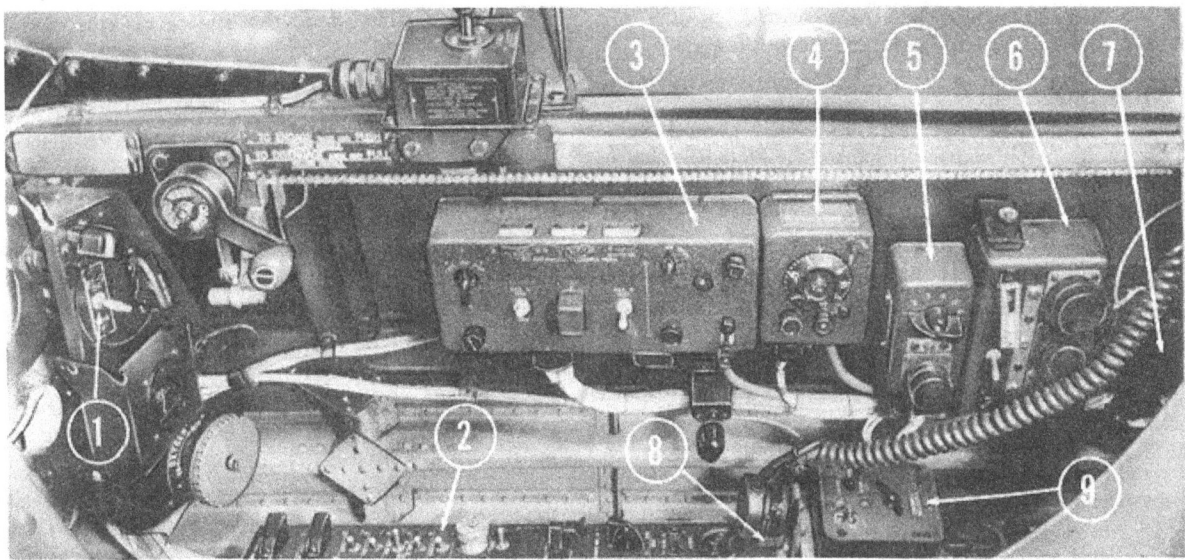

1. IFF Control Switches
2. Radio Master Switch
3. Receiver Control C-38/ARC-5
4. Range Receiver C-26/ARC-5
5. Selector Unit C-55/APX-1
6. Control Unit C-54/APX-1
7. Microphone Jack Box J-22ARC-5
8. Hand Microphone Clip
9. VHF Control C-45/ARC-1

Figure 55—Pilot's Communicating Controls (F7F-3 Airplane)

This receiver is controlled by the REC C switch on the pilot's C-38/ARC-5 control unit. With this arrangement the C-26/ARC-5 control and associated cables are not used.

(b) Provision is made in the receiver rack for the installation of an additional locktuned HF receiver. This additional receiver will be controlled by the REC B switch on the pilot's C-38/ARC-5 control unit—it will be necessary to remove the covers from the REC B toggle switch and sentivity control directly above.

(6) OPERATION.

(a) Insert the microphone and headset plugs into the jacks and make sure that they are completely engaged.

(b) Set battery switch and radio master switch (pilot's cockpit) to ON.

(c) TRANSMISSION.

1. The position of the ICS-VHF-MHF microphone selector switch on the C-38/ARC-5 pilot's control unit and on the C-39/ARC-5 radar operator's radio control will determine which component of the equipment will be used for transmission.

2. To operate the interphone system, set the microphone selector switch to ICS position, press the microphone switch, and talk.

3. To operate the MHF transmitter, set the microphone selector switch to MHF, press the microphone switch, and talk.

4. To transmit on VHF, set the microphone selector switch to VHF, set the rotary switches on the C-45/ARC-1 control, (pilot's cockpit), as desired. Press the microphone switch, and talk.

Note

The RT-18/ARC-1 equipment provides ten VHF channels and is so arranged that transmission and reception can be selected by the pilot on the C-45/ARC-1 as follows:

1

Position MAIN T/R.—Transmission and reception on the selected one of the nine main channels.

2

Position BOTH.—Transmission and reception on the selected one of the nine main channels and simultaneous monitoring of the GUARD channel.

3

Position GUARD.—Transmission and reception on the GUARD channel.

The following instructions assume that the microphone selector switch on the pilot's C-38/ARC-5 control is set to VHF and that the REC A toggle switch in the UP position.

1. To arrange the C-45/ARC-1 VHF control for transmission on any one of the nine main channels, rotate the three-position switch to MAIN T/R, rotate the channel selector switch to the channel desired, press the microphone switch, and talk.

2. Rotating the three-position switch to BOTH permits transmission and reception on any one of the selected main channels, and reception on the GUARD channel.

3. To arrange the C-45/ARC-1 control unit for transmission and reception on the GUARD channel, rotate the three-position selector switch to GUARD.

(d) RECEPTION.

1. GENERAL.—All receivers are always in the stand-by condition. The pilot only can select reception. Under normal conditions either or both of the REC A (VHF) or REC C (MHF) toggle switches on the pilot's C-38/ARC-5 control unit are set in the UP position.

2. INTERPHONE.—The interphone (ICS) system will always take precedence over any other message being received.

3. HF RECEIVER.—Reception on MHF is controlled by the REC C toggle switch on the pilot's C-38/ARC-5 control unit.

Set the toggle switch "C" on the receiver control unit in the UP position and set the sensitivity control above switch "C", marked "SET FOR MAX. TOLERABLE NOISE". Make certain that the toggle switch "A" on the receiver control unit is in the OFF position, and that the OUTPUT control knob on the receiver control unit is in the minimum position while thus setting the level; however, unless sensitivity control is set for "MAX. TOLERABLE NOISE", weak signals may not be heard.

4. VHF RECEIVER.—Reception on VHF is controlled by the REC A toggle switch on the C-38/ARC-5 control unit, and by the selector switch on the C-45/ARC-1 control unit, in the pilot's cockpit. Refer to transmission, paragraph (c) above for information on selecting any one of the ten channels provided. Set switch "A" on the receiver control unit in the UP position, the toggle switch "C" in the OFF position, and reception will be obtained only on the VHF channel selected.

(e) JOINT OPERATION.

1. The C-39/ARC-5 radar operator's radio control is equipped with a three-position microphone selector switch identical in function to the similar switch on the pilot's C-38/ARC-5 control. Each switch is independent of the other. The following operations permit the radar operator to transmit or receive:

a. Transmission on a VHF channel selected by the pilot; rotate the microphone selector switch to VHF, press the microphone switch, and talk.

b. Transmission on HF (independent of the pilot); rotate the microphone selector switch to HF, press the microphone switch and talk.

c. Transmission on ICS; rotate the microphone selector switch to ICS, press the microphone switch and talk.

d. Reception; the choice of reception is available only to the pilot—the radar operator will hear only on those channels selected by the pilot. The radar operator can adjust volume as he chooses.

(7) IFF EQUIPMENT.—The AN/APX-2 transmitter-receiver, RT-24/APX-2, is installed aft of Station 362. The pilot's control unit, C-57/APX-2 is located on the hydraulic control panel on the right side of the cockpit. The radar operator's control unit, C-56/APX-2, is located at the bottom center of his instrument panel.

(a) OPERATING INSTRUCTIONS.

1. TO START THE EQUIPMENT.—On the pilot control unit C-57/APX-2 rotate the master control switch clockwise away from the OFF position and set it in the desired operating position.

2. TO CHANGE SELECTOR SWITCH POSITIONS.—On the operator control unit, C-56/APX-2, rotate the selector switch to the position designated by the Commanding Officer. Unless otherwise designated, this switch is set and left in position "1".

3. FOR G-BAND OPERATION. — On the pilot control unit throw the G-Band switch to the ON position or flip it to the TIME position.

4. FOR INT OPERATION—On the pilot control unit throw the INT switch to the ON position or hold it momentarily in the PRESS position; or on the operator control unit hold the INT switch momentarily in the PRESS position.

5. FOR ROO OPERATION.— On the pilot control unit rotate the master control switch to the ROO position (only by specific direction of the Commanding Officer and only if a specified ROO adjust-has been made inside the receiver transmitter unit by the maintenance crew).

6. FOR DISTRESS OPERATION.—On the pilot control unit push the guard latch to the right (tilting it up) and rotate the master control switch to the EMERGENCY (extreme clockwise) position.

7. TO DESTROY THE RECEIVER-TRANSMITTER UNIT.—If possible, warn operating personnel to stand clear of the receiver-transmitter unit. On the pilot control unit raise the red guard cover breaking the safety wire, and throw the DESTRUCT switch to the ON position. This will explode all Type AN/MI Destructors in the unit.

8. FURTHER OPERATING PROCEDURES. —Information on further operating procedures must be obtained from the Commanding Officer.

9. TO STOP THE EQUIPMENT. — On the pilot control unit rotate the master control switch to the extreme counterclockwise position, marked OFF.

(b) ALTERNATE EQUIPMENT. — Control, wiring and space provisions are made for the alternate installation of the ABA-1 IFF equipment.

(8) RADIO ALTIMETER. — The AN/APN-1 radio altimeter is installed in the fuselage radio compartment on the right side, aft of the ladder bracket. The antennae are installed on the underside of each wing inner panel. The indicator and the limit indicator lights are on the right side of the pilot's instrument panel. The limit switch is on the pilot's lower right instrument panel.

WARNING

The high ranges of the altimeter must never be used when flying at altitudes within the low range or when landing. The high range is not calibrated for such use and an accurate zero altitude indication would not be obtained.

(a) Turn the power switch, located on the indicator, to "ON".

(b) The limit switch SA-1/ARN-1 should be set at the desired altitude.

(c) True indication of altitude will be given by the indicator, ID-14/APN-1, consecutively over the low and high ranges. (The effective high range starts at the upper limit of the low range.) Some fluctuation may be noticed in the indicator reading when flying over rough or uneven terrain or when flying through bumpy air. At an altitude considerably above the upper limit of each range the indicator needle may be expected to fall back from its full position.

(d) The limit indicator relieves the pilot of constant attention to the indicator scale. The indicator consists of three colored lamps, one for each of the three conditions of relay contact operation. The lamps are lighted as follows:

1. Red—indicates flight below the "pre-set altitude" (on Limit Switch).

2. White—indicates flight at approximately the "pre-set altitude".

3. Green—indicates flight above the "pre-set altitude".

d. RADAR EQUIPMENT—MODEL F7F-2N AIRPLANE.—AN/APA-32 and AN/APS-6 radar equipment is installed in the nose of the fuselage behind a radome, and in the fuselage aft of Station 318.

The pilot's indicator is installed on the centerline of his main instrument panel; the pilot's switch box, SA-38/APA-32, is located on the left side of the cockpit, outboard of the throttle.

The radar operator's indicator is installed on the centerline of his instrument panel; the radar main control, C-46/APS-6, is located on the lower left side of his instrument panel; his auxiliary control, C-47/APS-6, is outboard (to the left) of the main control.

Note

1

For additional information on the operation of APX, APN and APS equipment refer to applicable manuals and T.O.'s.

2

Reliable operation of the VHF and navigation equipment is generally confined to approximately line-of-sight distance as determined by height of the transmitting and receiving antennae, but since transmission at these frequencies depends on meteorological conditions, large deviations from the line of sight distance may occur. HF communication for ranges over approximately 40 miles depends on sky-wave transmission and the results depend on the frequency, time of day, the season and the other factors, rather than transmitter and receiver heights.

3

The curve (Figure 56) indicates the normal distance range of VHF communications when one antenna is at sea level and there are no intervening obstructions. Under favorable conditions the range, in nautical miles, will be equal to the indicated statute mile range.

e. COMMUNICATION EQUIPMENT—MODEL F7F-3 AIRPLANE.

(1) COMMUNICATING RADIO.—AN/ARC-5 and AN/ARC-1 receiving and transmitting equipment is installed in the fuselage between Stations 318 and 362.

The following controls are installed in the pilot's cockpit:

(a) RADIO MASTER SWITCH.—On top of electrical control panel.

(b) MASK MICROPHONE "PRESS-TO-TALK" SWITCH BUTTON.—On inboard (right engine) throttle handle.

(c) HAND MICROPHONE.—Stowed in clip on right side of cockpit.

(d) C-38/ARC-5 AND C-45/ARC-1 RECEIVER CONTROL UNITS.—On right side of cockpit.

(2) NAVIGATION RECEIVER. — An ARR-2A receiver is installed in the fuselage with the ARC-5 units; it is controlled by the communicating controls.

(3) FERRY RADIO.—An R-23/ARC-5 LF range receiver and associated tunable control C-26/ARC-5 is installed for ferrying use.

(4) TACTICAL RADIO.

(a) In service, the tunable LF radio range receiver and associated control can be replaced by a lock-tuned HF receiver. To put this HF receiver into operation, the plug in the middle position in the receiver rack must be removed and replaced by the plug stowed on the aft side of Station 318 bulkhead, directly in front of the receiver rack.

Section V
Paragraph 3

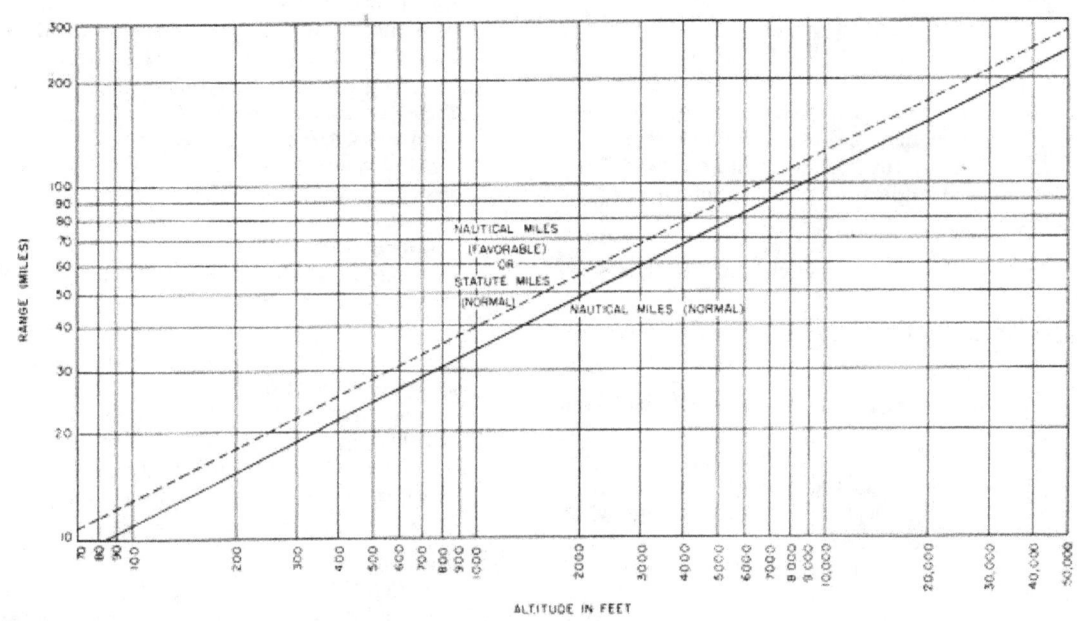

Figure 56—VHF Range vs. Altitude

This receiver is controlled by the REC C switch on the pilot's C-38/ARC-5 control unit. With this arrangement the C-26/ARC-5 control and associated cables are not used.

(b) Provision is made in the receiver rack for the installation of an an additional lock-tuned HF receiver. This additional receiver will be controlled by the REC B switch on the pilot's C-38/ARC-5 control unit—it will be necessary to remove the covers from the REC B toggle switch and sensitivity control directly above.

(5) OPERATION.

(a) Insert the microphone and headset plugs into the jacks and make sure that the plugs are completely engaged.

(b) Set battery switch and radio master switch (pilot's cockpit) to ON.

(c) TRANSMISSION.

1. The position of the VHF-MHF microphone selector switch on the C-38/ARC-5 pilot's control unit will determine which component of the equipment will be used for transmission.

2. To operate the MHF transmitter, set the microphone selector switch to MHF, press the microphone switch, and talk.

3. To transmit on VHF, set the microphone selector switch to VHF, set the rotary switches on the C-45/ARC-1 control as desired. Press the microphone switch, and talk.

Note

The RT-18/ARC-1 equipment provides ten VHF channels and is so arranged that transmission and reception can be selected by the pilot on the C-45/ARC-1 as follows:

1

Position MAIN T/R.—Transmission and reception on the selected one of the nine main channels.

2

Position BOTH.—Transmission and reception on the selected one of the main channels and simultaneous monitoring on the GUARD channel.

3

Position GUARD.—Transmission and reception on the GUARD channel.

The following instructions assume that the microphone selector switch on the pilot's C-38/ARC-5 control is set to VHF and that the REC A toggle switch in the UP position.

1. To arrange the C-45/ARC-1 VHF control for transmission on any of the nine main channels, rotate the three-position switch to MAIN T/R, rotate the channel selector switch to any one of the nine channels desired, press the microphone switch, and talk.

2. Rotating the three-position switch to BOTH permits transmission and reception on any one of the selected main channels, and reception on the GUARD channel.

3. To arrange the C-45/ARC-1 control unit for transmission and reception on the GUARD channel, rotate the three-position selector switch to GUARD.

(d) RECEPTION.

1. GENERAL.—All receivers are always in the stand-by condition. Under normal conditions either or both of the REC A (VHF) or REC C (MHF) toggle switches on the pilot's C-38/ARC-5 control unit are set in the UP position.

2. HF RECEIVER.—Reception on MHF is controlled by the REC C toggle switch on the pilot's C-38/ARC-5 control unit.

Set the toggle switch "C" on the receiver control unit in the UP position and set the sensitivity control above switch "C", marked "SET FOR MAX. TOLERABLE NOISE". Make certain that the toggle switch "A" on the receiver control unit is in the OFF position, and that the OUTPUT control knob on the receiver control unit is in the minimum position while thus setting the level; however, unless sensitivity control is set for "MAX. TOLERABLE NOISE", weak signals may not be heard.

3. VHF RECEIVER.—Reception on VHF is controlled by the REC A toggle switch on the C-38/ARC-5 control unit, and by the selector switch on the C-45/ARC-1 control unit. Refer to transmission, paragraph *(c)* above for information on selecting any one of the ten channels provided. Set switch "A" on the receiver control unit in the UP position, the toggle switch "C" in the OFF position, and reception will be obtained only on the VHF channel selected.

(6) IFF EQUIPMENT.—The AN/APX-1 transmitter receiver, RT-22/APX-1, is installed aft of Station 362. The control units, C-54 and C-55, are located at the right side of the cockpit on radio control panel. The "G" band switch and the Destruct switch are located on the lower right instrument panel.

(a) OPERATING INSTRUCTIONS.

1. TO START THE EQUIPMENT.—The toggle switch on control unit, C-54/APX-1, is thrown on.

2. TO CHANGE SELECTOR SWITCH POSITIONS.—On the selector unit, C-55/APX-1, rotate the rotary switch to the position designated by the Commanding Officer. Unless otherwise directed, this switch is set and left in position "1".

3. TO OPERATE THE "G"-BAND.—On the pilot's remote-switch panel throw the "G"-band switch to the ON position or flip it to the TIME position.

4. FOR DISTRESS OPERATION.—On the control unit, C-54/APX-1, lift the green EMERGENCY guard and throw the switch ON.

5. TO DESTROY THE RECEIVER-TRANSMITTER UNIT.—If possible, warn operating personnel to stand clear of the receiver-transmitter unit. On the pilot's remote-switch panel raise the red guard and throw the DESTRUCT switch to the ON position. This will explode all Type AN/MI destructors in the unit.

6. FURTHER OPERATING PROCEDURES.—Information on further operation procedures must be obtained from the Commanding Officer.

7. TO STOP THE EQUIPMENT.—On the control unit, C-54/APX-1, throw the toggle switch to the OFF position.

(b) ALTERNATE EQUIPMENT. — Control, wiring, and space provisions are made for the alternate installation of the ABA-1 IFF equipment.

4. RADAR OPERATOR'S COCKPIT.

a. COCKPIT HOOD.

(1) GENERAL. — The hood is hinged to the cockpit rail on the left side and held in place by latch-pins on the right side. A hinged plexiglas access plate for the removable reserve fuel tank fillerneck is installed in the top of the hood. A finger latch for opening the hood is installed in the frame on the right side, and a control handle to operate the latch is installed inside. An emergency release handle is installed on the left, inside the hood.

Section V
Paragraph 4

(2) OPERATION.

(a) To open the hood from the outside—lift the finger latch and lift the hood to open. The latch will not operate if the control handle is in the forward (locked) position.

(b) To lock the hood from inside—move the control handle on the right hand side full forward.

WARNING

Be sure handle is locked full forward prior to take-off.

(3) EMERGENCY EXIT IN FLIGHT.—Refer to Section IV paragraph 6, emergency exit from cockpits.

b. SEAT AND HARNESS.—The fabric seat is designed to take a life raft pack as a cushion and is not adjustable. This standard adjustable lap and shoulder type harness is attached to fittings on the cockpit floor (tank top) and on the armor plate back of the seat.

c. HEATER CONTROL.—A duct from the combustion type heater located in the fuselage nose carries air aft to an opening in the fuselage bulkhead forward of the cockpit, to the right of the centerline. The control is a cover plate equipped with a hand tab, which may be rotated to close off or regulate the amount of opening.

d. INSTRUMENTS.—The following flight instruments are installed on the panel.

(1) Airspeed indicator.

(2) Outside air temperature indicator.

(3) Compass indicator.

(4) Sensitive altimeter.

(5) Clock.

e. EQUIPMENT.

(1) MAP CASE.—A standard map case is installed on the right side of the cockpit—forward.

(2) CHARTBOARD.—A standard chartboard is stowed below the instrument panel. To use the board clear the securing clamp and pull the board out.

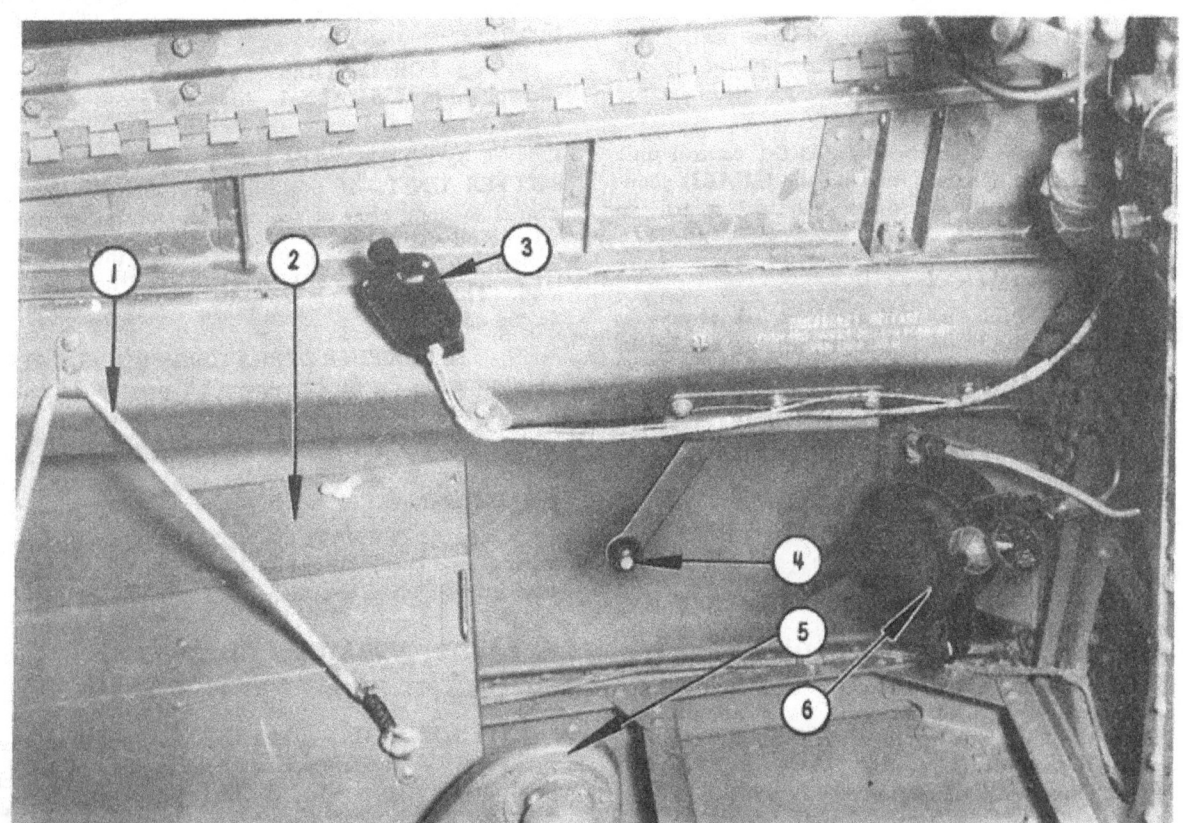

1. Emergency Equipment Kit Retainer
2. Cover—Oxygen Cylinder
3. Mask Microphone Switch
4. Emergency Hood Release Handle
5. Seat Stanchion
6. Oxygen Regulator

Figure 57—Radar Operator's Cockpit—L.H. Side

RESTRICTED
AN 01-85FA-1

**Paragraph 4
Section V**

CAUTION

Be sure that chartboard is secured in place for take-off and landing.

(3) PARACHUTE PACK STOWAGE.—A length of bungee cord is installed over a hook on the right hand side of the cockpit for stowage of a chest type parachute pack.

(4) EMERGENCY CONTAINER STOWAGE.—A length of bungee cord is installed over a hook on the left hand side of the cockpit for stowage of an emergency equipment container, above the oxygen bottle.

(5) RELIEF TUBE.—A relief tube is stowed in a clip below the seat.

f. ELECTRICAL EQUIPMENT.—This instrument panel is lighted by a reflector panel. The lighting is controlled by a rheostat switch (with circuit breaker) located on the right hand side.

Note

Rotate clockwise to ON and BRIGHT.
Rotate counterclockwise to DIM and OFF.

Spare lamps are stowed in a container on the left hand side of the panel.

g. OXYGEN EQUIPMENT.—A standard 514 cu. in. capacity oxygen cylinder, covered by a protecting plate, is installed in clamps on the floor to the left of the seat and the diluter-demand type regulator is installed on the left hand side of the cockpit, forward. A breathing tube and facepiece are attached. The oxygen flow indicator blinker is installed on the left side of the instrument panel. For operating information refer to paragraph 2., oxygen, above.

h. COMMUNICATING EQUIPMENT.—The following equipment is installed on the instrument panel:

(1) Scope indicator, 1D-32/APS-6, (on adjustable mount).

(2) Control unit, C-56/APX-2, with hand microphone in clip.

(3) Main controller, C-46/APS-6.

(4) Auxiliary control, C-47/APS-6.

For additional information, refer to paragraph 3., this section.

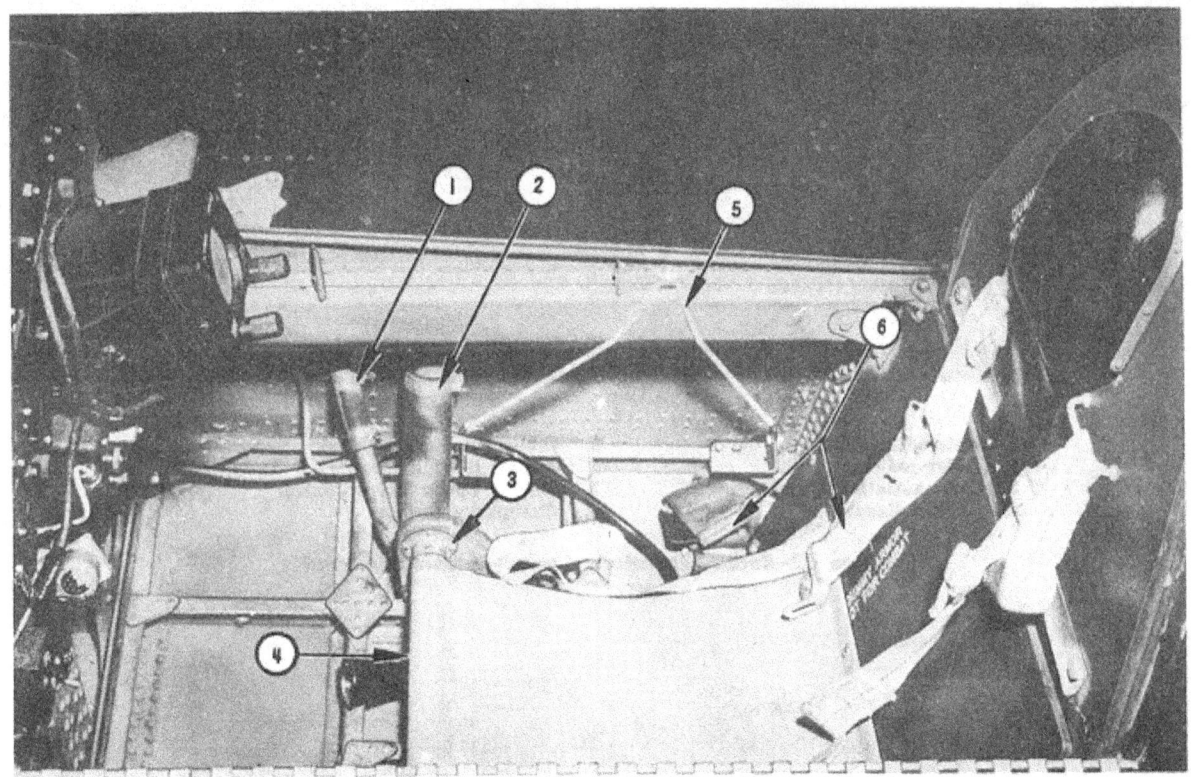

1. Reserve Tank Vent Line
2. Reserve Tank Fillerneck
3. Seat Stanchion
4. Seat
5. Parachute Pack Retainer
6. Lap and Shoulder Harness

Figure 58—Radar Operator's Cockpit—R.H. Side

SECTION VI
EXTREME WEATHER OPERATION

THIS INFORMATION WILL BE SUPPLIED WHEN AVAILABLE

THIS INFORMATION WILL BE SUPPLIED WHEN AVAILABLE

Appendix I of this publication shall not be carried in aircraft on combat missions or when there is a reasonable chance of its falling into the hands of the enemy.

APPENDIX I

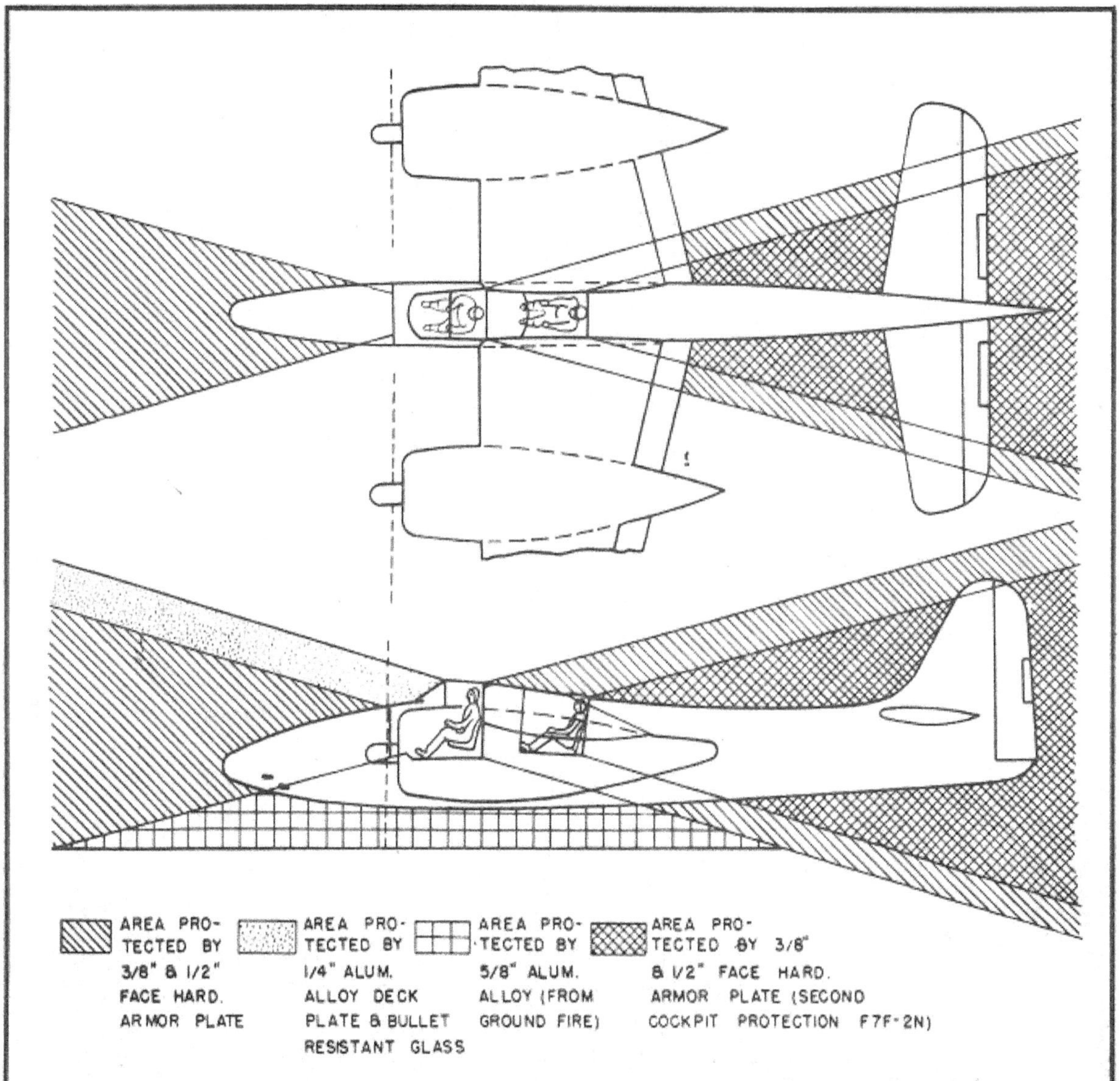

Figure 60—Protection from Gunfire Diagram

Appendix I of this publication shall not be carried in aircraft on combat missions or when there is a reasonable chance of its falling into the hands of the enemy.

AAF/NC-527
8-1-44

AIRCRAFT MODEL(S): F7F

ENGINE MODEL(S): R-2800-22W

TAKE-OFF, CLIMB & LANDING CHART

TAKE-OFF DISTANCE FEET

GROSS WEIGHT LB.	HEAD WIND		HARD SURFACE RUNWAY						SOD-TURF RUNWAY						SOFT SURFACE RUNWAY					
			AT SEA LEVEL		AT 3000 FEET		AT 6000 FEET		AT SEA LEVEL		AT 3000 FEET		AT 6000 FEET		AT SEA LEVEL		AT 3000 FEET		AT 6000 FEET	
	M.P.H.	KTS.	GROUND RUN	TO CLEAR 50' OBJ.	GROUND RUN	TO CLEAR 50' OBJ.	GROUND RUN	TO CLEAR 50' OBJ.	GROUND RUN	TO CLEAR 50' OBJ.	GROUND RUN	TO CLEAR 50' OBJ.	GROUND RUN	TO CLEAR 50' OBJ.	GROUND RUN	TO CLEAR 50' OBJ.	GROUND RUN	TO CLEAR 50' OBJ.	GROUND RUN	TO CLEAR 50' OBJ.
25800	0	0	1050																	
23725	0	0	875																	
21650	0	0	725																	
25800	17.3	15	760																	
23725	17.3	15	625																	
21650	17.3	15	510																	
25800	28.8	25	580																	
23725	28.8	25	470																	
21650	28.8	25	380																	

CARRIER

CARRIER

NOTE: INCREASE CHART DISTANCES AS FOLLOWS: 75°F + 10%; 100°F + 20%; 125°F + 30%; 150°F + 40%
DATA AS OF 12-15-44 BASED ON:

OPTIMUM TAKE-OFF WITH RPM, IN.HG. & DEG.FLAP IS 80% OF CHART VALUES

CLIMB DATA

GROSS WEIGHT LB.	AT SEA LEVEL				AT 5000 FEET					AT 10,000 FEET					AT 15,000 FEET					AT 25000 FEET					AT FEET				
	BEST I.A.S.		RATE OF CLIMB	GAL. OF FUEL	BEST I.A.S.		RATE OF CLIMB	FROM SEA LEVEL		BEST I.A.S.		RATE OF CLIMB	FROM SEA LEVEL		BEST I.A.S.		RATE OF CLIMB	FROM SEA LEVEL		BEST I.A.S.		RATE OF CLIMB	FROM SEA LEVEL		BEST I.A.S.		RATE OF CLIMB	FROM SEA LEVEL	
	MPH	KTS	F.P.M.	USED	MPH	KTS	F.P.M.	TIME MIN.	FUEL USED	MPH	KTS	F.P.M.	TIME MIN.	FUEL USED	MPH	KTS	F.P.M.	TIME MIN.	FUEL USED	MPH	KTS	F.P.M.	TIME MIN.	FUEL USED	MPH	KTS	F.P.M.	TIME MIN.	FUEL USED
25800	180	156	3065	28	181	157	2480	1.8		172	149	1960	4.0		167	145	1850	6.6		147	128	700	14.3						
23725	180	156	3605	28	181	157	3000	1.6		172	149	2450	3.3		167	145	2350	5.4		147	128	1100	11.1						
21650	180	156	4150	28	181	157	3500	1.4		172	149	2900	2.9		167	145	2800	4.6		147	128	1480	9.2						

POWER PLANT SETTINGS: (DETAILS ON FIG. 38 SECTION III):
DATA AS OF 12-15-44 BASED ON:

FUEL USED (U.S. GAL.) INCLUDES WARM-UP & TAKE-OFF ALLOWANCE

LANDING DISTANCE FEET

GROSS WEIGHT LB.	BEST IAS APPROACH				HARD DRY SURFACE						FIRM DRY SOD						WET OR SLIPPERY					
	POWER OFF		POWER ON		AT SEA LEVEL		AT 3000 FEET		AT 6000 FEET		AT SEA LEVEL		AT 3000 FEET		AT 6000 FEET		AT SEA LEVEL		AT 3000 FEET		AT 6000 FEET	
	MPH	KTS	MPH	KTS	GROUND ROLL	TO CLEAR 50' OBJ.	GROUND ROLL	TO CLEAR 50' OBJ.	GROUND ROLL	TO CLEAR 50' OBJ.	GROUND ROLL	TO CLEAR 50' OBJ.	GROUND ROLL	TO CLEAR 50' OBJ.	GROUND ROLL	TO CLEAR 50' OBJ.	GROUND ROLL	TO CLEAR 50' OBJ.	GROUND ROLL	TO CLEAR 50' OBJ.	GROUND ROLL	TO CLEAR 50' OBJ.

DATA AS OF BASED ON:

OPTIMUM LANDING IS 80% OF CHART VALUES

REMARKS: TAKE-OFF FIGURES FOR FULL FLAPS (-40°) CONDITION

NOTE: TO DETERMINE FUEL CONSUMPTION IN BRITISH IMPERIAL GALLONS, MULTIPLY BY 10, THEN DIVIDE BY 12

LEGEND
I.A.S. : INDICATED AIRSPEED
M.P.H. : MILES PER HOUR
KTS. : KNOTS
F.P.M. : FEET PER MINUTE

WP-8-41-44-10M

Figure 61 (Sheet 1 of 2 Sheets)—Take-Off, Climb and Landing Chart

Appendix I of this publication shall not be carried in aircraft on combat missions or when there is a reasonable chance of its falling into the hands of the enemy.

Appendix I

TAKE-OFF, CLIMB & LANDING CHART

AIRCRAFT MODEL(S):

ENGINE MODEL(S): R-2800-34W

TAKE-OFF DISTANCE (FEET)

HARD SURFACE RUNWAY

GROSS WEIGHT LB.	HEAD WIND		AT SEA LEVEL		AT 3000 FEET		AT 6000 FEET	
	M.P.H.	KTS.	GROUND RUN	TO CLEAR 50' OBJ.	GROUND RUN	TO CLEAR 50' OBJ.	GROUND RUN	TO CLEAR 50' OBJ.
20834	0	0	763	1214	917	1439	1095	1719
	17.3	15	515	820	633	994	766	1200
	34.5	30	303	482	384	604	480	752
	46.1	40	190	302	248	390	323	507
25000 2-150 GALLON DROP TANKS	0	0	1149	1800	1357	2110	1680	2607
	17.3	15	804	1260	974	1510	1220	1890
	34.5	30	505	791	621	967	811	1260
	46.1	40	340	533	364	670	576	894

SOD-TURF RUNWAY

	AT SEA LEVEL		AT 3000 FEET		AT 6000 FEET	
	GROUND RUN	TO CLEAR 50' OBJ.	GROUND RUN	TO CLEAR 50' OBJ.	GROUND RUN	TO CLEAR 50' OBJ.
	788	1240	942	1461	1143	1765
	532	887	650	1010	800	1235
	313	493	395	613	501	773
	196	309	255	396	337	520
	1178	1830	1375	2130	1725	2650
	825	1280	985	1530	1250	1920
	519	805	630	975	834	1280
	348	541	436	675	592	910

SOFT SURFACE RUNWAY

	AT SEA LEVEL		AT 3000 FEET		AT 6000 FEET	
	GROUND RUN	TO CLEAR 50' OBJ.	GROUND RUN	TO CLEAR 50' OBJ.	GROUND RUN	TO CLEAR 50' OBJ.
	836	1290	1000	1520	1223	1849
	565	870	690	1049	856	1294
	332	512	419	636	535	810
	208	321	271	412	300	545
	1275	1925	1520	2270	1918	2840
	893	1350	1090	1630	1390	2060
	561	847	696	1040	926	1372
	377	570	482	720	658	975

NOTE: INCREASE CHART DISTANCES AS FOLLOWS: 75°F + 10%; 100°F + 25%; 125°F + 30%; 150°F + 40%

OPTIMUM TAKE-OFF WITH _____ IN. HG. & _____ RPM. DEC. FLAP IS 80% OF CHART VALUES

CLIMB DATA

GROSS WEIGHT LB.	AT SEA LEVEL				AT 5000 FEET				AT 10,000 FEET				AT 15,000 FEET			
	BEST I.A.S.		RATE OF CLIMB F.P.M.	GAL. OF FUEL USED	BEST I.A.S.		RATE OF CLIMB F.P.M.	FROM SEA LEVEL	BEST I.A.S.		RATE OF CLIMB F.P.M.	FROM SEA LEVEL	BEST I.A.S.		RATE OF CLIMB F.P.M.	FROM SEA LEVEL
	MPH	KTS			MPH	KTS		TIME MIN. FUEL USED	MPH	KTS		TIME MIN. FUEL USED	MPH	KTS		TIME MIN. FUEL USED
20834	173	150	3330	28	169	147	3210	1.5 36	170	148	3000	3.1 45	170	148	2450	5.0 55
25000 2-150 DROP TANKS	180	156	2580	28	179	155	2530	1.6 39	179	155	2360	3.8 50	182	158	1710	6.1 63

AT 20,000 FEET				
BEST I.A.S.		RATE OF CLIMB F.P.M.	FROM SEA LEVEL	
MPH	KTS		TIME MIN.	FUEL USED
161	140	1790	7.2	66
173	150	1080	8.8	79

| FROM SEA LEVEL |
| TIME MIN. / FUEL USED |
| 9.7 / 77 |
| 12.5 / 100 |

FUEL USED (U.S. GAL.) INCLUDES WARM-UP & TAKE-OFF ALLOWANCE

POWER PLANT SETTINGS: DETAILS ON FIG. _____, SECTION III; BASED ON: _____

LANDING DISTANCE (FEET)

GROSS WEIGHT LB.	BEST IAS APPROACH		POWER ON		HARD DRY SURFACE						FIRM DRY SOD						WET OR SLIPPERY					
	POWER OFF				AT SEA LEVEL		AT 3000 FEET		AT 6000 FEET		AT SEA LEVEL		AT 3000 FEET		AT 6000 FEET		AT SEA LEVEL		AT 3000 FEET		AT 6000 FEET	
	MPH KTS	MPH KTS			GROUND ROLL	TO CLEAR 50' OBJ.	GROUND ROLL	TO CLEAR 50' OBJ.	GROUND ROLL	TO CLEAR 50' OBJ.	GROUND ROLL	TO CLEAR 50' OBJ.	GROUND ROLL	TO CLEAR 50' OBJ.	GROUND ROLL	TO CLEAR 50' OBJ.	GROUND ROLL	TO CLEAR 50' OBJ.	GROUND ROLL	TO CLEAR 50' OBJ.	GROUND ROLL	TO CLEAR 50' OBJ.

DATA AS OF _____, BASED ON: _____

REMARKS:

NOTE: TO DETERMINE FUEL CONSUMPTION IN BRITISH IMPERIAL GALLONS, MULTIPLY BY 10, THEN DIVIDE BY 12

OPTIMUM LANDING IS 80% OF CHART VALUES

LEGEND:
I.A.S.: INDICATED AIRSPEED
M.P.H.: MILES PER HOUR
KTS.: KNOTS
F.P.M.: FEET PER MINUTE

Figure 61 (Sheet 2 of 2 Sheets)—Take-Off, Climb and Landing Chart

Appendix I of this publication shall not be carried in aircraft on combat missions or when there is a reasonable chance of its falling into the hands of the enemy.

Appendix I

RESTRICTED
AN 01-85FA-1

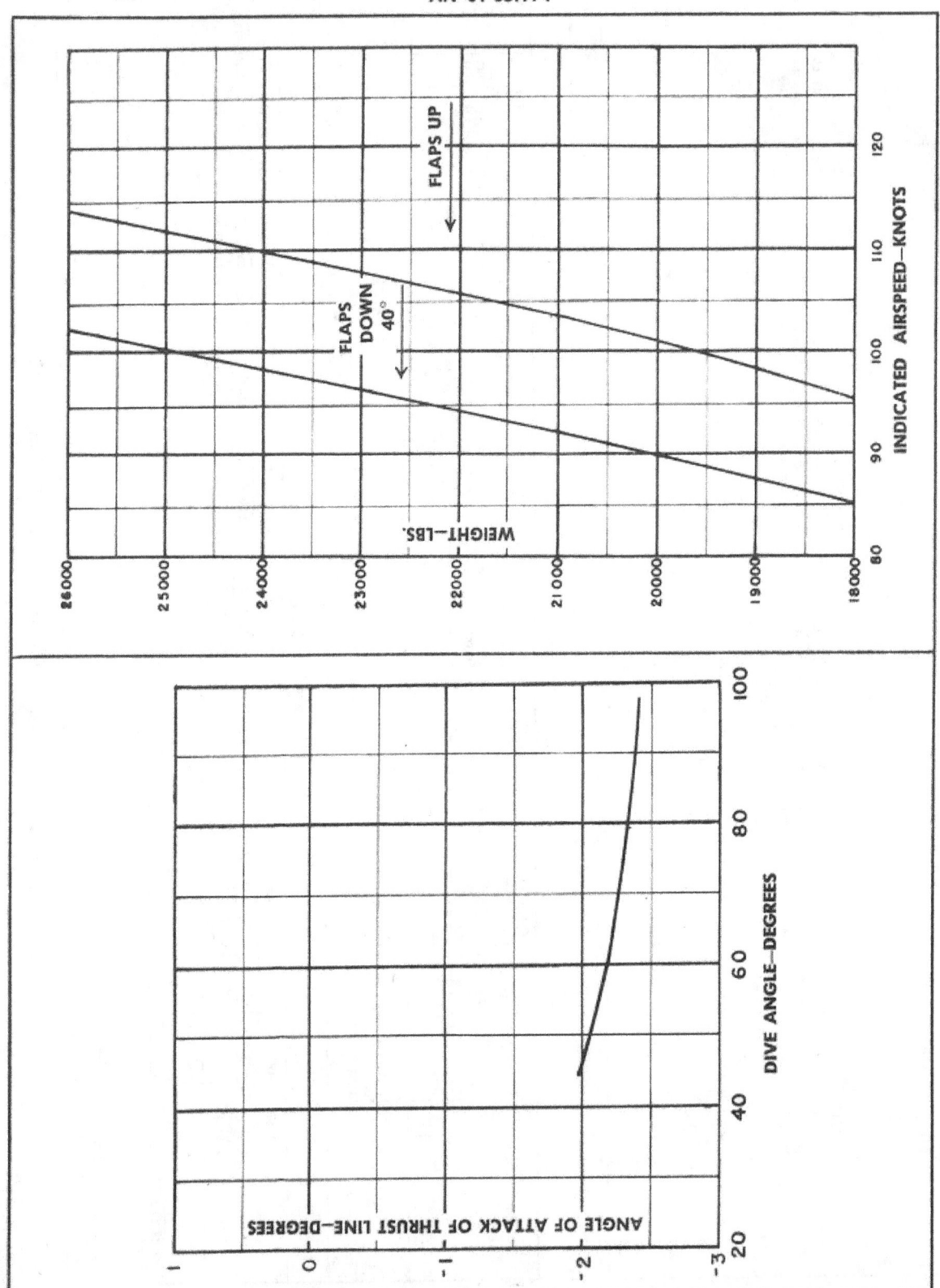

Figure 64—Stalling Speed vs. Weight (Power Off)

Figure 63—Dive Angle vs. Angle of Attack

Appendix I of this publication shall not be carried in aircraft on combat missions or when there is a reasonable chance of its falling into the hands of the enemy.

Appendix I

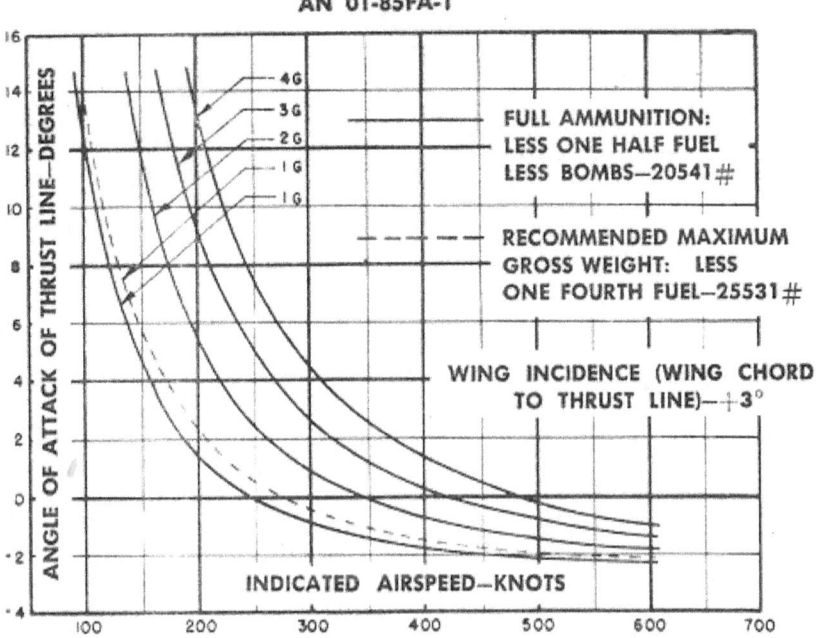

Figure 65—Angle of Attack vs. Indicated Airspeed (F7F-1 Day Fighter)

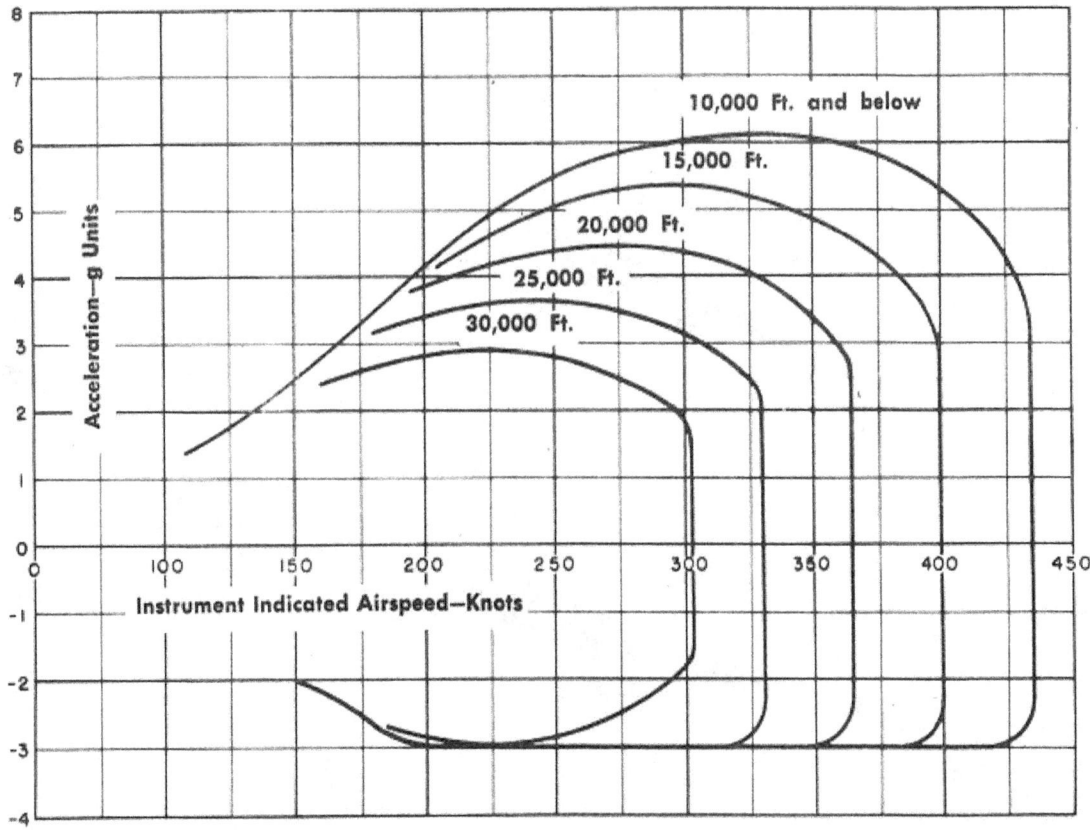

Figure 66—Operating Flight Strength Diagram (Gross Wt. 21,000 lbs.)

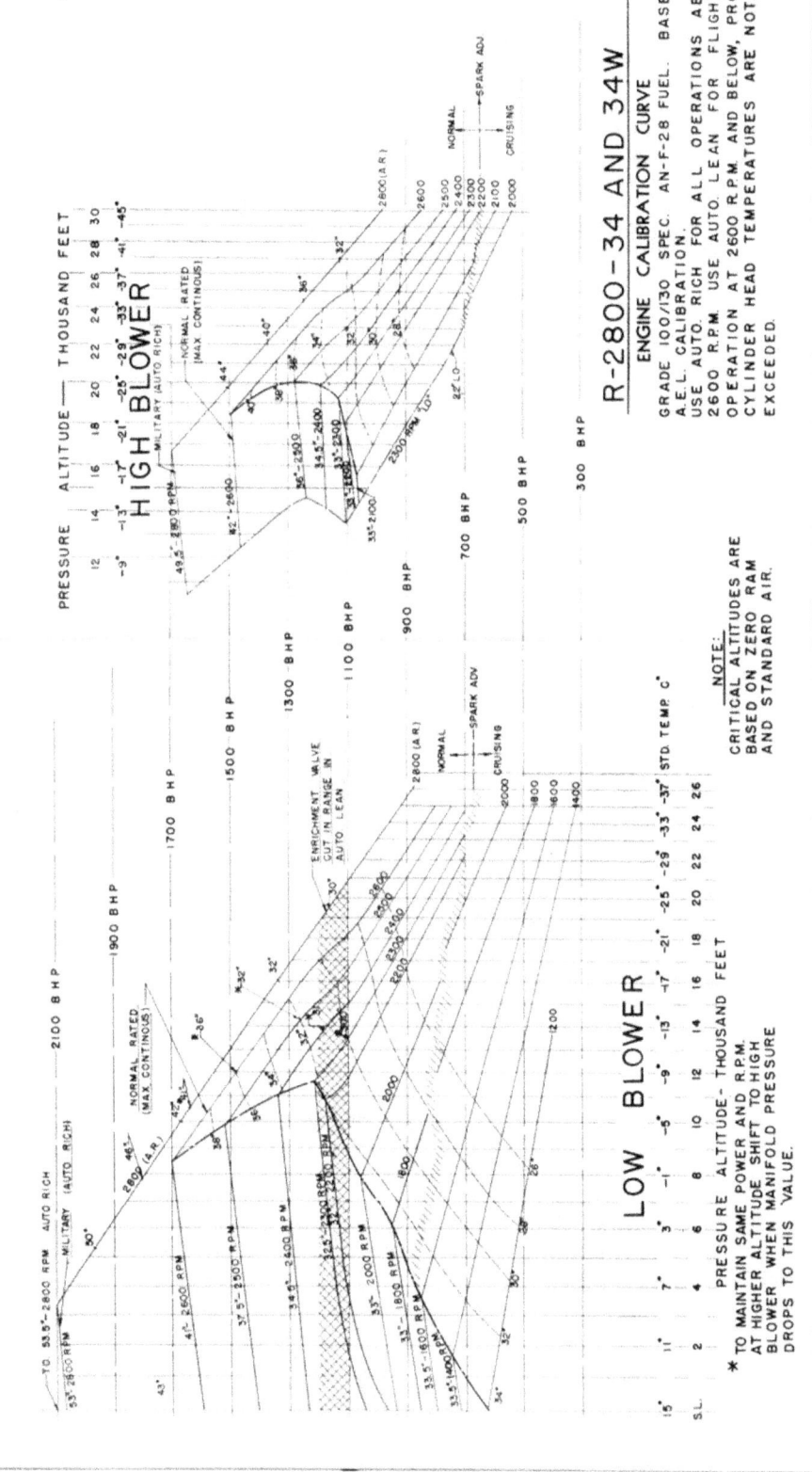

Figure 67 (Sheet 1 of 2 Sheets)—Engine Calibration Curves

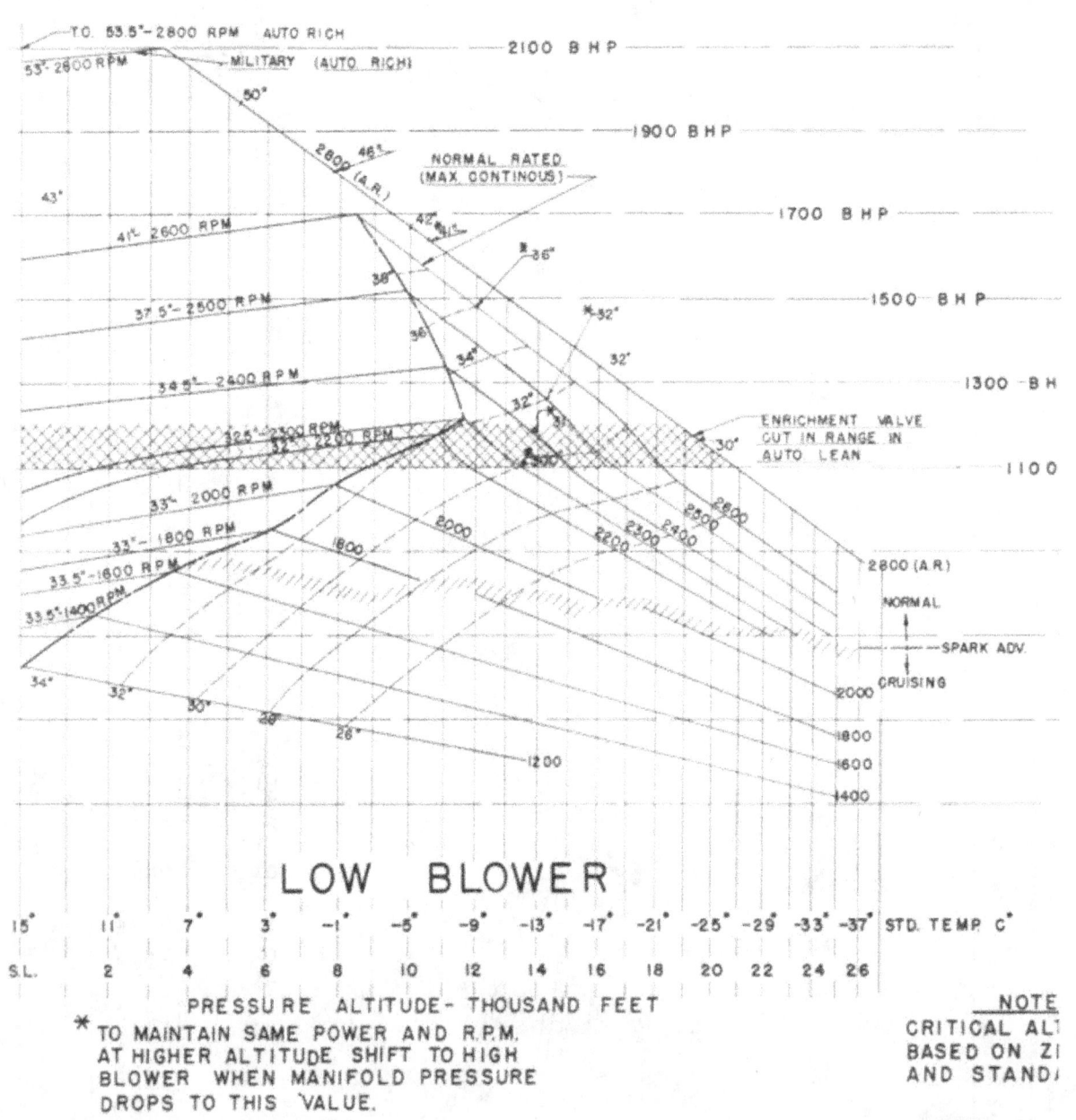

Figure 67 (Sheet 1 of 2 Sheets)—Engine Calibration Curves

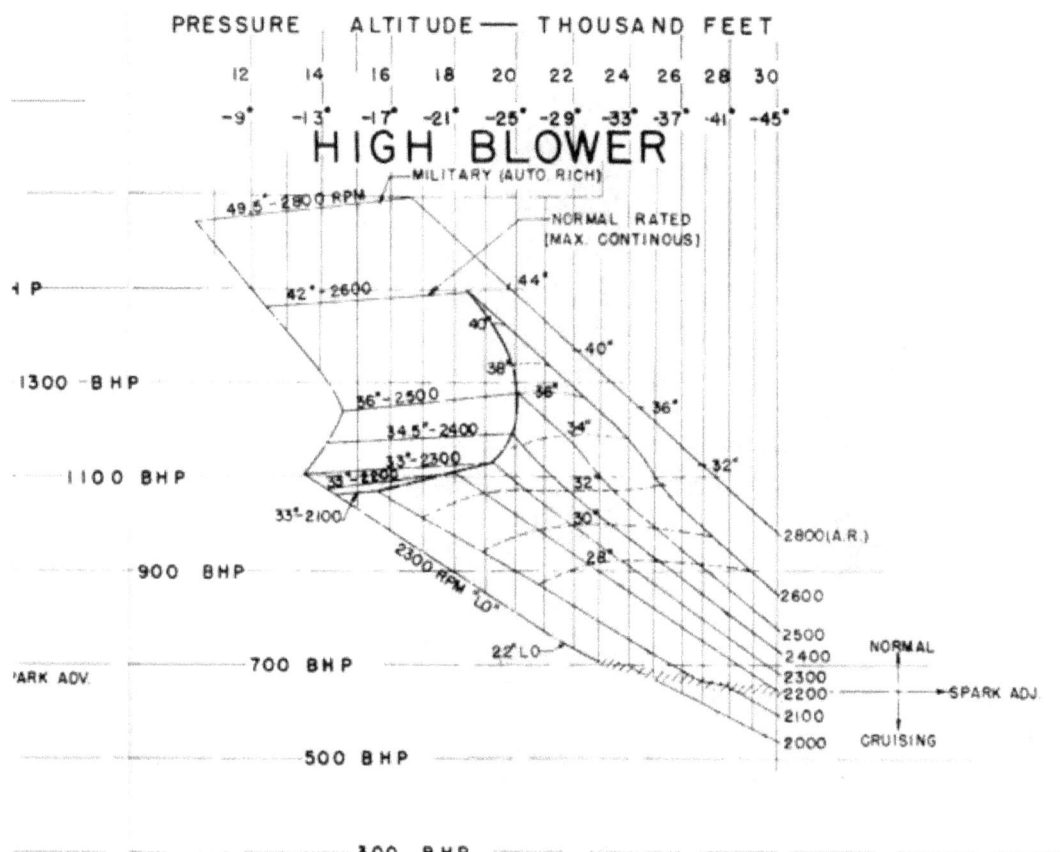

R-2800-34 AND 34W
ENGINE CALIBRATION CURVE

GRADE 100/130 SPEC. AN-F-28 FUEL. BASED ON A.E.L. CALIBRATION.
USE AUTO. RICH FOR ALL OPERATIONS ABOVE 2600 R.P.M. USE AUTO. LEAN FOR FLIGHT OPERATION AT 2600 R.P.M. AND BELOW, PROVIDED CYLINDER HEAD TEMPERATURES ARE NOT EXCEEDED.

NOTE:
ICAL ALTITUDES ARE
ED ON ZERO RAM
STANDARD AIR.

RESTRICTED
AN 01-85FA-1

This publication shall not be carried in aircraft or combat missions or when there is a reasonable chance of its falling into the hands of the enemy.

RESTRICTED
AN 01-85FA-1

APPENDIX II

PRELIMINARY ISSUE
SUPPLEMENTARY OPERATING INSTRUCTIONS
MODELS F7F-1, -2N, -3, -3N AIRPLANES

1. ORIGIN AND SCOPE OF DATA

The data presented in this preliminary issue of Model F7F-1, -2N, -3, -3N Airplanes' Supplementary Operating Instructions are based on the results of flight tests conducted on an F7F-1 airplane, BuNo. 80263, at the Naval Air Test Center, Patuxent River, Maryland. Fuel consumption is shown for AUTO LEAN operation in LOW BLOWER at calibrated airspeeds from 150 knots to 220 knots at gross weights ranging from 19,000 to 25,000 lbs. While the data were obtained with an F7F-1 airplane, it is considered that the differences in configuration between the listed F7F airplane models are insufficient to cause appreciable error when the data are applied to other airplanes of this group, equipped with either R-2800-22W or R-2800-34W engines and PR58E-2 carburetors having any of the following settings:

      Parts List Number 395516-11
      Parts List Number 395516-12
      Parts List Number 395516-13

2. CONDITION OF THE TEST

The test airplane was equipped with R-2800-34W engines and Stromberg Model PR58E-2 carburetors, Setting Parts List Number 395516-11. Complete data for both engines were recorded and the results reported here represent the average performance of the two engines. Fuel flows shown are total fuel consumed by both engines, and are based on averaged requirements of the two engines when operated in AUTO LEAN. Fuel flows obtainable by manual leaning were not determined, but instructions for manual leaning are included in this publication. Cooling was satisfactory with cowl and oil cooler flaps fully closed at the air speeds used during the tests.

3. USE OF DATA

(a) AIRPLANE WITH NO EXTERNAL DRAG ITEMS

The charts shown hold true for an airplane without external useful-load items and operating in standard air. The tabulated CAS and GPH will be obtained with the recommended MP and RPM only when flying such an airplane in an Outside Air Temperature corresponding to the Standard Temperature at the Pressure Altitude (1) flown.

Under Non-standard conditions close correlation between airspeeds and power settings should not be expected. Nevertheless if power is set up using calibrated airspeed and density altitude as a guide, fuel consumption predicted by the tabulations should check very well with actual fuel consumption.

(1) Pressure Altitude defined on page 6.

RESTRICTED

This publication shall not be carried in aircraft or combat missions or when there is a reasonable chance of its falling into the hands of the enemy.

APPENDIX II

RESTRICTED
AN 01-85FA-1

To use these tables, select the proper chart for the CAS to be flown. Enter the STD. ALT. column with Density Altitude (2) and for the particular GROSS WEIGHT, read off the MP, RPM, and GPH. Set up this MP and RPM, and when the airplane has settled down to constant airspeed, note whether this airspeed is lower or higher than desired. If the airspeed is low, advance the throttle to raise it, provided the MP is not over 32 in. In case the airspeed is still low after the throttle has been advanced to 32 in., or to FT, increase RPM until the desired airspeed is obtained. Do not use over 32 in. MP.

NOTE: At part throttle, an increase in RPM may cause the MP to drop. Advance throttle to raise it, and reduce RPM slightly, if necessary, in order to hold desired airspeed. At or near FT, an increase in RPM will cause a rise in MP which may require readjustment of the throttle to prevent exceeding 32 in.

If the airspeed is high and the RPM is over 1400, hold the MP at 32 in. (or use FT if 32 in. cannot be obtained) and reduce RPM. Do not use less than 1400 RPM. If airspeed is still too high at 1400 RPM, retard throttle as necessary.

EXAMPLE:

A flight is to be made at 23,000 lb. gross weight at 4000' Pressure Altitude. The OAT at that altitude is 15°C. What fuel flow may be expected, and what will be the approximate power settings?

The first step is to find the Density Altitude by using the Density Altitude Graph or the MK8A Computer, if available. At 4000 feet PA and 15°C, the Density Altitude is 5000 feet. With this altitude enter the column marked "STD ALT" in the chart headed "160 KNOTS CAS". Since this chart shows data for 4000 and 6000 feet, a simple interpolation is necessary. The predicted fuel consumption is 87.5 gallons per hour and the approximate power settings are 25 inches and 1400 RPM.

At a given weight and configuration, the power and hence, the fuel flow requirements of the airplane are fixed by the density altitude, and the CAS at which the airplane is flown. This is evident because the Airplane's True Airspeed depends on Density Altitude and CAS alone. Since, in this example, the airplane is actually flying at 5000 feet Density Altitude (although the altimeter reads 4000' Pressure Altitude), the fuel flow value will be 87.5 GPH at 160 CAS, as charted. On another day, if the temperature at 4000 feet PA is 8°C the Density Altitude will also be 4000'. On a colder day, at a PA of 6000' and a temperature of -5°C the Density Altitude will be 5000 feet and the airplane's fuel flow requirement will still be 87.5 GPH at 160 KNOTS CAS.

(2) Density Altitude defined on page 6.

This publication shall not be carried in aircraft or combat missions or when there is a reasonable chance of its falling into the hands of the enemy.

RESTRICTED
AN 01-85FA-1

APPENDIX II

It must be remembered that, at the same Pressure Altitude, for a given MP and RPM, an increase in air temperature will decrease the power output. The Charts give power settings to obtain certain Calibrated Airspeeds under standard conditions. Therefore on a day colder than standard, the Power Settings required will be slightly reduced, and on a warm day they must be increased.

(b) AIRPLANE WITH EXTERNAL DRAG ITEMS

An airplane flying in standard air equipped with external useful load items would require more horsepower to attain a prescribed CAS than a similar airplane in clean configuration, i.e., with no bombs, fuel tanks, or supporting racks externally attached; consequently, more fuel would be burned in carrying the drag items. Similarly, it may be considered that the addition of particular external loads would be equivalent to a definite reduction in CAS. For example: On the test airplane the parasitic drag of a MK-8 droppable fuel tank was found to be equivalent to a reduction in CAS of 7 Kts. within the range of speeds covered -- 150 to 220 Kts. Thus, to find the power settings and fuel consumption of a similar airplane flying at 150 Kts. CAS carrying a MK-8 droppable tank, it would be necessary to interpolate between the 150 CAS and the 160 CAS charts for 157 Kts. CAS. Similarly the parasitic drag of 2-1000 lb. General Purpose bombs on wing racks was equivalent to a reduction in CAS of 18 Kts., and the combined drag of the droppable tank and the bombs was equivalent to the sum of the two or 25 Kts. reduction in CAS.

4. AIRSPEED CALIBRATION

The airspeed calibration of the test airplane, Figure 1, indicates that the difference between indicated airspeed and calibrated airspeed is large enough to be considered of importance within the speed range covered by these charts. However, this calibration may not be representative of other F7F airplanes, and therefore, all airplanes should be checked for airspeed calibration unless recent data are readily available. Pacing the airplane to be calibrated against another airplane of known calibration should yield satisfactory results.

5. MAXIMUM RANGE AIRSPEED - AUTO LEAN

Maximum range airspeeds in AUTO LEAN have been calculated for three configurations as follows:

      (a) Clean configuration (no external load items) - 180 Kts. CAS.
      (b) MK 8 - 300 gal. droppable fuel tank on fuselage - 170 Kts. CAS.
      (c) MK 8 - droppable tank on fuselage and 2 x 1000 lb. General Purpose bombs on wing racks - 165 Kts. CAS.

6. MAXIMUM RANGE AIRSPEED - MANUAL LEAN

Although the AUTO LEAN Setting of the carburetor is designed to provide a mixture at fuel-air ratios near best economy above a certain power output, at relatively low airspeeds in part-throttle conditions, the power require-

Section V
Paragraph 4

1. Instrument Panel
2. Radar Indicator
3. Communicating Controls
4. Oxygen Regulator
5. Tubing to Oxygen Mask
6. Cockpit Hood Emergency Release Handle
7. Oxygen Bottle Valve Control
8. Microphone Switch

Figure 59—Radar Operator's Cockpit—Looking Forward

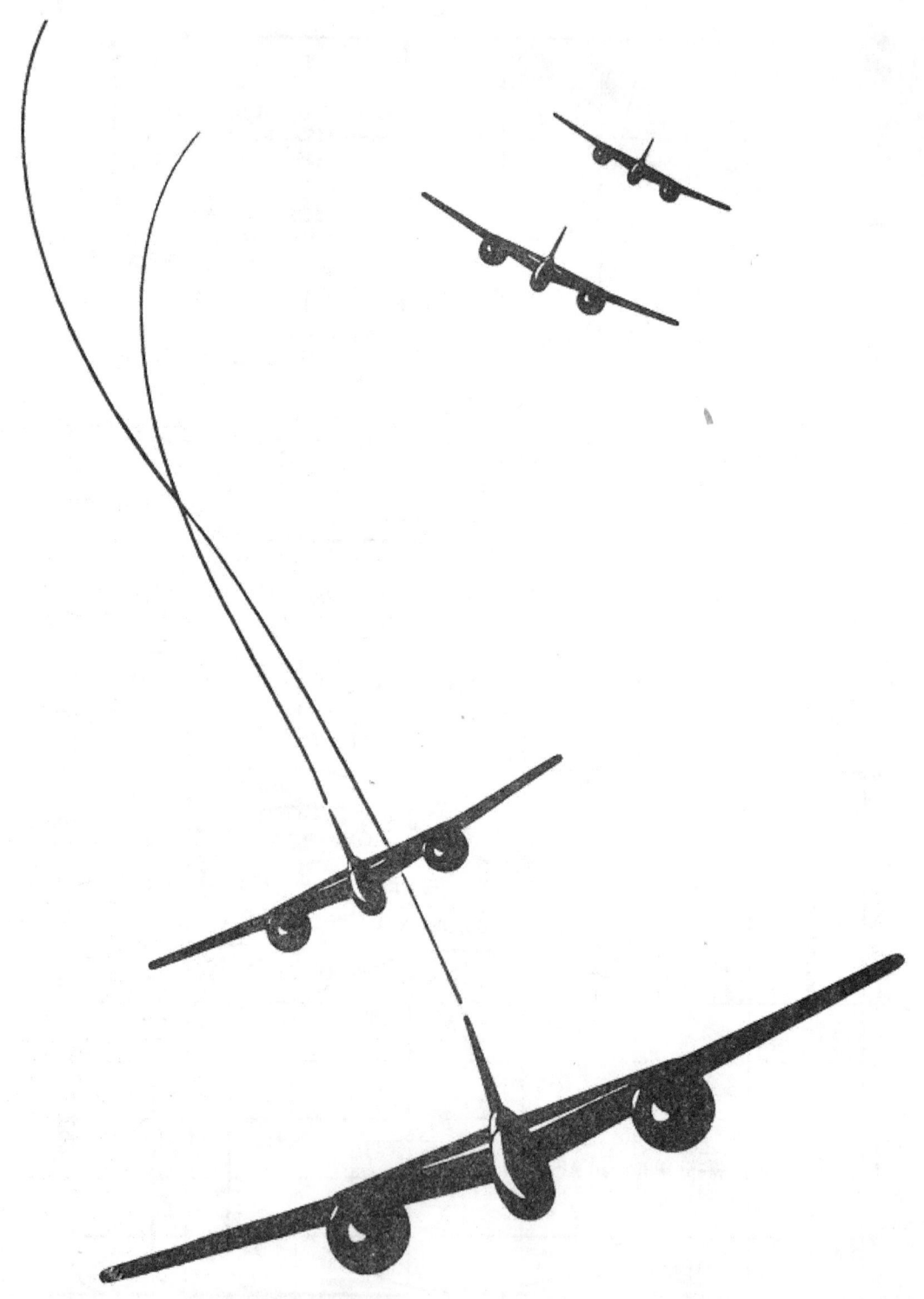

This publication shall not be carried in aircraft or combat missions or when there is a reasonable chance of its falling into the hands of the enemy.

APPENDIX II

RESTRICTED
AN 01-85FA-1

ments of the F7F Airplane are of such a value that the carburetor will provide excessively rich mixtures due to idle enrichment. The results are analogous to ground operation at idling RPM's where the idling jets of the carburetor meter the fuel at fuel-air ratios higher than best economy in order to provide satisfactory engine cooling.

In flight, however, where engine cooling is not critical at cruising powers, operation in the idle enrichment range results in a waste of fuel. The idle enrichment in this engine-carburetor combination begins to take place at approximately 630 BHP with the mixture control in AUTO LEAN, and becomes progressively worse at lower powers. It must be emphasized here that engine operation in AUTO LEAN in the idle enrichment range is entirely satisfactory EXCEPT from the standpoint of fuel economy.

The region in which MANUAL Leaning is permissible is shown on the accompanying charts. The line of demarcation below which Manual-Leaning may be performed represents the conditions where idle enrichment begins. No improvement in fuel economy would result in Manual-Leaning above this power.

Pending results of Manual-Leaning flight tests now being undertaken at NATC, Patuxent River, the following technique for Manual-Leaning is suggested. Use the power settings for AUTO LEAN operation determined by the procedure outlined in Section 3. Retard the mixture control smoothly toward the Idle Cut-Off position until the first indication of engine roughness is felt or heard. (During the leaning-out process the power output of the engine will necessarily change. Therefore, in order not to confuse RPM changes due to changes in power with engine roughness due to excessively lean mixtures, retard the mixture control smoothly enough to permit the propeller governor to maintain constant RPM.) Advance the mixture forward as far as needed to resume smooth engine operation. This will require a very small movement if the leaning-out process has been done carefully.

Since the variation in power during the leaning-out process will result in a change in airspeed, the power settings must be readjusted, as outlined in Section 3 (a), to regain the airspeed desired.

Excessive leaning-out will result in engine speed instability and an unsteady power output. Under most conditions best economy mixtures will be obtained before engine instability is reached. A mixture setting slightly richer than that obtained at the limit of stability is therefore desired.

The fuel flow values appearing on the charts are AUTO LEAN values. Because of the many variables involved it is not possible, with the evidence at hand, to predict what manual leaning flow values would be. The results obtained in one airplane, by one pilot, should not be used for planning purposes for the entire squadron. However, the range (air miles per gallon) of any particular airplane may be increased as much as 50% by manual leaning especially at low gross weights and altitudes.

This publication shall not be carried in aircraft or combat missions or when there is a reasonable chance of its falling into the hands of the enemy.

RESTRICTED
AN 01-85FA-1

APPENDIX II

To obtain maximum air miles per gallon fly at 160 Knots CAS, and manual-lean as described above. This airspeed has been calculated to be the optimum for all weights and altitudes in the clean configuration only.

7. CYLINDER HEAD TEMPERATURE LIMITS
   (R-2800-22, -22W, -34, -34W)

Take-off	AUTO RICH, 5 min.	$260^\circ C$
Military Power	AUTO RICH, 5 min.	$260^\circ C$
Normal Rated Power	AUTO RICH, One Hour	$260^\circ C$
	AUTO LEAN, No Limit	$232^\circ C$
Maximum Cruise and Lower Power	AUTO LEAN, No Limit	$232^\circ C$

AUTO RICH must be used for all operation above 2600 RPM, and for take-off, landing, landing approach, for all ground operation, and whenever cylinder head temperatures cannot be maintained within limits in AUTO LEAN.

AUTO LEAN may be used for all flight operation (except take-off, landing and landing approach) at 2600 RPM and below provided cylinder head temperature limits are not exceeded.

8. BLOWER SHIFTING

During these tests no attempt was made to find the optimum blower-shift altitude for powers below Maximum Cruise. All tests were conducted in Low Blower and AUTO LEAN mixture up to and including 20000 feet. The data available at present indicate that better fuel economy in High Blower would probably be realized at altitudes of approximately 14000 feet and above.

Pending results of flight tests Manual-Leaning must not be attempted in High Blower.

APPENDIX II

RESTRICTED
AN 01-85FA-1

DENSITY ALTITUDE GRAPH

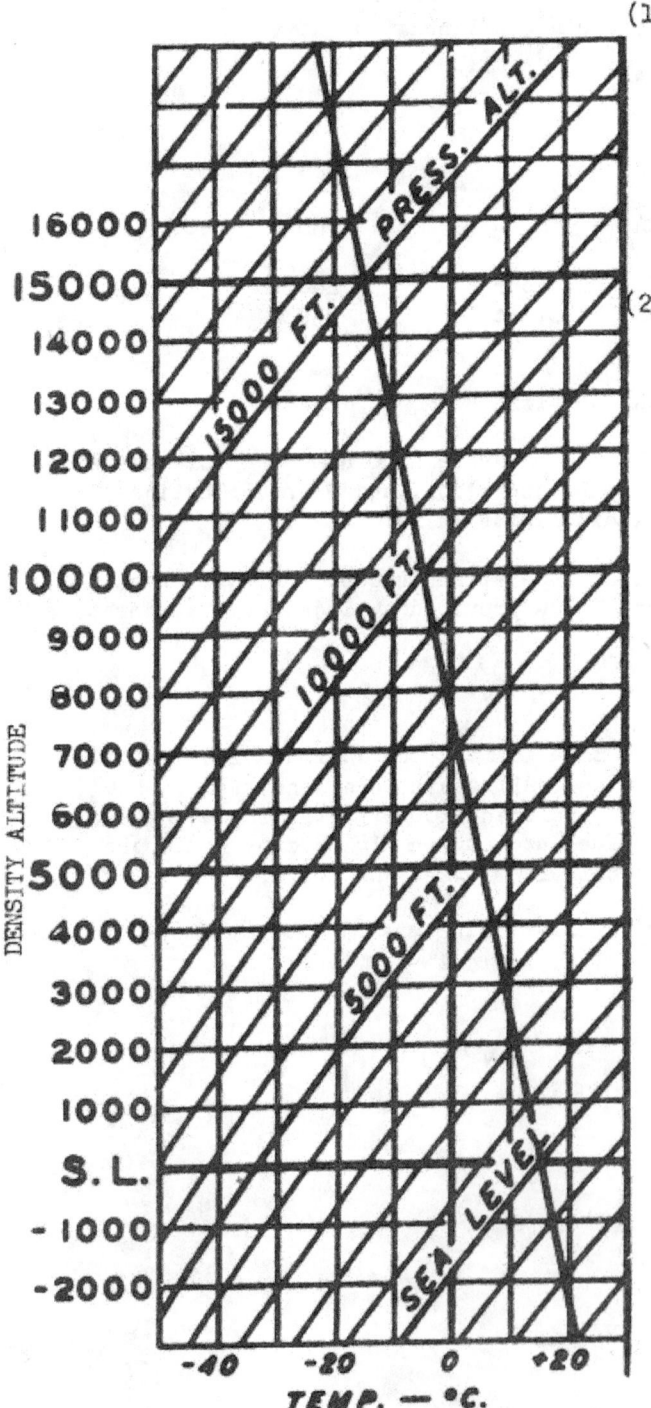

OUTSIDE AIR TEMPERATURE

(1) To obtain PRESSURE ALTITUDE -
Adjust the altimeter setting ("window number") to 29.92. The altitude indicated by the altimeter, after correction for instrument errors, will be Pressure Altitude. Pressure Altitude lines are inclined upward to right; Density Altitude lines are horizontal; Outside Air Temperature lines are vertical.

(2) To determine DENSITY ALTITUDE -
Enter graph with Pressure Altitude and Outside Air Temperature; locate the intersection, and read off Density Altitude.

EXAMPLES:
1. Press. Alt. = 6000 ft.
   OAT = 20°C
   Read Dens. Alt. = 8000 ft.

2. Press. Alt. = 9,500 ft.
   OAT = 5°C
   Read Dens. Alt. = 10,500 ft.

This publication shall not be carried in aircraft or combat missions or when there is a reasonable chance of its falling into the hands of the enemy.

RESTRICTED
AN 01-85FA-1

APPENDIX II

150 KNOTS CAS

Clean Configuration
Auto Lean
Low Blower

PR 58E2 Carburetors
Parts List No. 395516-11

Cowl and Oil Cooler Flaps closed.

25,000 lbs.			23,000 lbs.			Std. Alt.	Std. Temp. °C.	21,000 lbs.			19,000 lbs.		
RPM	MP	GPH	RPM	MP	GPH			RPM	MP	GPH	RPM	MP	GPH
1880	FT	113	1790	FT	102	20,000	-25	1680	FT	94	---	---	---
1760	FT	108	1680	FT	98	18,000	-21	1570	FT	91	---	---	---
1650	FT	103	1570	FT	96	16,000	-17	1470	FT	89	---	---	---
1550	FT	99	1480	FT	93	14,000	-13	1400	22.0	87	---	---	---
1450	FT	97	1400	24.0	90	12,000	-9	1400	21.5	86	---	---	---
1400	25.5	94	1400	23.5	89	10,000	-5	1400	21.5	85	---	---	---
1400	25.5	91	1400	23.5	88	8,000	-1	1400	21.5	84	---	---	---
1400	26.0	89	1400	24.0	86	6,000	3	1400	22.0	83	---	---	---
1400	26.5	88	1400	24.5	85	4,000	7	1400	23.0	83	---	---	---
1400	27.0	87	1400	25.5	84	2,000	11	1400	23.5	82	---	---	---
1400	27.5	86	1400	26.0	84	S. L.	15	1400	24.5	82	---	---	---

MANUAL LEANING PERMISSIBLE BELOW THIS LINE

ABBREVIATIONS:

CAS - Calibrated air speed
MP - Manifold pressure
FT - Full throttle

GPH - Gallons per hour, both engines
STD. ALT. - Standard altitude
Std. Temp. - Standard temperature

IMPORTANT - FOR MAXIMUM RANGE IN CLEAN CONFIGURATION USE MANUAL LEAN AND FLY AT 160 KNOTS CAS.

RESTRICTED

This publication shall not be carried in aircraft or combat missions or when there is a reasonable chance of its falling into the hands of the enemy.

APPENDIX II

RESTRICTED
AN 01-85FA-1

160 KNOTS CAS

Clean Configuration
Auto Lean
Low Blower

PR 58E2 Carburetors
Parts List No. 395516-11

Cowl and Oil Cooler Flaps closed.

25,000 lbs.			23,000 lbs.			Std. Alt.	Std. Temp. °C.	21,000 lbs.			19,000 lbs.		
RPM	MP	GPH	RPM	MP	GPH			RPM	MP	GPH	RPM	MP	GPH
1930	FT	118	1840	FT	108	20,000	-25	1750	FT	98	1640	FT	91
1790	FT	114	1720	FT	103	18,000	-21	1630	FT	96	1540	FT	89
1680	FT	108	1610	FT	99	16,000	-17	1530	FT	93	1440	FT	88
1580	FT	104	1520	FT	97	14,000	-13	1430	FT	90	1400	21	86
1490	FT	99	1420	FT	94	12,000	-9	1400	23.0	89	---	---	---
1400	26.5	96	1400	24.5	91	10,000	-5	1400	22.5	87	---	---	---
1400	26.5	94	1400	24.5	89	8,000	-1	1400	22.5	86	---	---	---
1400	26.5	92	1400	25.0	88	6,000	3	1400	23.0	84	---	---	---
1400	27.0	89	1400	25.5	87	4,000	7	1400	24.0	84	---	---	---
1400	27.5	88	1400	26.0	86	2,000	11	1400	24.5	83	---	---	---
1400	28.0	87	1400	26.5	85	S. L.	15	1400	25.0	83	---	---	---

MANUAL LEANING PERMISSIBLE BELOW THIS LINE

ABBREVIATIONS:

CAS - Calibrated air speed
MP - Manifold pressure
FT - Full throttle
GPH - Gallons per hour, both engines
STD. ALT. - Standard altitude
STD Temp. - Standard temperature

IMPORTANT - FOR MAXIMUM RANGE IN CLEAN CONFIGURATION USE MANUAL LEAN AND FLY AT 160 KNOTS CAS.

RESTRICTED

This publication shall not be carried in aircraft or combat missions or when there is a reasonable chance of its falling into the hands of the enemy.

RESTRICTED
AN 01-85FA-1

APPENDIX II

170 KNOTS CAS

Clean Configuration
Auto Lean
Low Blower

PR 58E2 Carburetors
Parts List No. 395516-11

Cowl and
Oil Cooler
Flaps closed.

25,000 lbs.			23,000 lbs.			STD. ALT.	STD. TEMP. °C	21,000 lbs.			19,000 lbs.		
RPM	MP	GPH	RPM	MP	GPH			RPM	MP	GPH	RPM	MP	GPH
2000	FT	123	1910	FT	116	20,000	-25	1820	FT	106	1710	FT	96
1850	FT	120	1780	FT	111	18,000	-21	1700	FT	101	1590	FT	93
1730	FT	116	1670	FT	107	16,000	-17	1590	FT	98	1500	FT	90
1630	FT	112	1570	FT	101	14,000	-13	1500	FT	95	1400	FT	89
1550	FT	106	1470	FT	98	12,000	-9	1400	FT	92	1400	22.0	87
1440	FT	101	1400	26.0	96	10,000	-5	1400	24.5	90	1400	21.5	86
1400	27.5	98	1400	26.0	93	8,000	-1	1400	24.5	89	1400	21.5	85
1400	28.0	96	1400	26.5	90	6,000	3	1400	24.5	87	1400	22.5	84
1400	28.0	93	1400	27.0	89	4,000	7	1400	25.5	86	1400	23.5	83
1400	28.5	90	1400	27.5	88	2,000	11	1400	26.0	85	1400	24.0	83
1400	29.0	89	1400	27.5	87	S. L.	15	1400	26.5	84	1400	24.5	82

MANUAL LEANING PERMISSIBLE BELOW THIS LINE

ABBREVIATIONS:

CAS - Calibrated Air speed
MP - Manifold pressure
FT - Full throttle
GPH - Gallons per hour, both engines.
STD. ALT. - Standard altitude
STD. TEMP. - Standard temperature

IMPORTANT - FOR MAXIMUM RANGE IN CLEAN CONFIGURATION USE MANUAL LEAN AND FLY AT 160 KNOTS CAS.

RESTRICTED

This publication shall not be carried in aircraft or combat missions or when there is a reasonable chance of its falling into the hands of the enemy.

APPENDIX II

RESTRICTED
AN 01-85FA-1

180 KNOTS CAS

Clean Configuration
Auto Lean
Low Blower

PR 58E2 Carburetors
Parts List No. 395516-11

Cowl and
Oil cooler
Flaps closed.

25,000 lbs.			23,000 lbs.			STD. ALT.	STD. TEMP °C.	21,000 lbs.			19,000 lbs.		
RPM	MP	GPH	RPM	MP	GPH			RPM	MP	GPH	RPM	MP	GPH
2030	FT	134	2000	FT	124	20,000	-25	1920	FT	116	1850	FT	109
1930	FT	129	1850	FT	120	18,000	-21	1780	FT	112	1730	FT	104
1790	FT	124	1750	FT	116	16,000	-17	1680	FT	107	1620	FT	100
1700	FT	120	1640	FT	112	14,000	-13	1580	FT	102	1520	FT	96
1600	FT	115	1540	FT	106	12,000	-9	1480	FT	99	1430	FT	94
1500	FT	110	1440	FT	101	10,000	-5	1400	26.0	96	1400	25.0	92
1400	FT	105	1400	27.5	98	8,000	-1	1400	26.5	93	1400	25.0	90
1400	29.5	100	1400	28.0	96	6,000	3	1400	26.5	91	1400	25.5	88
1400	29.5	98	1400	28.5	93	4,000	7	1400	27.0	89	1400	26.0	87
1400	30.0	95	1400	28.5	90	2,000	11	1400	27.5	88	1400	26.5	86
1400	30.5	92	1400	29.0	89	S.L.	15	1400	27.5	87	1400	26.5	85

ABBREVIATIONS:

CAS - Calibrated air speed
MP - Manifold pressure
FT - Full throttle

GPH - Gallons per hour, both engines
STD. ALT. - Standard altitude
STD. TEMP. - Standard temperature

IMPORTANT – FOR MAXIMUM RANGE IN CLEAN CONFIGURATION USE MANUAL LEAN AND FLY AT 160 KNOTS CAS.

MANUAL LEANING PERMISSIBLE BELOW THIS LINE

RESTRICTED

86

This publication shall not be carried in aircraft or combat missions or when there is a reasonable chance of its falling into the hands of the enemy.

RESTRICTED
AN 01-85FA-1

APPENDIX II

190 KNOTS CAS

Clean Configuration
Auto Lean
Low Blower

PR 58E2 Carburetors
Parts List No. 395516-11

Cowl and Oil cooler Flaps Closed

25,000 lbs.			23,000 lbs.			STD. ALT.	STD. TEMP. °C	21,000 lbs.			19,000 lbs.		
RPM	MP	GPH	RPM	MP	GPH			RPM	MP	GPH	RPM	MP	GPH
2180	FT	145	2100	FT	137	20,000	-25	2020	FT	128	1970	FT	121
2030	FT	140	1970	FT	132	18,000	-21	1890	FT	124	1830	FT	117
1890	FT	136	1820	FT	127	16,000	-17	1770	FT	119	1720	FT	113
1800	FT	130	1720	FT	122	14,000	-13	1670	FT	115	1620	FT	108
1680	FT	126	1620	FT	118	12,000	-9	1570	FT	110	1510	FT	102
1580	FT	122	1520	FT	114	10,000	-5	1470	FT	105	1420	FT	99
1490	FT	117	1430	FT	109	8,000	-1	1400	28.0	100	1400	27.0	97
1400	FT	113	1400	30.0	104	6,000	3	1400	28.5	98	1400	27.5	94
1400	31.5	108	1400	30.0	100	4,000	7	1400	29.0	95	1400	27.5	91
1400	32.0	104	1400	30.5	97	2,000	11	1400	29.5	92	1400	28.0	89
1430	32.0	100	1400	31.0	94	S. L.	15	1400	30.0	90	1400	28.5	88

ABBREVIATIONS:

CAS - Calibrated air speed
MP - Manifold pressure
FT - Full throttle

GPH - Gallons per hour, both engines
STD. ALT. - Standard altitude
STD. TEMP. - Standard temperature

IMPORTANT - FOR MAXIMUM RANGE IN CLEAN CONFIGURATION USE MANUAL LEAN AND FLY AT 160 KNOTS CAS.

MANUAL LEANING PERMISSIBLE BELOW THIS LINE

APPENDIX II

RESTRICTED
AN 01-85FA-1

200 KNOTS CAS

Clean Configuration
Auto Lean
Low Blower

PR 58E2 Carburetors
Parts List No. 395516-11

Cowl and
Oil Cooler
Flaps closed.

25,000 lbs.			23,000 lbs.			STD. ALT.	STD. TEMP. °C.	21,000 lbs.			19,000 lbs.		
RPM	MP	GPH	RPM	MP	GPH			RPM	MP	GPH	RPM	MP	GPH
2270	FT	156	2200	FT	150	20000	-25	2150	FT	143	2050	FT	136
2120	FT	152	2060	FT	144	18000	-21	2000	FT	137	1950	FT	132
1980	FT	146	1920	FT	138	16000	-17	1870	FT	132	1800	FT	126
1830	FT	140	1800	FT	134	14000	-13	1750	FT	127	1710	FT	122
1770	FT	136	1700	FT	129	12000	-9	1650	FT	124	1620	FT	116
1640	FT	131	1600	FT	125	10000	-5	1570	FT	119	1530	FT	112
1560	FT	126	1510	FT	121	8000	-1	1470	FT	115	1430	FT	108
1470	FT	123	1430	FT	116	6000	3	1400	30.5	110	1400	29.5	104
1490	32.0	120	1400	32.0	113	4000	7	1400	31.0	105	1400	30.0	98
1560	32.0	116	1450	32.0	108	2000	11	1400	31.5	100	1400	30.5	96
1630	32.0	112	1520	32.0	104	S. L.	15	1400	32.0	96	1400	31.0	94

NO MANUAL LEANING PERMISSIBLE

ABBREVIATIONS:

CAS – Calibrated air speed
MP – Manifold pressure
FT – Full throttle

GPH – Gallons per hour, both engines
STD. ALT. – Standard altitude
STD. TEMP. – Standard temperature

This publication shall not be carried in aircraft or combat missions or when there is a reasonable chance of its falling into the hands of the enemy.

RESTRICTED
AN 01-85FA-1

APPENDIX II

210 KNOTS CAS

Clean Configuration
Auto Lean
Low Blower

PR 58E2 Carburetors
Parts List No. 395516-11

Cowl and
Oil Cooler
Flaps Closed.

25,000 lbs.			23,000 lbs.			STD. ALT.	STD. TEMP. °C	21,000 lbs.			19,000 lbs.		
RPM	MP	GPH	RPM	MP	GPH			RPM	MP	GPH	RPM	MP	GPH
2390	FT	174	2340	FT	166	20000	-25	2290	FT	160	2230	FT	153
2240	FT	168	2180	FT	160	18000	-21	2150	FT	153	2080	FT	147
2090	FT	161	2030	FT	154	16000	-17	1980	FT	147	1950	FT	141
1970	FT	156	1900	FT	148	14000	-13	1850	FT	141	1800	FT	137
1840	FT	150	1800	FT	142	12000	-9	1770	FT	137	1730	FT	133
1740	FT	144	1690	FT	137	10000	-5	1650	FT	132	1630	FT	128
1630	FT	140	1580	FT	133	8000	-1	1570	FT	128	1530	FT	124
1610	32.0	136	1540	32.0	129	6000	3	1480	FT	124	1440	FT	120
1720	32.0	133	1590	32.0	125	4000	7	1510	32.0	120	1430	32.0	116
1810	32.0	130	1700	32.0	123	2000	11	1580	32.0	118	1490	32.0	112
1850	32.0	128	1800	32.0	120	S. L.	15	1680	32.0	115	1570	32.0	108

NO MANUAL LEANING PERMISSIBLE

ABBREVIATIONS:

CAS - Calibrated air speed
MP - Manifold pressure
FT - Full throttle

GPH - Gallons per hour, both engines
STD. ALT. - Standard altitude
STD. TEMP. - Standard temperature

This publication shall not be carried in aircraft or combat missions or when there is a reasonable chance of its falling into the hands of the enemy.

APPENDIX II
RESTRICTED
AN 01-85FA-1

220 KNOTS CAS

Clean Configuration
Auto Lean
Low Blower

PR 58E2 Carburetors
Parts List No. 395516-11

Cowl and Oil Cooler Flaps Closed

25,000 lbs.			23,000 lbs.			STD. ALT.	STD. TEMP. °C	21,000 lbs.			19,000 lbs.		
RPM	MP	GPH	RPM	MP	GPH			RPM	MP	GPH	RPM	MP	GPH
2490	FT	193	2440	FT	185	20,000	-25	2420	FT	178	2390	FT	174
2370	FT	186	2300	FT	178	18,000	-21	2270	FT	172	2240	FT	168
2210	FT	180	2160	FT	171	16,000	-17	2120	FT	166	2090	FT	161
2070	FT	173	2000	FT	164	14,000	-13	1970	FT	159	1970	FT	156
1940	FT	166	1890	FT	158	12,000	-9	1870	FT	153	1840	FT	150
1830	FT	160	1790	FT	152	10,000	-5	1770	FT	148	1740	FT	142
1790	32.0	155	1680	FT	148	8,000	-1	1660	FT	143	1630	FT	140
1850	32.0	152	1780	32.0	144	6,000	3	1670	32.0	139	1610	32.0	136
1900	32.0	148	1830	32.0	140	4,000	7	1770	32.0	136	1720	32.0	133
1960	32.0	145	1890	32.0	138	2,000	11	1840	32.0	134	1810	32.0	130
1980	32.0	142	1930	32.0	136	S. L.	15	1880	32.0	131	1850	32.0	128

NO MANUAL LEANING PERMISSIBLE

ABBREVIATIONS:

CAS - Calibrated air speed
MP - Manifold pressure
FT - Full throttle
GPH - Gallons per hour, both engines
STD. ALT. - Standard altitude
STD. TEMP. - Standard temperature

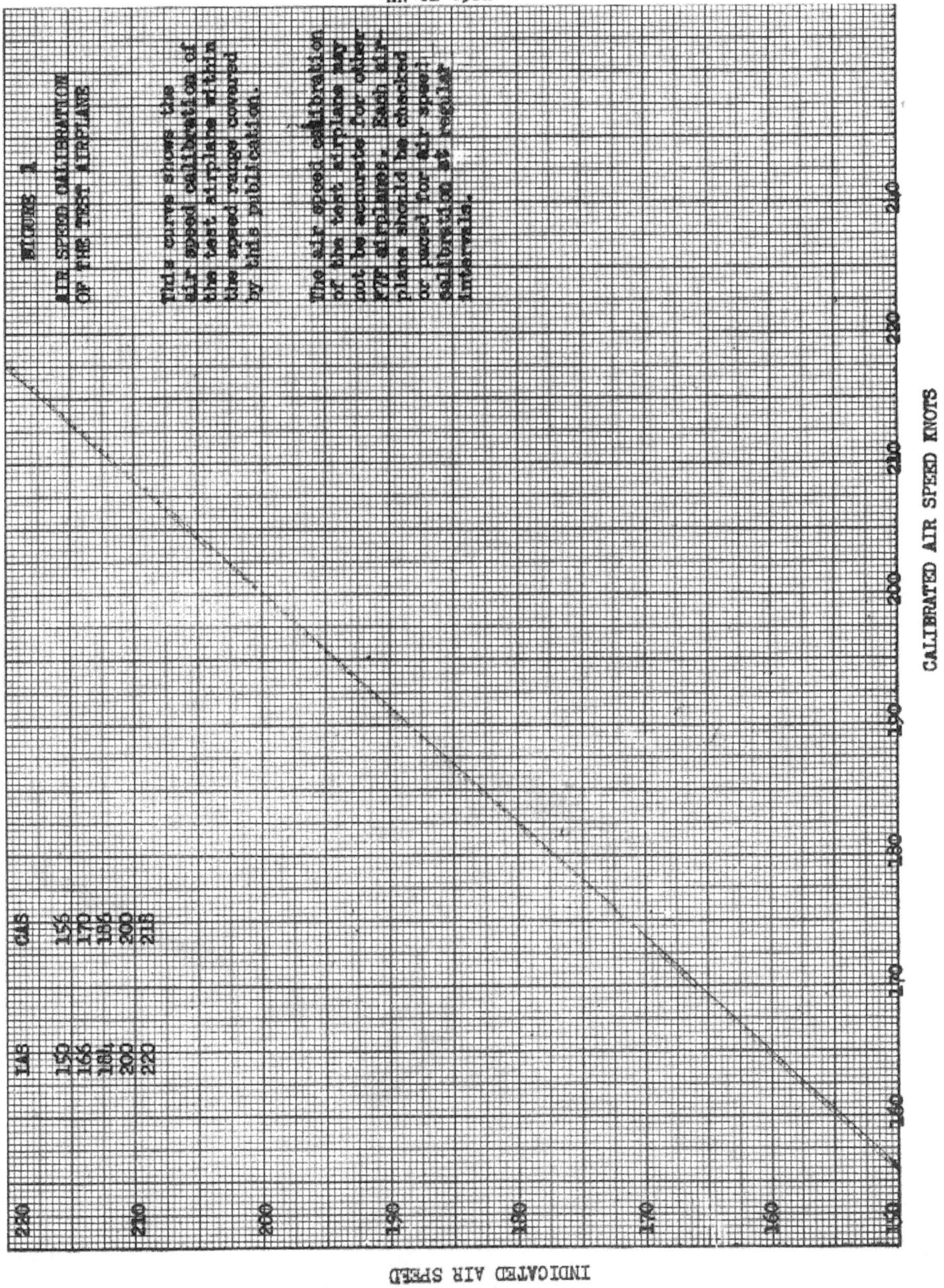
FIGURE 1
AIR SPEED CALIBRATION OF THE TEST AIRPLANE
This curve shows the air speed calibration of the test airplane within the speed range covered by this publication.
The air speed calibration of the test airplane may not be accurate for other F7F airplanes. Each airplane should be checked or paced for air speed calibration at regular intervals.
IAS CAS
150 156
165 170
184 186
200 200
220 218
150
160
170
180
190
200
210
220
230
240
CALIBRATED AIR SPEED KNOTS
INDICATED AIR SPEED

RESTRICTED
AN 01-85FA-1

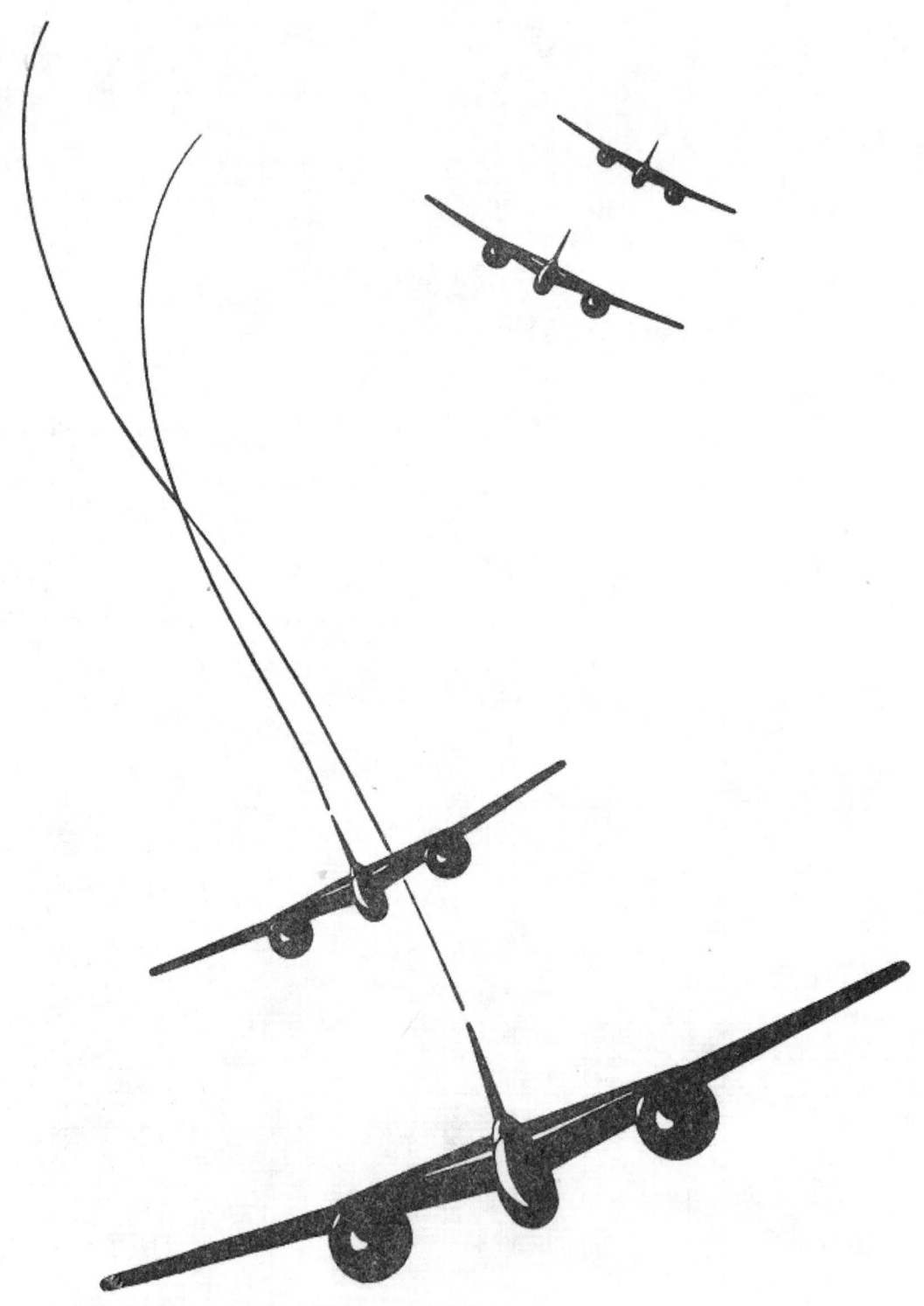

RESTRICTED

This publication shall not be carried in aircraft or combat missions or when there is a reasonable chance of its falling into the hands of the enemy.

RESTRICTED
AN 01-85FA-1

APPENDIX II

CONDENSED OPERATING INSTRUCTIONS

F7F

LOW BLOWER AUTO LEAN

CRUISE POWER SETTINGS

DO NOT EXCEED 232 °C

HOLD 32 IN. (OR FULL THROTTLE IF 32 IN. CANNOT BE OBTAINED) AND CONTROL AIRSPEED BY ADJUSTING RPM IN THE RANGE

1400 TO 2200 RPM.

IF NECESSARY HOLD 1400 RPM

AND REDUCE MP BELOW 32 IN.

1400 RPM — MINIMUM RECOMMENDED

THE ABOVE CARD MAY BE CARRIED BY THE PILOT OR POSTED IN THE COCKPIT.

NASA PROJECT GEMINI

FAMILIARIZATION MANUAL
Manned Satellite Capsule

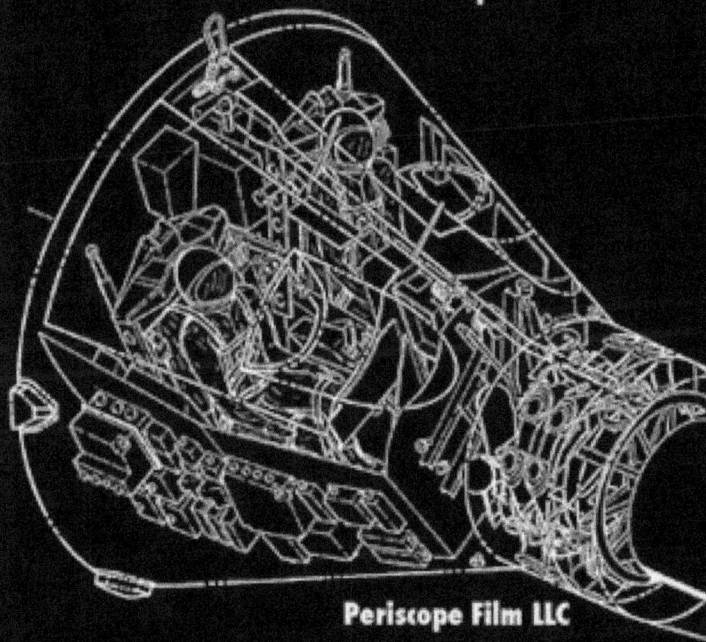

Periscope Film LLC

Aircraft At War DVD Series

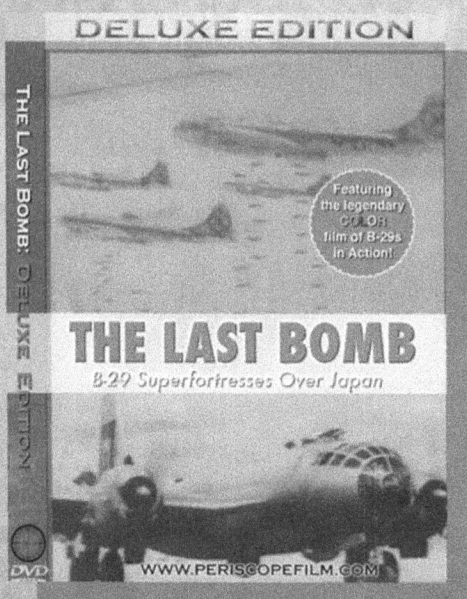

Now Available!

SPRUCE GOOSE
HUGHES FLYING BOAT MANUAL

RESTRICTED

Originally Published by the War Department
Reprinted by Periscope Film LLC

NOW AVAILABLE!

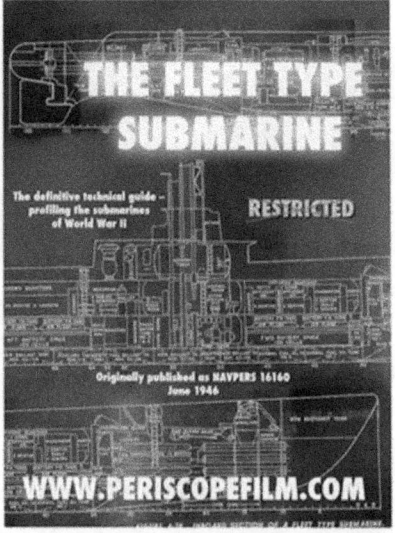

ALSO NOW AVAILABLE
FROM PERISCOPEFILM.COM

©2008-2011 Periscope Film LLC
ALL Rights Reserved
WWW.PERISCOPEFILM.COM
ISBN# 978-1-935700-72-2

www.ingramcontent.com/pod-product-compliance
Lightning Source LLC
Chambersburg PA
CBHW080517110426
42742CB00017B/3146